Stormy Monday

Stormy Monday

The T-Bone Walker Story

Helen Oakley Dance

With a Foreword by B. B. King

A DA CAPO PAPERBACK

Library of Congress Cataloging in Publication Data

Dance, Helen Oakley, 1913-
   Stormy Monday: the T-Bone Walker story / Helen Oakley Dance;
with a foreword by B. B. King.
      p.   cm. — (A Da Capo paperback)
   Originally published: Baton Rouge: Louisiana State University Press,
c1987.
   Discography: p.
   Includes bibliographical references and index.
   ISBN 0-306-80413-1
   1. Walker, T-Bone, 1910-1975. 2. Blues musicians — United States —
Biography. I. Title.
[ML419.W27D3   1990]   90-38859
782.42'1643'092 — dc20   CIP
[B]   MN

The author makes grateful acknowledgment to the following
individuals, publications, and publishers: Gregmark Music Company, Los
Angeles, California, Lester Sills, President, for permission to reprint
the music and lyrics of "Call It Stormy Monday" © 1963; *Soul Bag*
magazine, Jacques Périn, Editor, for permission to reprint the T-Bone
Walker discography published in *Soul Bag*, No. 100 (September–October,
1984); Pete Welding, for permission to reprint excerpts from liner notes
for the Blue Note reissue album of T-Bone Walker recordings; Sheldon
Harris and Arlington House for permission to reprint data from *Blues
Who's Who* (New Rochelle, N.Y., 1979); and Norbert Hess, for access
to his research data on T-Bone Walker.
All illustrations, except where noted, are reproduced courtesy of
Vida Lee Walker and Bernita Walker Moss.

This Da Capo Press paperback edition of *Stormy Monday: The
T-Bone Walker Story* is an unabridged republication of the edition
published in Baton Rouge, Louisiana in 1987, supplemented with
author emendations. It is reprinted by arrangement with Louisiana
State University Press.

Published by Da Capo Press, Inc.
A Subsidiary of Plenum Publishing Corporation
233 Spring Street, New York, New York 10013

Manufactured in the United States of America

*This is not a treatise on the range
of expertise developed in the art of
guitar-playing. Rather, it is the story of
one of its most innovative and
charismatic performers.*

*This book is a memorial to T-Bone
Walker and the blues giants who
preceded him. It celebrates his kindred
spirit in artists like B. B. King, John
Lee Hooker, Junior Wells, Eddie
Vinson, Son Seals, Otis Rush, and
many others whose dedication and
commitment help propagate the blues.*

Contents

Illustrations

Foreword

B. B. King

For me, the blues is more than music: it's a way of life. And a story, too, that began in the fields a long time ago. As people got freer and more knowing, so did the blues. The blues never deserted the South, but they came up north besides. When they surfaced in the cities, they had turned into urban blues.

But don't misunderstand—bluesmen aren't always down in the mouth. They sing shouts as well. When I'm feeling good, I have to shout sometimes. And people relate to that, too.

One thing about the blues—they always tell a tale. Good deals, bad deals, no-good women, gambling men. They come to life in the blues, because the blues singers stay on top of what is going on. In my "Why I Sing the Blues," I end up,

> And everybody want to know why I sing the blues,
> Well, I've been around a long time, I've really paid my dues.

Meaning there's all kind of trouble in life, and a heap of blues artists were needed to keep track of all that. In this tradition and way out in front was T-Bone Walker. I think he was one of the greatest guitarists we've ever had. He got a sound all his own, and if I could have played like him, I would have. We thought alike. T-Bone said: "Blues is just gospel turned around. It's feeling great, and feeling sad right on, besides." I kept digging Bone until it was his turn to go. But you can hear him still, on the records he made, and know that the blues were what made life different for him.

After nearly fifty years of playing them all over the world, I feel the blues should be recognized as a universal language. But at times

I feel bad because I think today's pop fans are ignoring a heritage that should mean a lot to them. It's funny that people in Europe seem to care more about blues than folks at home. But maybe that will change, because nowadays I'm often invited to tell how the blues started up and how they kept traveling to reach the point where they are today.

When life seems a drag, the blues can make you feel good. That's a message that has been relayed and welcomed all over the world. Listen to T-Bone, and you will understand.

Acknowledgments

I am grateful to T-Bone Walker's widow, Vida Lee, to members of his family, and to his many friends whose memories have so enlivened this account of his life. It is sad that other friends, like Muddy Waters, Joe Turner, and Pee Wee Crayton, are no longer with us. Like T-Bone, they will be sorely missed. I am also grateful to my daughter, Maria Lindley, for her dedication and the superior skills she exhibited in the preparation of the manuscript, and I owe much to Mary Boone for the exceptional care she took in the transcription of tapes. In addition, I am indebted to the staff of Louisiana State University Press, especially to Beverly Jarrett and Catherine Barton for their unfailing support and guidance and to John Easterly for his thorough editorial work. My greatest debt, however, is to my husband. His background knowledge of the subject and uncompromising standards have been a constant source of enlightenment and inspiration.

Stormy Monday

Introduction

Although our main endeavor has been oriented to jazz, my husband, Stanley, and I have always had an abiding allegiance to the blues. Over the years we paid close attention to T-Bone Walker's career, impressed by his talent and also by his recorded output, which successfully bridged the worlds of both jazz and the blues.

As a blues man his eminence is secure. He ranks at the top, with male artists like B. B. King, Muddy Waters, John Lee Hooker, Robert Johnson, Elmore James, Sonny Boy Williamson I and II, Freddie King, Bill Broonzy, and Otis Rush, and with ladies like Bessie Smith, Ma Rainey, Memphis Minnie, and Clara Smith. As a jazz artist he performed in concert and on records with outstanding instrumentalists such as Johnny Hodges, Clark Terry, Lester Young, Buddy Tate, Illinois Jacquet, Arnett Cobb, Tyree Glenn, Dizzy Gillespie, Count Basie, Ram Ramirez, Jay McShann, Jo Jones, Sidney Catlett, and Red Callender, to name only a few.

He was not, however, the only blues guitarist to be respected and welcomed by the jazz community. Lonnie Johnson, for example, had recorded with Duke Ellington and Louis Armstrong in the twenties, but for the most part those who had ventured into jazz were accomplished pianists, possibly because their instrument lent itself so admirably to both genres. The talents of Pete Johnson, Memphis Slim, Roosevelt Sykes, Albert Ammons, Meade Lux Lewis, Joshua Altheimer, and Little Brother Montgomery attest to this. Other artists, in a kind of neutral territory, drew inspiration from both areas. This category is exemplified by musicians like Jelly Roll Morton, James P. Johnson, Count Basie, Duke Ellington, Mary Lou Williams, Jay McShann, Kenny Kersey, Ray Bryant, Horace Silver, and Thelonious Monk.

With the approach of the forties, the dual role the piano had
played was challenged on both fronts by the guitar. Charlie Christian, when he joined Benny Goodman in 1939, opened up new ave-
nues for this instrument, which until then had been relegated
primarily to the rhythm section of a band. Not to be contained in
so limited a sphere, Christian's improvisatory gifts and compelling
beat made him an innovator in his field. No less endowed, and also
a pioneer of the electric guitar, T-Bone Walker similarly took the
jazz world by surprise when he came east with the Les Hite band in
1940.

Both men became identified with the swing era and made remarkable contributions to it. Both were born in the Southwest,
T-Bone in Dallas in 1910, Charlie in Oklahoma in 1916, and became friends in their teens. They liked jamming together and
shared the same teacher, Oklahoman Chuck Richardson, who
helped shape their techniques. Their paths, however, diverged.
Since Charlie's brothers were jazz musicians, he naturally gravi-
tated to a band setting, while T-Bone, equally naturally, continued
as a single in the way he had begun.

As a child he and his cousin danced in the streets and circulated
a cigar box after a group of relatives, playing homemade string instruments, had entertained. T-Bone originally modeled his vocal
style on that of pianist Leroy Carr, a popular blues artist of the day.
Later he was influenced by Lonnie Johnson's more sophisticated approach. Soon, however, he was on his way to fashioning an individual repertoire enhanced by a distinctive sound that by the early
forties was being emulated from coast to coast.

As artist and performer, T-Bone was accurately evaluated by
blues authority Pete Welding, who produced the Blue Note album
of reissues in 1976. His notes for the album include the following
remarks.

Anyone who has enjoyed the music of B. B., Albert or Freddie King,
Eric Clapton, Buddy Guy, Jimi Hendrix, Albert Collins, Duane Allman, Mike Bloomfield, Earl Hooker, Johnny Winter or any of a host
of other contemporary blues and blues-influenced players has heard
T-Bone as well.

The reason is simple: he is one of the deep, enduring wellsprings of the modern blues to which they and so many others have turned and continue to return for inspiration and renewal. T-Bone Walker is the fundamental source of the modern urban style of playing and singing blues and is widely regarded as having started it all back in the late 1930s when, almost alone, he forged the fleet, jazz-based guitar style that has since become the dominant approach for the instrument and, with it, the blues itself. In a very real sense the modern blues is largely his creation. The blues was different before he came onto the scene, and it hasn't been the same since, and few men can lay claim to that kind of distinction.

He participated in and contributed to virtually every development black vernacular music has witnessed in the last half-century. A number of them he initiated as well. In length of service, adaptability and continuous creative activity, perhaps only Coleman Hawkins or Duke Ellington have matched him; nor are such comparisons forced or undeserved, for his contributions to American music are demonstrably, significantly comparable to theirs, though manifestly of a different order. Among blues artists he is *nonpareil:* no one has contributed as much, as long, or as variously to the blues as he has.

Also reflected in their white counterparts, the developments in black vernacular music paralleled the progress of blues from country to urban settings. In time the term *rhythm and blues* defined a further mutation that owed a great deal to earlier jazz and blues forms. In the 1950s white audiences acclaimed the advent of rock, and later black audiences embraced music identified as soul. Blues qua blues lost some of their appeal, and they languished until the sixties, when, ironically enough, English groups like the Rolling Stones and John Mayall's band developed styles based on those of postwar electric blues and turned fashion around. Following an example set by Elvis Presley and Bill Haley, who, incidentally, were harvesting financial rewards far in excess of the dreams of those they copied, young white Americans acclaimed the work of such artists as Muddy Waters, Memphis Slim, John Lee Hooker, Lowell Fulson, Big Mama Thornton, Gatemouth Brown, and Hound Dog Taylor. Groups like the Allman Brothers, Canned Heat, the Doors, and White Trash, as well as performers like Janis Joplin, Jimi Hendrix, and Eric Clapton, emulated their styles. "It's rough on us blues men," T-Bone observed, "but we're happy just doing our thing."

This was a viewpoint difficult to maintain, however, when he learned that a million copies had been sold of the Allman Brothers album featuring his composition "Stormy Monday," while his own version was allowed to go out of print. Still, thousands of teenagers, many of whom now heard his name for the first time, applauded wildly when his song was announced at rock festivals and jamborees. Overnight the number became a blues anthem and has remained a standard ever since.

Acclaim came too late. T-Bone's physique had been undermined both by drinking and a lifelong battle with ill health. For a time, backed by a small band, he continued to play one-nighters, performing on the piano when he found it too difficult to support the guitar. Ultimately even this proved too much. On December 31, 1974, he suffered a stroke. "It's just a setback," he told friends later. "You think this time it's for real? Don't count on it! A cat like me has got ninety-nine lives."

But T-Bone's luck had run its course. When his death was announced on March 16, 1975, a thousand mourners gathered in Los Angeles to pay homage to him. T-Bone's innovations are now basic, incorporated in the twin idioms of blues and jazz. His records, nourishing successive generations, are deemed a legacy impervious to time.

One

Down the Katy Track

"We were in Chicago, years back, and my uncle was gambling," said R. S. Rankin, T-Bone Walker's nephew. "He'd sent me to do the show at the Crown Propeller at Cottage Grove and Sixty-third. I was billed as T-Bone, Jr., and he wanted to break me in to where I could do a show by myself. The act was like a father-and-son thing. That's what the man had hired us to do. So I came on with half the act, nervous and sweating. Maybe I did OK, I don't know. I was trying the best I knew how. I made a few mistakes, but they didn't say anything, not till the show was over. Then the man came and said: 'Junior, where's your dad? I want him up here on the stage. You go find him.' This had happened a couple of times before, and I would run around the corner to the hotel and say: 'Bone, you got to come along, man. We have to do the last show *together*.'

"So this particular day, when I was going up in the elevator to fetch him, what did I do but forget the keys to his room! I'd already called him out from the crap game he was in—and then I had to go back down to the desk. I would always be forgetting because I was so nervous about the show. So this night when the elevator took me up again and let me out, here were these two guys with a great big ol' gun! With my mind on the show, I figured they were jiving. To me, it was a joke."

"Some joke!" T-Bone broke in. "A guy with a German Luger automatic gets in my face when I come away from the game! I see there are two of them, with stocking caps pulled over their heads. And there am I, hands full of bills. More than four thousand dollars, I'll bet, and I hadn't so much as stowed it away. I decided I'd give them *nothing*. But right away this guy cocked his pistol and said, 'I don't want to kill you, T-Bone, but if you don't hand over, it's what I'll have to do.'

"So then I guessed it was a planned thing of some kind, a sort of plot. I'd come in from Detroit, and I'd been gambling, because Detroit was a wide-open town. I'd been living there awhile, working different spots. The Frolic Bar, the Flame Show Bar, a lot of places like that. When I arrived in Chicago to open up my gig, Sugar Ray was in town for the championship fight. That meant the folks from Detroit came over to bet and watch him go for the title. So I think half the people staying in the hotel must have been friends of mine.

6

But not all, because maybe I'd been *too* lucky. There were games all over the place, and this one had been going on all day. A lot of money was tied up there, and a good bit come my way. But I had to bow out because I had my show to do. Either the guys had this figured, or word had gone round and someone on the outside was waiting for me."

"Well, T-Bone was standing there," R. S. continued, "clutching those bills. 'Don't do nothin',' he told me. 'These guys'll kill you, son!' I'd been about to cross over to him when I caught sight of the elevator boy, hands in the air, and then I dug what was happening. 'Don't move,' T-Bone said, and with that, one of the guys hit me upside my head with his .45. They grabbed the money and cut out real fast." He turned to T-Bone. "With the ring from your finger, remember?"

"Not mine. I'd won it off Jimmy Jones. When he'd run out of dough, he'd gambled his ring. But the way that guy grabbed for my finger, you could think it might be someone who'd taken that kind of fall. Well, Chicago's a gambler's town. You know, there's guys hang around there would steal you blind if they could."

This was my introduction to T-Bone Walker's world. His house on West Forty-third Place in Los Angeles was filled with relatives and friends. "It's often like this," T-Bone's wife, Vida Lee, told me. "People stop by all the time. We look for it when my husband's home. You should first meet M'Dear, my mother-in-law. She's over there on the couch beside my sister Mattie."

Movelia, T-Bone's mother, white-haired and frail, allowed me to shake her hand, and then T-Bone started introducing his friends. "T-Bone sat by me in school," said Patty Jack Lott, who had been raised alongside him in Dallas. Stymie Beard, a younger man who was presented next, said: "I haven't known him that long. Just since he came to L.A."[1]

"That's right," T-Bone nodded. "But I owe Stymie a lot. He showed me the ropes. Then Lester Skaggs here," he continued, "is just a cat

---

1. As a child Matthew "Stymie" Beard had starred in Columbia Pictures' "Little Rascals" movie shorts.

like me. That's why Mama likes him, I guess. He rooms in her place back of mine and watches out for things." Holding onto my elbow, T-Bone began to steer me across the hall. "It's quieter in here," he said.

We entered a long, narrow room Vida Lee had fixed up for him. Two of the walls were mirrored with aluminum tiles ceiling high. They reflected four stools pulled up to a semicircular bar with a red-formica top and chrome sides. Cartons of old photographs and publicity shots were stacked on the floor, and the Gibson guitar stood in the corner in a battered case. In front of windows that faced on the street, there were upholstered chairs, and a couch along the far wall completed the set. Stymie and Patty Jack followed us in, and the latter, going back of the bar, flattened a newspaper and fetched up a jam jar half full of pot. Shaking it loose, he started to roll.

"Count me out," Stymie said, and T-Bone smiled.

"He's playing it straight today. Columbia Pictures called. Now that we get those reruns of 'Our Gang' on TV every day, Stymie is in heavy demand."

"Come off it," Stymie said. "Look, R. S. is cutting out."

"Everything is under control," R. S. indicated on his way out the front door. "Skaggs will stay back and keep an eye on M'Dear."

"OK." T-Bone was satisfied. Although her wits were sharp, his mother was nearly eighty, and when she came over from her place, he saw to it she had company in his. "Well, let's get started," he said, testing the mike and handing it to me.

"Hold it a minute," Vi called from across the hall. "Here are some sodas you might want after a while."

"Fine. And let's ask Mama to join us," T-Bone directed.

A moment later Vi smiled as she watched her mother-in-law step carefully into the room, erect, and wary as a bird. Her eyes were lively as she looked around at us all.

"What you want?" she asked.

"Tell about Grandpa," T-Bone suggested.

"Well, you *know* your grandpa's name. It was Edward Jamison, and he answered to Ed. Mother's name was Martha. I don't know

why, because she was full-blooded Cherokee. She and my daddy
were strict churchgoing folk. The Bible, with our names written in
it, was the onliest book we ever read. I had a heap of sisters, and
brothers too. My daddy worked for Grogan Brothers, because they
were the first ones hired him to work in a lumber camp. Grogans
located their mills outside a whole lot of towns in northeast Texas.
Where I was born was called Sulser. It was near Texarkana, I guess.
Part was in Arkansas, too, and for a while we lived there as well.
Then they took the mill to Biven, and when they'd cut the wood
out of there, it was Winnsburg next. We were moving down the
Katy track." She smiled, probably remembering the blues song
about a local on the Missouri-Kansas-Texas line, "I Thought I
Heard the Katy Whistle Blow."

"Soon as the land was cleared, the workers struck camp, moving
farther on. Timpson, Kildare, Conroe, and Linden, where T-Bone
was born. My daddy lived to be ninety and was a lumber stacker all
his life. He had fourteen children, but a lot of them died. I had
three sisters to live—Ella, Leola, and Berte. The eldest girl, she died
of typhoid, and another, a baby, got hives. Bold hives, they called
them, and that's what killed her, I guess. I don't rightly remember
the others, but four brothers have lasted—William, Edgar, Nate,
and Jack. Jack was the youngest and always poorly. Now we have
him fixed up nearby. Vi sees him every weekend, and he comes for
dinner Christmas. My dad started work at sunup. We'd bring breakfast out to him later, and sup with him some, my sisters and I. One
time he got four wheels and cut down a sapling to make us a cart.
The places where we lived, people called them shotgun houses. Because you could see clear through. Through the front, to the bedroom and the kitchen at the back." Hesitating a moment, she
looked at T-Bone, and they exchanged smiles.

"You don't want to be shy," he said.

"All right. Behind that was the outhouse," she declared. "Everywhere the same. We'd stay three, four years, and move on to the
next place. Daddy didn't visit the juke joints like the other men,
Saturday nights. Not even when fellows came in off the road, playing piano for people to dance. Low-down, Mama called that. She

and Daddy were real strict. Every Sunday we were handclapping and singing hymns all day long." Mischief surfaced in her voice as she addressed T-Bone directly. "You know I had my fill a long time ago.

"I don't go to church," she said, addressing me, "and that don't sit right with Vi, because T-Bone's the same. He don't go with her either."

"The only churchgoing that got to me was back in Dallas," T-Bone said, "there in the Holiness church, near where we lived. Some guys are big-time about sanctified religion. Not me. Those people are true believers. If you hang in there long enough, some of it rubs off on you . . . all that singing and shouting. They go on about bad times, all that sorry stuff we have to go through. Then after a while they get lighthearted. Joyful is more like it.

"When I was a kid, I'd crouch by a window and peep once in a while. The preacher knew how to stir them up, and the hall came alive when he got going real good. People jumped and shouted and everyone hollered 'Amen!' With the deacons whipping him, he'd be calling on the Lord, and when the handclapping started, the spirituals would begin. I'd be kneeling in the dirt, my heart pounding. Their time was so *great*. It was joyful, all right, but it was pitiful, too. If I hadn't been hearing the blues from Mama, I'd have learned them right then."

"Sure." His mother nodded. "T-Bone always knowed the blues, and I could strum and sing before I ever married his dad. I'd pick myself up like that, after minding younguns all day. Then I had a mind to be free, so I married Rance Walker. His kin came from Conroe, sharecroppers mostly, but he was stacking lumber at Grogans' right then. We stayed close to my folks till the baby was born [on May 28, 1910], moving to Lawrenceville after, and picking cotton for a time. Rance wanted to settle in Conroe and go on the land for himself, so that's what he did when I left.

"My mind was set on moving to Dallas and carrying T-Bone along. No need of him working out in fields all his life. Rance had a sister in Dallas who took us in. Soon I was cooking and cleaning for whites in another part of town, and we started renting in Oak Cliff so I could catch the streetcar to work. A lady living near us had a family half grown, and that was good for my boy. There were brothers and sisters that kept a sharp eye on them all."

"Aunty was close by, too," T-Bone reminded her.

"That's right. And the way he hit it off with his cousin Ellie Mae put my mind at rest. I'd walk down to the Bottoms real early each morning and cross the railroad tracks so I could board the trolley. By time I got back, it would be dark. I had to fix supper at work before I could quit. Except Saturdays. We dished early then. Sunday I could go home after the noonday meal. I guess I held together for a piece because I was young. And then T-Bone's stepdaddy showed up."

"He was good to me," T-Bone said. "Marco Washington could play every kind of instrument. Everyone in his family knew some kind of music, and they'd formed a group that played together, with mandolins, guitars, and violins. Mama played guitar, pretty good, too. Good enough to fall in with Huddie Ledbetter more than once.[2] When he visited Dallas, Leadbelly would stay some days, spending them with his sister who lived on Central and Allen. When he came by our place, if he felt like it, he would play. It was before he teamed up for a time with Blind Lemon Jefferson, I guess.[3] Blind Lemon I remember well. Though I was only a kid, he had me to lead him around. He kept the guitar strapped on his chest, a tin cup on the neck, and on Central Avenue people stopped to listen, clinking coins so he could hear them drop. Afterwards, I'd guide him back up the hill, and Mama would fix supper. She'd pour him a little taste, and they'd sit quiet for a while. Later on, if they played, Marco and I would listen, or Marco would get out his bass.

"Lemon sang things he wrote himself about life—good times and bad. Mostly bad, I guess. Everyone knew what he was singing about. There's nothing *new* in the blues. It's everything that's going

2. Country blues singer Huddie Ledbetter was a legendary figure in the first half of the century whose work is described by John and Alan Lomax in *Negro Folk Songs as Sung by Leadbelly* (New York, 1936).

3. Blind Lemon Jefferson, who was born in 1897 and died prematurely in 1930, exerted a tremendous influence not only on the blues men of his day but on those who came after. His verses and motifs and the songs he recorded in the twenties became the idiomatic currency of the genre.

on. You've heard it all before, maybe a whole lot of times. There's some fellow who landed in jail or a guy whose old lady got knifed. There's a home underwater or a field full of blight. It's hurricane time, or maybe it's drought. One thing in particular is the root of the songs most fellows sing: women, and women's ways. When you start messin' with that, you may be singing all night and still not get through."

"No, love ain't never out of style. Not yet," his mother said. "That's how come T-Bone stayed with the blues."

"But when the family went out," T-Bone reminded her, "it wasn't only blues that we played. Plenty of requests would come in, and we played fast things as well. Back then it seemed everyone we knew was living in South Dallas. Right around the Bottoms in the same shotgun houses Mama told you about. On the weekends all who could play would go with Marco and his folks and parade through the streets. Jesse Hooker had a saxophone and a clarinet, but he was the only one had a horn. The others had mandolins, guitars, and bass, and some had homemade strings. The first stop, maybe, would be at a root-beer stand."

"Will Green would be doing the singing," his mother remembered. "Then the younguns danced, and afterwards T-Bone and his cousin Casey would go to the parked cars for requests. They passed the cigar box at the finish, and there'd be like a dollar fifty there!"

"I couldn't play good back then," T-Bone added, "but I had learned to dance. Casey, too."

"You could always dance," M'Dear agreed. "And we had a friend would stand up by you and teach you new things."

"Frank Evans," T-Bone nodded. "He said I caught on easy, and I learned stands and splits and spins. That's what put change in the kitty most times. When I got older, maybe twelve, I could play the ukulele, and I worked up an act. I would sing anything they asked. I entertained at church picnics or at Riverside Park."

"He played hooky a lot," his mother said. "So I got me a switch and whipped him sometimes. For going off riding horseback or staying in the water too long."

"I never talked back, that's one thing," T-Bone said. "I came up that way. We all did. You didn't fight your own, not like now. And the one time I knew no better, I had to pick myself up when Mama got through!"

"I taught him different, though, if trouble came from outside," his mother said. " 'Fight back,' I would say, 'and don't you dare cry! Hit 'em back!' That's what I'd tell him."

"Had to anyhow," T-Bone said. "An undersized guy has to learn to fight. I never grew that big."

"Big enough to steal a pony for a ride," his mother said, "and bring him tumbling down."

Two

The Blue Hole

"I loved to ride," T-Bone said. "I couldn't help myself, I just had to borrow a pony sometimes. There was one I used to ride a lot that belonged to a friend of mine, Charlie Griffin. The Griffins had settled in Oak Cliff before us. They had a bunch of pretty daughters, so I hung out with Charlie and practically lived in their house. Mr. Griffin was the type of man who was crazy about kids. He didn't mind letting me ride the pony some days. But he wouldn't let me ride all the time. I can't tell you how I felt those days when I wanted to ride so bad.

"Sometimes, when they wouldn't let me, I'd just go on and steal! I'd put the bridle on that pony and ride him up to school. We were in grade school then, and instead of being there, I was on the pony. But what happened next was rough. I guess this one time I must have ridden him too hard—for the kind of shape he was in. We got to Cliff and Richardson, and he just keeled over and died. In front of Dave Clark's house. My leg was pinned underneath, and they had to send for help before I could get out. I wasn't hurt. I was scared, scared of what Mr. Griffin would do. He was mad all right, but he wouldn't have me arrested. He was that sort. I'd been like one of the family, underfoot all the time."

"But do you remember the time a policeman did come 'round?" His mother gave him a look.

"You mean do I remember some guys at school robbing a store? And by me being the youngest, I had to sit on the curb and keep watch. When the fellows came out with the money, they loaded the candy on me. I didn't know what to do with it, so I ran home and put it on Mama's bed. But I had a lesson coming, because she showed up and beat the daylights out of me."

His mother nodded. "Unless I knew where it came from, he couldn't bring anything home," she said. "So he had to go back with this candy."

"The law came after me then," T-Bone said, "trying to round up the gang. But I was through with those fellows. After the whipping I'd got, I figured they were bad to be running around with."

"The neighbors would ask me how come T-Bone was never in trouble for stealing." M'Dear permitted herself a faint smile. "I'd tell them, 'I'll kill him if he steal.'"

16

"But Mama never had real bad trouble with me," T-Bone said. "There was too much going on in my head. I wanted to dance, and I wanted strings real bad. My first guitar was an old cigar box I fixed up with nails and strung wire between. I got a few tones like that. Some of the fellows used rubber bands, but this was better because I got to bend the notes, like Mama did. When I was small, I used to listen to her when I was supposed to be in bed. She'd give me the chills sometimes, so I aimed at gettin' hold of some of those notes. I was about twelve, I guess, when she loaned me her guitar a time or two. The big day came when Marco walked me to the store, and I picked out a banjo and paid for it with the change I'd put by. I'd take that thing and go to the downtown hotels, and it got so they all knew me. At the Adelphi, maybe, or the Baker, they'd let me go in to where a band was at work. After I made it onto the floor and went into my dance, the people would throw money. I'd come home with five, six, sometimes ten dollars.

"I did lots of things to make money. There was a little girl called Tiny Durham who used to dance with me sometimes. When she was along, we could make a few extra dollars. Near where I lived, there was an ice arena that meant plenty of jobs. On Monday nights they let the paid help skate, but no one knew how. We had a ball trying. But it was comical, really, and one time I broke my leg. A kid in front of me fell, and I tried to get past, but I wasn't used to tall skates. My ankle keeled over, and I heard it crack, so I lay where I fell, and people came out to help and brought a stew pot along. Everyone that skated by put change in it for me because they knew I wouldn't be dancing for a time.

"Later there was Dr. Breeding. He had like a medicine show, and he hired me and another boy, Josephus Cook, to ballyhoo for him. When we were out of school for the summer and the weather had turned good, Dr. Breeding took the show on the road, and we went from town to town. The stuff he was selling was black and evil-tasting, but it turned the people out! So they bought it, fifty cents a time." T-Bone smiled. "Doc called it 'Elixir' and taught Seph and me to work up some patter about it and climb on the back of a panel truck to drum people in. I'd play and feed jokes to Seph, and he'd start in to dance. I'd pick up from there, and we built on our breaks. Then we'd stack up the bottles, and Doc would come on. Behind the crowd he'd have someone, maybe his wife, yell something that made people laugh.

"'Don't be shy!' Doc would shout, 'Try my B and B tonic. It's a wonderful dose, and you won't need but one!'

"'Amen, brother!' someone would holler down front, and first thing you knew, we'd be handing down bottles and Doc would be collecting a fistful of coins. Seph and I rode and slept on the truck. Doc and his wife drove a tin lizzie old as sin and set up at night in a tent. He had a fellow in charge of the truck who would build a fire and dish up some food. Of the fifteen dollars I got, I sent ten back to Mama, but if business was bad, we went hungry sometimes."

"He'd always want to go," M'Dear remembered, "but it only lasted two summers because once he got into his teens, there were too many calls for affairs at home—like church outings and picnics, or amateur shows. Someone's at the door," she said, interrupting herself.

"I'll catch it." Stymie got to his feet. "I'm on my way out."

"It's my sis," Patty Jack told T-Bone, watching Marguerite Seymour shrug off her coat. "Where's your old man, Margy?" he asked.

"Oh, you know, the usual trip up here. He's at the garage. Carburetor, I guess." She grimaced.

"San Diego's too far to come if your engine ain't right," T-Bone told her, though he knew she and her husband would find a way to see him and Patty regardless, because they'd been friends for years. "You timed it just right, girl," he smiled. "See, it's Memory Lane."

"Good. One thing I can remember," Margy said, "and maybe Brother can, too. Time I was no more than eight, and I knocked you out cold. Threatening to tell Willie Mae you'd seen me hand in hand with a boy, T-Bone! Willie Mae," she explained to me, "was my mother. When she was alive, she would have whipped me, hearing that. Rather than get it myself when I reached home, I turned round and punched T-Bone hard. I thought he was still coming behind me till I looked back and saw them pouring water on his head. Good God! I was a tomboy, yeah, but I didn't think I'd hit him *that* hard." She laughed. "I went back and fanned him with his cap until he came to. Then I asked, 'You still gonna tell?'

"But that was only one time. Mostly we had a ball, because T-Bone was very tight with my brothers Patty, J. W., Raymond, and Joe. Before Willie Mae passed, I used to run with the boys. Then I had to take her place, because they were wild, drinkin' that chock or whatever moonshine they could get. A man called Hicky lived downhill in the Bottoms. The boys would sneak a drink from him and tell about how nasty it was, made out of dried fruit and stuff. They said he put a dirty sock in the bottom and that would give it a kick! When they'd been gone awhile, someone would come up the hill.

"'You better go down there,' they'd say, 'and see about T-Bone and Patty. They high on that stuff.'"

T-Bone and Patty exchanged amused looks.

"Black Gal is tellin' it like it is," Patty said. "She took good care of us."

"We lived on Church Street," Margy went on, "and T-Bone and M'Dear lived on Ninth, so we went to school together at Northwest Hardee up till seventh grade. Everyone had their own way of going, and upwards of a hundred kids would show up. Our bunch had a shortcut between the outhouses and down Anthony Street. Willie Mae, not four foot eleven, had to whip the boys because they played hooky so much. Ours she could handle. T-Bone got his at home. They liked to go off swimming, down to the Blue Hole, out a piece from the Bottoms below the school yard, maybe eight or nine blocks along Dentley Drive. After that it was into the country a little, because it was a gravel pit once and deep and dangerous, we heard. But the water was clear, so they named it Blue Hole.

"I knew people had drowned there, and I nearly drowned there myself. It was Patty's birthday, and some girls from North Dallas were with us. My uncle had a ball club and a bus he hauled the ball boys in, so he let us use it that day. We were on our way to Lake Wahoo, and we had two big No. 3 tubs of lemonade and fried chicken. Something went wrong with the bus, and it wouldn't go fast, so we headed for the Blue Hole instead.

"This boy, I. J. McNamara, got to fooling with me. Probably he felt kind of mad because in the dance marathon my brother and I had beaten him and his girl. He was hell on land, he said, and hell in water, too. He didn't want anyone to beat him any kind of way.

"I was sitting at the lower end of the hole where there was a tree with branches hanging down near the water. I. J. came over and picked me up, and though I was kicking and kicking, he staggered around with me. Bone and my brothers were swimming down at the other end, but they heard me holler, 'Keep your hands off me!' I couldn't swim, you see, and I knew he couldn't either. But he got us out on some rocks and dropped me in the water. Then I guess he overbalanced himself.

"I was choking and going down fast when my brothers ran up, and Austin Brown dove in. When I came to on the bank, I asked could they see I. J. They looked out, and about this much of his hand was sticking out of the water. We stared at each other, because none of us knew how to save someone drowning. Next to I. J., Caesar Phelps was the biggest, and so he went in first. I. J. threw an arm round his neck and they went down together. Caesar had a time knocking himself loose, but finally friends pulled him out. I remember Bone, who was the smallest, standing there shaking beside me as we watched some of the others dive back in and search. After a while somebody called the police. They brought divers along but found nothing either, although I. J.'s hat was still spinning around right over where he went down.

"When the firemen showed up, they brought this big long thing, like a fisherman's net. I never want to see one of those things again. They kept dragging till they found him. I. J. was always dark-skinned, but he seemed much darker now—swallowed so much water, I guess. The pond had no bottom to it. It was a disaster area, the police said. They didn't want anyone coming there again. They put up a sign—NO SWIMMING—and we all returned to the bus. Everything was back in the baskets, but nobody ate. That was an outing I'll never forget.

"I can't forget the walkathon either, because my brother J. W. and I were the winners that year. They put it on at the Ice Palace, and you walked forty-five minutes, and after that, you rested for fifteen. You couldn't sleep then, somehow. Days would go by before you could really sleep. But when two weeks passed, that fifteen minutes felt like an eight-hour stretch. The time we beat I. J., the walkathon lasted ten weeks. Everyone had sponsors who would buy you shoes because you went through them so fast. We wore blouses and pants, and a number was printed on everyone's back. We had lots of sponsors since we were a brother-sister team, but people knew me anyway because in the beginning, during rest time, I used to dance in the show. There were musicians around day and night, and when they played the intermissions, different people danced out on the floor and made the people shout.

"One time when T-Bone was playing he hollered, 'Marguerite Lott, leave your partner and do the mess-around!' So then I messed around. 'Do the pinetop,' he called then, and I did that, too. 'All right now,' he shouted, 'get *real* low-down!' My fingers and the top of my head went down to hit the floor, and when I started doing that, it looked like everything quieted down, although the place was jam-packed. Suddenly somebody called out to me, 'Up!' T-Bone was so tickled he nearly fell off his stool, because that was my mother. I could never have guessed she'd be there, but T-Bone had seen her and figured he'd get his own back for once.

"'Why didn't you tell me she was there?' I asked him later. 'You know good and well how she's gonna do me now!' Well, she whipped me, but it didn't stop me from dancing, because we danced at home till our feet fell off, though no more snakehips, I guess.

"The last marathon I danced, I'd already left school and could get paid each day and night. My mother had passed, but my father came down with me, and with all the sponsors I had, some nights I picked up pretty near two hundred dollars. There was always a doctor and a nurse on hand, and the announcer was Joey Preston, who worked wrestling matches and fights. He wore a white tuxedo and was so handsome it made me want to win real bad. Twenty couples would start off, and it went on till the couple before last fell out. Whoever was left standing was the winner. We used to win, J. W. and I, but he didn't always do right. In his fifteen minutes, he'd sneak out for chock, and afterwards I would have to let him stand on *my* feet. I didn't want to fall out, so for forty-five minutes I'd hold him up. I thought I'd die."

"There were a lot of big-time dancers in those days," T-Bone observed. "I was on the same stage as Bill Robinson once. Real early on the program, but the act went over fine, though I was only fifteen. That was the biggest thrill I'd ever had in life.

"Pretty soon afterwards I ran away from home. I was a freshman in high school, but I'd fallen in love with a girl called Dorothy in the Ida Cox show.[1] Her dad played tuba in a band in San Antone. Because I followed her everywhere, in the end Miss Cox put us onstage together, dancing. Jesse Crump was married to Ida then, and he got me the job. They let me play banjo, too. But then the sheriff in Albany, Texas, made me go home. I'd gone to talk to him myself after an argument with Miss Cox. I said us kids in the show weren't being treated right. We were getting practically nothing. But Miss Cox had gotten there first.[2] I'd forgotten I'd quit school. They knew and made me turn around and go home.[3]

"Dorothy wasn't the first girl I'd been crazy about, so Mama didn't get on to me too bad." T-Bone smiled at M'Dear, and it was clear they were alike. "No, Mama's never let me down. I repaid her one time, though, and nearly got myself killed. See?" His hand went to his cheek and a scar that extended to his chin and then reappeared on his neck at the collarbone. "This happened in 1929, on Juneteenth, always a big day in Texas for blacks. Marco said it marked the date blacks were set free.

"The celebration was at the park, and I had a team in the Little League series, so we had a ball game going, and there was a picnic

1. Ida Cox was born in 1896 and died in 1967. She began recording in 1923 and made eighty-eight sides for Paramount over the next six years, often accompanied by outstanding instrumentalists. She was touring with her own show when T-Bone appeared with the company.

2. "I liked Ida fine, though," T-Bone said later. "She wasn't the only one that did people like that. A whole lot did the same. And still do."

3. T-Bone had worked briefly around that time for another well-known blues singer of this era, Ma Rainey. He was hired to perform with her show when it appeared for three days at the Coliseum in Houston.

besides. You know how talk starts. Somehow Mama heard a woman intended to pick a fight with my aunt, claiming she was going steady with someone else's man. Aunty weighed no more than ninety pounds, so Mama was alert. When we finished our game, we walked up to the clubhouse for some fun just about the time Mama showed up. I didn't know, because I was fooling at the piano and had my back turned, but I heard a fight start. I jumped up from the stool, and there they were. I tried to separate them, but this woman had a razor and had already cut Mama's face. That made Mama so mad she slashed back with a knife she'd got into her hand. I barged in between, trying to break it up. First I got hit in the arm, and then they were fighting over my head. When I came up, I got the razor in my face, and it stopped a half inch from my jugular vein. Mama was cut, too, and you can still see the scar. 'Aren't some people lucky!' the doctor said when the ambulance came.

"For a good while after that I mostly stayed around home. I was playing gigs with our high school band like I'd been doing ever since grade school. The bunch of us had come out of Booker T., but I didn't finish, although the others did. I could always make money and figured there wasn't time enough for school. Lawson Brooks was our leader and played saxophone. We had sixteen pieces, and I played banjo to be heard. We didn't have mikes back then, and acoustic guitar got drowned. When I sang, I stood up front and used a megaphone. After a time a Jewish fellow called Hymie got us a job at the Tip Top on Central Avenue. He told us he owned us and said we sounded good, so we came to look on the place as our home.

"Some of the guys, like T. W. Pratt and Mike Lacy, could arrange, and we even got up enough nerve to try some of Ellington's stuff. We rehearsed three times a week and played almost every night. Later on Hymie fell out with Lawson and tried to get Nat 'King' Cole to take over. After a while I left, and Charlie Christian took my place for a time, and they got Buddy Tate out of Sherman to come in on tenor. I was sorry to leave, but there was always work to be had, and I liked being free. Anyway, Mama was alone again now. It was only her and me, and so I didn't want to go out on the road.

Later it was different, when Lemuel Randall came around and she
married again.[4]

"In those days I was kind of wild. If there was going to be a celebration, I would hock my guitar and buy chock. We drank a lot of
that stuff, and it burned your insides right out. Later if I had a gig
to play, I'd go by Margy's house and look for her dad. When he got
through cussing me out, he'd go to the pawn shop with me. 'I know
damn well why you hocked it,' he'd grumble. 'You gotta quit gambling, you boys.' He was wasting his breath, because it was his sons
I was hanging out with. Patty Jack can tell you. We'd shoot craps all
night. I'd travel all over town for a game, I was always crazy to
gamble. Well, that's how I *used* to be," he corrected himself, smiling mischievously at Vi, who was entering the room. "Anyway, I
did quit after a while, but at that time I'd be going out to the golf
club to caddy. As a kid I was always trying to make it with the
older fellows out there. They'd get some terrific games going, and
whoever wasn't caddying would be back there shooting dice. I didn't
really have an in though, until Cab Calloway had me out with his
show. It was that did the trick.

"When Cab came through Dallas and played the Majestic Theater, I won first prize in the amateur show they put on. I couldn't
believe my luck, because part of the deal was a week's work with
the band. When he carried me to Houston, Cab let me have a whole
bit to myself. By then I'd worked up an act, like playing the banjo
while I went down in the splits. Sometimes Cab even let me do one
of his numbers—'Minnie the Moocher,' I guess. I suppose I got a
little fame from that, because this fellow from Columbia Records
showed up in town and approached me. I knew nothing about making a record, but he had me go into this room where there was a
piano with Douglas Fernell sitting at it. I played two original
things, and believe it or not, that's a record I never owned, never
even heard till this year. Robert the Hippy says it's worth money
now. The label says Oak Cliff T-Bone. I guess they figured that was
OK, since I was living there. I named my blues 'Trinity River,' and
the other I called 'Wichita Falls.'

4. After Movelia Walker married, the family knew Lemuel Randall as Uncle Dink.

"For a while after that I was at home again, going out to the golf club regularly because I picked up quite a few gigs there. A lot of the members had plenty of money to spend. If they wanted to party in another town, they'd hire a train for their guests and get me and a few other guys to entertain and play the party as well. It was still Prohibition, but those people always had plenty to drink, and it was the first time we found out what real whiskey was like.

"I met Count Biloxi at the club because I was caddying for him. After a couple of days he suggested I go with him as part of his act. I don't know how long he had been over, but he was a White Russian who was fronting a band out of Hollywood that used to tour the Southwest. He wasn't a musician, but he had a gimmick, like Ted Lewis. And I was his shadow, I guess. They mostly played top spots, and the pay was good. But one thing bothered me: I was the only colored guy in the band. Everything would have been all right except for what happened on the girl singer's account. She was regular and treated me just like the rest, but you could tell the audience didn't go for that. One time when we were playing Blossom Heath in Oklahoma City, some roughnecks came backstage. We were in the dressing room, she and I, just kiddin' around. Suddenly things got scary, so two of the musicians went down the fire exit with me, and we managed to call a cab. I was supposed to lie low, but instead I lit out for Kansas City, where I figured I had good friends and should be OK."

"Friends that would party day and night, spend your money, and leave you sick as a dog," M'Dear said sharply. "You were nicely messed up. I had to borrow where I worked to get train fare to bring you home. And when you stepped down from that car, we carried you to hospital straightway."

"Yeah, that's right," T-Bone pulled a face. "That was the first time, maybe, but it sure wasn't the last. I'll bet I've stretched out in bed in whatever city you want to name. Ulcers sure drag you down. Seymour knows all about it," he said, smiling. Turning to me, he asked, "Why don't you ride back to San Diego with him and Margy tonight?"

Three

Freight Train Blues

Photograph by the author

"My wife Margy has been knowing T-Bone longer'n me," Clarence
Seymour said. "That's because I went to school in northern Dallas,
where I was born, and he went to Hardee. But T-Bone used to fool
around up our way, too, and I met him when I was about fifteen and
he was a couple of years older, I guess. Patty Jack and J. W. used to
be with him, and that's how I met them before Margy.

"But one day J. W. was so drunk that me and my gang had to carry
him home. We were standing around on the sidewalk outside the
Lotts' house when he just slid down and was out cold. Chuffie
Hans, one of the fellows in my little bunch, started going through
his pockets. Chuffie could sing like Louis Armstrong. Satchmo
even let him trade verses with him sometimes when he happened
to be playing the North Dallas Club, on top of Smith Brothers'
drugstore across from the State Theater. Chuffie was a guy who
never let anything bother him, and since he didn't know J. W. was a
good friend of mine, he was patting him over.

"Right then Marguerite came down the steps looking for her
brother. She gave Chuffie such a stare that he moved to one side,
and she went over to J. W. and slapped him upside his face two or
three times. 'Come along, boy, get up from there,' she said, and
right away we laughed.

"'Wow! Your ol' lady done caught up with you,' we said.

"'He's my brother, fool,' Margy said, and her eyes lit on me. Afterwards I found out that J. W. wasn't the only one that she would do
that way. If T-Bone would be with him and likewise drunk, she
would slap them both. They'd open their eyes and say, 'Oh, Margy!'
because they knew no one else would come and get them like that.

"But her uncle was the one I used to hang out with most. His
name was Black Cat, and he was a good cardsharp and gambler. He
was a slick black man, tall and dark, with nice ways but a nasty
mouth. I was younger than he, but I liked the life and had the temperament for it. I didn't have the need, because my family was back
of me. To me it was kicks, but my folks disliked all kinds of fast
living, and it was a great big no-no to them, so I had to hide my
ways. I enjoyed Black Cat, though, and if you kept him off the whiskey, everything was all right. When he drank too much, everything

came apart. He was a terrific con man. He could sell anything at all. I swear one time he sold Dallas City Hall to a sucker and got a down payment in cash. Several thousand dollars!

"He could carry three or four pair of dice in one hand and switch them whenever he got ready. I never was a dice shooter, but I liked to carry the money and loan or give out. I did that for Bone, too. I'd be in on the game and know what was happening, and that way I could keep some of the weight off him. See, if he were in a game with three or four guys, they could be putting loaded dice on him. Or if it was a card game, they might be manipulating the cards, dealing from the bottom or slipping one out some other way. A guy like Bone would be watching usually, but a gambler would sometimes use psychology to distract attention, and the minute you were thrown off, he would be doing his thing!

"Bone loved to shoot dice, and he was pretty good at it. It's not only luck. You have to know what you're doing. Then there's the fact somebody may have had the dice made. In Vegas they use good square dice, and they're precision made. You can't hit over three or four times on good dice. But some guys get real proficient. Like Black Cat could bump the wall and control them. He'd take the dice in his hand, bounce them up against the wall, and make them come out right. Both would hit the wall at the same time and same way they hit, that's how they came back out. He could make anything he wanted, anytime he got ready.

"Then guys have their own games they like to play. Like you have thrown a four—three and one. So the fellows may say, 'Make four the hard way!'—meaning two deuces.

"Another guy will make a side bet by saying, 'Bet you'll make four—ace trey—before you make it two deuces!' You may take him up on that bet, although your point is ace trey. That's the bet you've got on the board with the people you're playing with, but the money may not mean as much as that side bet.

"You pick up the dice to shoot, and some other guy may say, 'I think he's gonna make it,' and his friend will tell him, 'That's a bet!' Then they've got something going, too. And if you say, 'I bet I do!' It begins to get complicated and you may need protection. If you've got four or five different bets on the table at one time, it's hard to decide where you're going. So if it should be T-Bone, he'll maybe tell me, 'Keep up with this for me.'

"I'll say: 'OK, all good bets come over here! $6 to you? $20 for you? And $50 to you? OK. Don't worry about it.' Then if Bone hits his point, he may have lost a packet, but a guy or two on the other side will have lost to him, too. It may even out.

"What happens is, you throw the dice till you fall off. You throw and get a point, say a six. Then you throw till you make that point again. And after that, if you throw a seven or an eleven, you can go again. You try to hit as many times as you can, but if a seven comes up before you've made your six, or whatever your point is, then you've fouled up and you've got to hand over the dice.

"But anytime you make your point, you're entitled to say, 'Let the money ride.' And if you throw a seven after that, you can say it again. Same thing if you throw an eleven. By this time the money may be getting big, and before you shoot for the next point, you might think of drawing some down. You should draw at least as much as you ventured in the first place. Say you started off with $20 and you won. You let it ride and that's $80. One more time. Now the party's $160. Unless everybody's got a lot of money and you think you know what you're doing, it's best to take the biggest slice out, say the $100, and then you might let the $60 ride. Because they have to meet you every time, even if they have to get together to cover your pot.

"If they don't want to cover you, you can withdraw all your money and say, 'All right, I'll throw for $20.' But you hope they'll come back with, 'Aw, that's too high.' Or maybe another man will tell you, 'Pass the dice!' Somebody will grab hold of them, saying, 'Give him another set of dice.'

"They're figuring somethin's out of line with the dice you are using. You may have dropped one of your own in there. So the dice get checked out. Sometimes you can tell by the feel or by the way the spot lies. They can do a lot of crazy things to a good pair of dice—they might be one-thousandth of an inch off. A rough hand would never feel it, but a good, supple hand—a fellow with a hand like that, when he picks them up he can *feel*.

"If you've been winning a long time, one thing you do—you give to the different players to keep them from being broke. If a few guys have been losing, you maybe say, 'Hey, let's all go out to breakfast, and this is on me.' First place, you don't want *all* the money. Afterwards I see you, and I say, 'Aw, man, here's $50.' And to another fellow I give something as well, so he has something to wake up to. With that $50 the first guy may go somewhere else and make money. It's a code of ethics. You just don't wipe a guy out and leave him clean.

"T-Bone liked to play cotch, which is strictly a Negro game. It's not complicated. It's psychology, really. All the time you're trying to figure out what the other guy has got, and if you think you know, you say, 'Cotch, dick and bet.' Patty plays it. He's a good gambler and knows how to dicker. Patty, T-Bone, and J. W. used to have gambling sessions at the golf course as well. And they'd make money, though they'd only be shooting a dime at a time. There were guys out there who could shoot a thousand hits if it was for a dime. But the minute you said, 'Let it ride up to a dollar,' they'd get nervous and couldn't hit. Betting a dime, they could shoot all day long.

"After a while it got so I used to hang out with Bone a good deal, but somehow I never saw Margy again. Not till one time when we were all hanging around the tracks on Central and Elm because T-Bone was working there with Lawson Brooks' band upstairs at the Tip Top. Elm Street was the dividing line between north and south Dallas, and there was an area there where the old train station used to be, but afterwards no buildings were left. Instead, all the buildings were on the righthand side of the tracks, going south. So that big vacant lot was where all the blues singers, guitar players, and con men would work. Farther down were the Palace and Elm picture houses. Across the street was the Tip Top, and this time when I saw her, Margy had just got through there, waiting tables. When I spotted her, she was leaving the place, on her way home, I guess, and she looked *foxy*—About a hundred and fifteen pounds, and fine, big gams.

"I don't know what came over me, but I crossed the street and told her, 'I'm gonna get you, little girl, if it's the last thing I do.' The way it turned out, she had terrific influence over me. It looked like I'd do things for her I wouldn't do for anybody else. Because at that time in Dallas, I was an uptown slicker who liked to get away with murder. But she could pretty near make a sucker out of me. Like the night this girl was on her way out to my place, carrying money for me. She was wearing a beautiful fur coat and was fixing to stay the night. But Marguerite was there in the bedroom with me. Not doing right, either. She was only kidding around. Yet I had to leave that girl sitting outside my place in the cold. She'd let her cab go back, and where we were, the streetcars had stopped running, and she was going to have to wait till they started up the next day." Seymour looked over at Margy to see if she was keeping a straight face. "It wasn't funny. She was half frozen," he informed her.

"I told you then, 'Let her come in,'" Marguerite said, and by now she was smiling. "*I* wasn't going out in the snow, so I said, 'Call her in, and *you* can sleep in the middle!' But if I'd been in her shoes, I'd have kicked the door down!"

"Margy had me tied in knots," Seymour continued. "So after a while I left town. I went first to St. Louis and then on to New York. There I got into trouble and couldn't stay. Back in St. Louis, I couldn't get her off my mind. I figured I'd better go back home and check up. When I got there, I couldn't find her till Black Cat let me know where she was.

"'I'm on the run,' I told her when we got back together. 'I'm going to California for keeps.' She was game. All she said was, 'OK.' So I gave her my money and sent her on ahead. Then I hopped a freight and followed her to L.A., where T-Bone had already gone in 1936.

"'Man, why don't you quit fooling around?' T-Bone asked when I arrived at his place. 'Go on and marry Black Gal! Ain't that what you want?' I was surprised. Didn't he figure I might panic? After the solo life I'd led? But in the end that's just what happened, after my freight ride into town.

"When you're riding the freights, you spend quite a bit of your time sleeping. Up on top of the cars, not tied or nothing. You gradually adjust to what's happening. First time I saw the Grand Canyon I was traveling like that. In the beginning, when the car moves you're scared of toppling over, but after a while you don't give it much thought. But sometimes you run into trouble, like we did on one trip, another boy and me.

"We'd been going a little better than a day when something alerted one of those railroad dicks who walk the train, and he decided to shake the train down. When they stopped a little farther down the line and told everyone to get out, we weren't aboard. We'd hopped off earlier, and I'd got away and holed up under a lady's house—along with her dog. She had this big ol' bad dog, but he didn't do nothing, so I stayed under there with him. I was hungry, and because it was cold, I came out early next morning hoping to catch another train and make up for lost time.

"I had a lot of money on me, so I tried to buy some food from the lady. But she wouldn't give it to me, because I'd been up under her house and she hadn't known I was there. So I asked her nicely again if she wouldn't go back in the kitchen for something. She came out with some cabbage so sour you could *hear* it bubbling—swish, swish, swish. But that was the *greatest* cabbage! I ate it and never got sick. I was in need, you see.

"When those railroad guards walk the top looking for you, you get down inside a 'reefer.' That's the refrigerator car, where they put the produce. On a car like that, there's a part that raises so that when all the stuff aboard is unloaded, it can be opened and aired out. Well, when you climb down onto the reefer, if you don't know what to do, the guard can close the top on you and you can smother to death in there, because it's airtight. So you take a spike with you and jam it so that whatever he does on top, it won't go down, and neither will it go back up—or only if you remove the spike. A lot of times he guesses what has happened, but it's a moving train, and he's got to worry about his movements, too. Still, once you get able to walk on top, you can end up running just as easy as on the sidewalk. Your equilibrium adjusts, and you learn to jump from car to car. That's about as far as taking a good long step. And you never look down. If you look down and see the ground moving that far away, then you fall.

"The reason I know is because of what happened sometime before to a bunch of us while we were still kind of young—Budd and

Keg Johnson and two other guys besides me.[1] When it comes to boarding, the guys that can run fastest catch the train last, because if you can't hop on trains good, you get on first while it's still going slow. You got to know what you're doing when it picks up speed, or you'll go under.

"So Budd and this guy Moore get on at one end of the train, and Slick Hart, Keg, and I board the other end. We are all going to one car in front where it's open and we can be on the inside, and we're all going across the top. There's a ring at the end of each car you can catch onto when you need to climb. So when Moore reached that far, he was going to grab hold of this ring, put his foot on the coupling, and then go up. But it had been raining, and when he stepped out, his foot slipped. Now, he's hanging!

"We see him and start running, Slick and I. Though we got to him and grabbed him as he went down, what was left of his foot was hanging there from the top of his shoe, but he'd have been cut up total if we hadn't got there when we did. Slick was bigger than me, so he gripped him by the pants. I got the opposite leg, and by then Moore had got his hands on top.

"It happened the brakeman had seen it. You know how they sit in the caboose and look out. First thing, he pulled the cord for the train to stop, and then he came after us over the top. So when the train slowed right down, we all got onto the ground and tied up Moore's leg.

"When we reached the next town, the cops were waiting, and they carried Moore to the hospital and telephoned home. Our folks got real excited, because we were only fifteen. My mother wanted to drive up, but the cops weren't going to let us off that easy. They aimed to discourage us, I guess. But I must have been immune, because that wasn't the last time. The last time was when I came out here to join Margy, and got hitched up for good."[2]

1. Texans Budd and Keg Johnson later won fame on tenor sax and trombone, respectively, in bands such as those of Earl Hines and Fletcher Henderson.
2. Clarence Seymour died on September 13, 1985.

Four

Married Man

"It was in the cards," T-Bone told me. "Seymour and Margy, they were well matched, and both were crazy at times."

"Black Cat was crazier, though," Patty observed. "Remember he used to take us round to see Percy, who kept whiskey in the bathtub? You'd go in there and drink whiskey from a gourd he'd bring out. And if the police raided the joint, he'd step inside and pull the plug to let the whiskey run away."

"Many's the whiskey I downed like that." T-Bone grinned. "We were too cheap to buy by the drink," he explained. "Percy's whiskey sold for $1.25 a half gallon, and we went in and helped ourselves. Remember the time I went with Skinner to some lady's house and the gang tagged along? There we were, drinking her whiskey, and after a while everybody excused themselves and went out the back. I didn't notice, and nobody said anything to me. They might have been headed for the can, I suppose. But all the time they were going through the door and climbing the fence. When I finally started to wonder, there wasn't a soul left to take care of that bill but me!

"Shall we let Vi in on something?" T-Bone suggested. "Tell her about ol' lady Coulson? Remember, she lived out in the woods a little ways past the Blue Hole?"

"Where we would dive off that railroad trestle, stark naked, into water seventy feet deep?"

"Yeah, but before that. We were kids and playing in the woods when somebody thought of that ol' lady's chock. We were sitting on the ground, backs against those trees, fire burning good, and nothing to drink! No money, and not old enough in any case. We decided to go to Mrs. Coulson, but we plotted the thing first.

"'That ol' lady's got some good chock,' we told each other. 'How we gonna get it?'"

Patty hitched forward in his chair. "Yeah, we had to think something up. But it was mean, what we did. We went along to the house to where she had the still out in back and told her the revenue men were headed her way. We'd overheard them talking in town."

"In no time," T-Bone continued, "we were in charge of that crock. It was heavy, and we only just made it back to the woods. There we

36

were, hunched over it like Indians, leaves banked for camouflage, and the police miles away."

"We just sat and drank that up. Poor old lady! And she trying to make a living selling home brew. She had to make a living some-how," Patty concluded, "because that daughter of hers was the ugli-est in the world. I've been everywhere, and you couldn't find worse. You'd let her keel over dead before you'd give her a drink. And big as a bull, like Buster Lloyd, eh, Bone?"

"Uh-huh. Then there was the guy with a brother called Coot, who used to take snuff. Coot was a gambling man, and when some-one made a point, he'd blow snuff in his face. There in the alley he kept a billy goat by his side while he sold us his chock."

"The stuff that made everyone sick?"

"He'd put tobacco in it," T-Bone nodded, "a big slab. We'd be drinking and drinking, not knowing what made us high as a kite. I pretty near killed him when I found out."

"How come I married you?" Vi said, shaking her head before going back to the kitchen, where she had a pan of greens on the stove. "Our meal's not ready," she told me. "I could come talk if you like. How I met T-Bone years back.

"In my family seven of us were girls. We were living in Waxa-hachie, forty miles southeast of Fort Worth. All of my sisters were older, and they'd married and left home by the time my mother passed, but Emma had stayed back to take care of me. I was the baby, and spoiled. They had all fussed over me, especially Mattie, because she and I have been close all our lives. She lives with Rob-ert, just four doors down from us now. That's how come T-Bone settled on West Forty-third Place.

"Mattie and Robert were in Fort Worth in 1934 and hadn't been married very long. Mattie had a job waiting table at the Gem Hotel, where they lived. T-Bone stayed there, too, because he was with a small band that played every night and was a featured attraction. Every so often he'd stand out on the floor and go into his act. I was so young Mattie hardly thought to watch me, but I'd have had to be blind not to see how women shined up to this man. My sister frowned on that, and I never brought up his name.

"The following year, when I'd graduated, Mattie persuaded Emma to let me come to Fort Worth. She'd put aside money for me to learn a trade. I could have been a beautician, I guess. Mattie'd come up the hard way, and she didn't want that for me.

"So I stayed with her, and T-Bone began singling me out. I wanted to tell her I liked him, but right from the start Mattie's mind was made up. T-Bone would stop by and say, 'Hey, Mattie, I want to ask you about your little sister.'

"'No, T-Bone. Just let her alone,' Mattie would answer. 'She's too young for you. Go on along.'

"'Can't we play cards one day?' T-Bone would say. Seeing my face, Mattie would hesitate and then hedge.

"'You can play cards with her one day, but *I'll* be around.'

"T-Bone kept coming, and we still played cards even when she wasn't there. I was thrilled, but nervous, I guess. Then he started taking me to the picture show. When we got away with that, he came more often. He was very good looking, you know, and I was scared every date was the last."

Vi got to her feet and crossed the hall to her room. "Come see his photograph and see how he looked then," she called out. "With his hair straightened and slicked right back. The look in his eyes says watch out. He wasn't heavy or anything, and since I was small myself, we paired up just right. He was a real sharp dresser and looked great in his act. His dancing, even the splits, came off easy because he was that strong.

"We hadn't been going together very long before he went overboard one night. 'Let's get married!' he said. Right then I was scared he'd run out the door. And I was worried about Mattie. We needed money to buy a ring, so I lent it, but it was hers. If I'd waited, you know, I'd have lost out right there. He felt that uncertain about marriage. But I was 100 percent about him, and that saw us through.

"After we got our certificates, we looked for a justice of the peace, and when we needed a witness, T-Bone sent for his saxophone man. Once we were married, there was just money enough left for us to ride home in a cab.

"Back at the hotel I started worrying about Mattie's money that had been saved for my schooling. Still, it was me leaving her she'd mind most. I prayed she might come around when I told her how happy we were. There was a party for us that night, and I forgot to be frightened till I walked in and saw the long table all set with JUST MARRIED on it. Then I was scared. I knew I should have talked to Mattie first. I knew someone else would have let the cat out of the bag.

"It was Mrs. Cooper who told her. She and her husband owned the Gem and cared about Mattie because she'd been there a good while. 'Have it annulled,' Mrs. Cooper advised. 'She's still a baby and you have your rights.' At that Mattie couldn't stop crying, and Robert was in a fit trying to get her to quit. After a while he persuaded her to show up downstairs. Right then we were having fun at the table, but soon as I saw her poor face, my tears started to roll.

"'Why, baby?' she kept saying. She couldn't understand, no matter how I tried to explain. But finally things got better when we said we'd stay with them later in the bigger apartment Robert promised to find.

"After T-Bone had finished his engagement, the Coopers let him keep his room for a time so I could stay while he was on the road. It was exciting being on my own for the first time in my life, and when he got back, we went to Dallas for me to meet M'Dear.

"'Let me see your license,' she told T-Bone as soon as we walked in. I reached in my bag and handed it over, and she looked at it and smiled. We've been close ever since.

"When we got back to Fort Worth, T-Bone left for the road again, and I suddenly came down with a rash and was feeling real bad. One of the waitresses got alarmed and called a doctor in. Mattie came too, worried to death.

"'I'm sorry,' the doctor told her, 'but it's scarlet fever she's got. Don't move her, she's got it bad.' Mattie couldn't bide by that. She brought Robert to the hotel, and wrapping me in a blanket, they carried me out to the car. My head was so fuzzy I didn't know what was going on. Otherwise I'd have told her T-Bone would be mad when he got back. He was, too.

'You were wrong,' he told Mattie later, 'spiriting my wife away like that.' I'd never seen him so put out. 'But we ain't gonna break up that easy,' he said. 'You wait and see.' He stayed beside me, holding my hand that night, but next day he had to leave to go back out on the road. Each night he would call, and later M'Dear came to see me, riding the bus in from Dallas. Though Mattie agreed that was nice, her mind was made up. She took the fever for a sign.

" 'T-Bone's fine, but not right for you,' she said. 'Not the marrying kind.' She started me thinking I was holding him back. She even got to him and unsettled his mind, too. So after a time he stopped visiting and got his own place in town." Vi was silent a moment. "Then I knew what to do. I couldn't lose my husband like that! He wasn't home when I located his room, but his landlady let me in. Finally I heard his step on the stairs, and I held my breath when he opened the door.

" 'So my baby's home,' he said. I knew right then we'd remain together no matter what anyone said."

THE *New* "CLUB ALABAM"

TWO BANDS

42nd AND CENTRAL, - LOS ANGELES CALIF.

Five

Little Harlem

It was hard for me to get T-Bone away by himself. Company amused him, and people came and went all the time. Vi had left him a lot of ground to cover. To fill in the gaps, T-Bone needed to backtrack five years to the time his son Aaron, Jr., was born while he and his girlfriend were still in school. When her time came, her folks were mad, and she ended up taking Junior to Shreveport to live. M'Dear was angry almost a year, then she dropped the subject, and T-Bone, still in his teens, was once again happy-go-lucky and broke more often than not.

When he married, he was afraid that everything would have to change. But if Vi stayed at the house, he thought, they might do all right. She and his mother hit it off from the start. So Vi did not make it hard on him—she wasn't like that. Nothing was so different, though they needed more money, of course. He thought he would have to work harder, that was all. But if his health held up, it would be OK to play gigs around home and still have a ball. He could go out of town as well.

In places like Sherman and Wichita Falls, four of them—a pianist, drummer, a horn player, and himself—could work three-day weekends and have forty-five or fifty dollars to split. They had a chance to blow, and when he went into his act, a lot of customers tossed change his way. Other weeks he worked the sawmill towns as a single, showing up in juke joints where local talent hogged the piano bench and hammered out an accompaniment on battered keys. If things got too noisy, his feet took over. The dance routines got as good a hand and were safer, because sometimes a good blues meant a fight would break out. Whoever was back of the bar would dim the lights and close up, shoving everyone outside. He didn't care. If he had made enough in tips, he would go somewhere and shoot dice.

"In a lot of those games the dice were loaded," he recalled. "But I never turned a game down, and in some towns fellows would be waiting for me to show up. I found that out when I was touring with Bee Kelly, because I was headlining his show. This break meant more to me than a whole lot of stuff that came later. We started out in Corpus Christi, going from club to club. We picked up so good, Kelly got to book us out on the road. He was a funny guy and did comedy bits. I was head dancer and the blues guitar man. Believe it or not, I was making a name as a dancer. Guys came into bars where I was working to steal my stuff. In the show I'd be playing and singing and then have to jump up right away because someone had called for me to dance.[1]

"It was a lot of fun, and Vi said don't worry. Mama had a place, and it was our home, too. I didn't have to fuss about Junior even, because after a while he was there in the house with us. It looked like his mother couldn't make it, so after a time M'Dear said her piece. He was eight years old, and she was his grandmother, see. So after Vi and I were married, he moved in, too.

"But finally I got to thinking. I wasn't making enough bread, and there was no sense kidding myself. So that's how I got things off the ground. If I hadn't needed the money, I'd have never gone to L.A. I'd have been fooling around still.

"What was that company ferried automobiles—was it Munch? In 1936 they were going to relocate in L.A., and there was a fleet of cars to be moved. I went in when they were looking for drivers, and they took me on. That's how I came to the West Coast. Whoever was driving never got paid but got a free ride. There was a whole bunch of fellows, although I didn't know any of them, and we each drove a car and towed one in back. I had a dollar in my pocket when I landed in L.A.! Now you can see why Vi had had to stay back.

"Wait a minute," T-Bone interrupted himself to bang on the front window, beckoning to a friend in the street. "I'm going to get hold of Phace Roberts. We worked together back then." He opened the door, ushering Roberts in.[2] "I was just fixing to tell about Little

1. Walker's claim to fame as a dancer was confirmed by blues man Tom Courtney in *Living Blues*, No. 20 (March, 1975): "I learned to dance from the head dancer in Bee Kelly's show—T-Bone Walker. I used to slip into bars and see T-Bone when I was younger, back in Waco. He was the best dancer around, and known all over Texas. Through most of the forties I stayed around Lubbock and worked in the honkies with T-Bone and others. He and I would play a while, and then we'd dance. Later I told him how, when I was little, I stole all his steps. He said, 'I knew you was doin' it!' Afterwards we were at a place in Lubbock called the Greasy Spoon which he opened up at 10:00 P.M. and didn't close till the next day."

2. In the 1930s Henry Roberts worked with a top-level dance act called the Three Rockets, which was especially popular on the West Coast, where it was based for a long time.

Harlem. You could do it better. You were in Los Angeles longer than me."

"Sure thing. Be glad to." Phace took a chair next to mine. "Well, you had mud streets in Watts back then," he said, "and the Brown sisters' place was out in a field. But Bone could be heard wailing before you made your way through the crowd. 'You're a dirty mistreater, Mama,' he'd be singing, 'but that's all right for you.'

"Us Rockets were working the Club Alabam then, and soon as our show was through, everyone in the place raced over to catch what Bone was laying down. Weekends you had a time getting near. Things were always jumping, and the chicks would be excited. You'd see them crossing the floor, climbing the bandstand, and handing Bone money. Fives and even tens! When he went into the splits, they'd kneel beside him, counting out their bills, putting them in his pockets or guitar! They'd call out requests and snap their fingers as they strutted on back to their seats. People went wild. We never let him quit till the wee, wee hours."

"It didn't start out like that," T-Bone said. "I had to break in, you understand. The day I arrived, I met a guy that took up with me. 'I'll take you around,' he said. And there at Little Harlem they didn't even know I played. Big Jim Wynn had some cats on the stand, and he had a good little band. Later he told me: 'I didn't need no more guys. I had Zutty Singleton on drums. He was a show in himself.'[3]

"Well, they told me to dance," T-Bone went on, "and that was fine by me. I needed the bread. And like I said, in the territory I did dance routines at times. If I couldn't be *heard.* So I danced, on the table and all. Later I grabbed the table corner in my mouth and whirled the thing around. This was a trick I'd learned that people went for every time. When the Brown sisters saw so much change roll onto the floor, I had me a job. And pretty soon Wynn let me play."

"At first you didn't have no guitar," Phace remarked.

3. New Orleans drummer Zutty Singleton gained a national reputation when he played with Louis Armstrong in the twenties. Jim Wynn, on baritone saxophone, headed the group that backed Walker later on.

"Because it didn't cut through like the banjo," T-Bone explained. "No amplification back then."

"You used to come up slow from the splits, hittin' the strings 'way up in the air, and Zutty swore each time you got through there'd be fifty dollars more in the kitty. And people lining up to lay out the cash! Wow!"

T-Bone glanced at him, amused. "I needed a stake for the game going on in back, remember?"

"How can I forget? But there in that dressing room I would leave the gambling to Bone," he said, turning to me. "Four- and five-hundred-dollar stakes—that was nothing, you know. I couldn't stretch out like Bone because his money was heavier than mine. And for a while there, he was on a winning streak. Sometimes on the way to work he would stop at a club and take up, or maybe drop, three hundred dollars in a single game. This was no kind of small stuff, like playing with the cats in the band. Those games featured big-time gamblers like Black Dot or Tricky. Nelson Crosswell, too. And Nelson would have furs he'd be selling as well."

"Rich Baker was another," T-Bone said. "Remember the racehorse bookie who hung out in that shack on Central Avenue?"

"Sure. Everyone went by there," Phace recalled, "because they had the big dice table and smaller ones, too. At times they'd all be crowded. Plus you'd have racehorse bookies, and then the money men. Bookies were the big thing in L.A. that year. Fellows would be shooting craps and placing bets, and when T-Bone wandered in, he would go straight to wherever the big money was. Like I say, sometimes he'd lose." Phace sighed. "We'd be wailing with him, but he'd stay cool. 'Tomorrow,' he'd say, and mean just that.

"If luck went with him in the dressing room that night, T-Bone would party. That meant everybody. Chicks would line up outside waiting for the Blues Balladeer." He grinned. "T-Bone pulled all the pretty girls. You could count on that, and it brought fellows into the club. But those Sweethearts of Rhythm were your favorites, huh?"

"They were my pets," T-Bone nodded, "and those chicks could

swing! I never playacted when they were out front. They always came by, wherever I was playing. Eddie Durham wrote their arrangements and traveled with them, remember? [4] He was hell on guitar, and he stayed with the Sweethearts a long time. They could blow, and he knew it."

"They stirred up Wynonie, too, don't forget," Phace glanced at T-Bone out of the corner of his eye.

"That crazy man!" said T-Bone, to Phace's satisfaction. Wynonie Harris was a dynamic blues singer whose popularity on the West Coast rivaled that of T-Bone's for a time. "Are you talking about the Alabam, on Central Avenue?"

"The Alabam, sure, or the Plantation. Any of those spots that made money featuring you and Wynonie in a 'battle of blues,'" Phace said. "And remember how he'd fool around backstage, turning the mike down if he thought you were grabbing the crowd?"

"Wynonie would do anything, don't care what," T-Bone replied. "And he had a bad mouth, too."

"I saw Durham awhile back, and we were talking about him," Phace said. "Eddie took Wynonie on the road, you know. 'You would never believe,' Eddie told me, 'how that guy carried on, but I had him brainwashed, like a preacher. I didn't drink, and he respected that. Nobody got along with him but me. And there were times he'd trick *me*, too. We'd hit the intro and there'd be no Wynonie. We'd hit again. He'd be out drinking somewhere. So maybe I'd get down off the stage and go out in the audience. He would be drinking in a bar across the street and would have heard the introduction, so here he comes, walking in at the front of the house. And right when they put the lights on him, he'd step out, snapping his fingers. The audience loved it, so it got to be an act. We just kept it in,' Eddie told me.

"When I got through laughing," Phace said, "Eddie told me about a club they were playing on Long Island where the lady had had a

4. Eddie Durham was the guitar player and trombonist in the Count Basie band thought to have pioneered the electric guitar as early as T-Bone himself. "T-Bone was the first I heard playing it," Durham said, "though I'd been fooling with it, too. But Bone was as big in blues as Charlie Christian was in jazz, the greatest I ever heard."

sign carrying Wynonie's name put up on the roof. He went down there one night when no one was about and, getting some paint, he changed it around. Instead of WYNONIE HARRIS, KING OF THE BLUES, it read, WYNONIE HARRIS, HOUSE OF BLUES AND BOOZE." This tickled T-Bone so much Phace had to break off for a moment.

"But listen," he went on, "the lady was so mad they got rid of Wynonie altogether, and still he would come in the bar, ordering whiskey, telling the bartender, 'This is *my* place, you know.'"

"He was crazy," T-Bone agreed. "You know he couldn't drive a car? He didn't have a license, not in any state at all. Because what he'd do was like one time in Ohio. He parked a car in a NO PARKING zone, right out on the boulevard in front of the theater. When a cop left a ticket, he walked out and, with everyone's eyes on him, tore it up and threw it in the street."

Phace laughed, and T-Bone picked up again. "That's not all. He got about twenty tickets like that before he left town! The management found him a chauffeur, but that made no difference. All over the country he got tickets like that. So he was barred from the wheel! That's what happened. Take my word."

"Eddie told me something else, but it had to be earlier, I guess," Phace remembered. "He said Wynonie liked to get him a couple of blondes to fill up his car. He'd set off downtown, maybe in Jersey or even in New York and pull up halfway along a one-way street, turn his car around the wrong way, get out and leave. He'd be long gone by time the police arrived, and the cop would explode.

"'Whose car is this? Wynonie Harris'? Oh, yeah!' And later Wynonie would plead, 'I get my publicity like that.'"

Phace shook his head. "But there's more. There was a bass player in the band, a big West Indian athlete named Chris who used to be a bouncer one time. When Wynonie got out of line, this cat was supposed to whip him. Wynonie *had* to be scared, because the guy was a giant. Wynonie would take out a date and get drunk, and Chris would go to his room and break down the door. He'd snatch him right out of bed! So help me! He'd pack up his clothes and run outside with him. That was his job. Eddie paid him extra. And what's more, it got to where Wynonie *liked* it. 'Let me get on my clothes,' he'd be saying, 'before this son of a bitch comes in here. I got a bodyguard, you know. Woman, get going!' When Chris arrived, he'd throw Wynonie in the car and drive off."

"He was one poor guy," T-Bone said.[5] "But he wasn't the only one knew how to hustle. How about the gig I played in L.A. where the bread wasn't right—short bread, man, remember? We had to make a little on the side. So what to do? It was a ballroom we were play-ing—no hard liquor allowed."

"So we smuggled them half-pints in!" Phace proclaimed. "It was summertime and we had no topcoats, so your guitar case was elected. The guard searched me, and I was clean. I watched him later scratching his head, trying to figure how the people got so happy off Coke and orange soda. I was over there on the bandstand, with my friends lined up behind. I had no more to do than just reach in Bone's case. I sure as hell was a popular cat that night."

"That was way back, still in the depression," T-Bone said. "Not as bad as in the East, maybe, but L.A. had felt it, too."

"How could I forget? In the club where we were working, we got seventy-five dollars for the week, and there were three in the act. Some of my pals worked projects for the WPA, and nobody was too big to call on Father Divine. 'Peace, it's wonderful!' That was God's truth. It was wonderful, man, because Father opened places in every city, you know. He kept a lot of folks from going hungry. Listen, if you had twenty-five cents you had yourself a meal. No questions asked. No smokes, no drinks, no cussing—those were the rules. 'Peace, brother, sit and eat.'"

T-Bone quit laughing when Phace gave him a look. "Maybe you didn't need it," he said. "I guess you could always get to your beans and rice with a few little bones on the side. But Father fed many a soul. He fed me more than once!"

---

5. Before he died in Los Angeles in 1969, Wynonie Harris had lost everything, including his home and his car.

Six

Marili

In the Central Avenue neighborhood T-Bone's popularity continued to grow. In three years, in and out of clubs like the Alabam and the Plantation, he had acquired a considerable following. The year 1940 brought a change, when Marili Morden (Marili Stuart at that time) set in motion a chain of events that owed much to the Jazz Man Record Shop, which Marili and her husband, Dave, had opened the previous year. The Jazz Man had established a reputation right away as a rendezvous for musicians and fans.[1]

"Some of these friends took me to see T-Bone at Little Harlem," Marili recalled. "Had this been in the twenties, it would have been a roadhouse, you know. A raffish-type building, tumbledown and tilted, and very dark out there at 114th Street and Central Avenue— quite as far out as you'd want to go in those days. Naturally the clientele was primarily black. I remember one occasion, though, when it was mixed, and with unpleasant results, because this was prehistoric times. Four or five whites were seated next to our group at a table bordering the floor, and they were men getting drunk. In addition to T-Bone, Little Harlem starred a girl called Little Bits. She was a belly dancer, with a barefoot act. When she appeared, these drunks got so excited they flung their drinks at her, out on the floor. When the glasses broke at her feet, things heated up. Jesse, the bouncer, came across right away and had them outside in minutes, but there were angry looks in our direction. We were not only shamed but scared we'd have to go. T-Bone shook his head, and the Brown sisters returned Jesse to his place at the door.

"T-Bone had the run of Little Harlem. He packed the place every night, and those wide little ol' ladies going in and out of a small office at the front knew what a gold mine they had. They themselves were legends. This club was new. The original had been their own quarters across the way, but after T-Bone came, their clientele had trebled and new premises were needed. T-Bone was the apple of

1. Stuart later transferred his interest to a Hollywood art gallery, and the partnership broke up. Marili subsequently married Nesuhi Ertegun, who later, with his brother, Ahmet, founded the Atlantic record company. T-Bone's Atlantic album, released much later, in 1955, featured an original composition he entitled "Blues for Marili."

their eye. They were very gracious, really, and in the end I got along
with them fine. But we tangled at first.

"I wasn't all that great at it, but I loved to dance. If I was invited
onto the floor by a good dancer, we'd have a fine time. My escorts
were usually musicians, and since it's hard to get them to dance, it
was OK. But after a time one of the sisters asked me to stop by her
office. 'You're very welcome here,' she said, 'but please—no mixed
dancing.'

"I gaped. Growing up in Oregon I was raised to think we lived in
a democracy. I really believed it! In Los Angeles my eyes were
opened a bit, but I hadn't run into anything like this before. 'My
God,' I thought, 'now I know how it feels.'

" 'Wait a minute,' I said, 'You don't like me?'

" 'That's not the case.' She shook her head.

" 'Then you feel I'm not good enough for your customers?'

"She didn't know what to reply, so she smiled, and nothing more
was said after that.

"Watching T-Bone, I began thinking how stupid it would be for
him to remain in Watts all his life. I hadn't expected to prefer the
electric guitar to acoustic, but the way T-Bone played was fantastic.
It was new to us all, and I was dumbfounded. The only thing I didn't
like was the show-biz bit when the guitar went back of his head.

" 'That's not necessary,' I told him.

" 'But it's my act,' he objected. The musicians had asked him
over, and he had pulled up a chair.

" 'When I worked in Texas, I used to pick up a table with my
teeth,' he added.

" 'Good God!' I shook my head. He needed direction, and I wondered if I couldn't start him off right.

" 'What if I could get you a job on the Strip?' I asked. 'You'd make
lots more money in Hollywood.'

"Naturally he was excited, and though the details aren't clear in
my mind, I think I got him an interview with someone at Music
Corporation of America. I've forgotten who. They figured on booking him into the Trocadero. 'Dandy,' I thought. 'Start at the top.' It
was what I had in mind.

"'I can just see it, yes,' the agent said. 'He comes out on the floor in overalls and a straw hat. Guitar on his back . . .'

"'Oh, no!' I interrupted, and T-Bone said I glared at the man. 'Nothing like that,' I told him. 'Handle this like any big-time act, like Calloway or Ethel Waters. Present him in tails. He'll deliver. Don't worry.' And he did, naturally. So this was a first for the Troc, and for a time it was the talk of the Strip. Great for every act that followed.

"Later I approached Billy Berg about the club on Vine Street. He didn't need much persuading. The place was rather small, but there was a balcony as well as the downstairs floor. Opening night was fine, but when I checked again at the end of the week, I saw what was happening. Fans from Little Harlem were being shunted upstairs.

"Down in Billy's office, I said, 'I'm sorry, but this is not it. You knew T-Bone had a following when you hired him. You have a chance now to make a lot of money. The word should go out that you're running your club right—everyone welcome. Something new for the West Side!'

"Well, he jammed the place, and they had to move to a new spot. Same policy, of course. This opened up Los Angeles. Occasionally a black single had done well, but never big business like that. I tried to set standards for T-Bone. He had eyes for show biz, but he couldn't help that, I guess. You don't cut loose from your background that easily. But he learned as the stars stopped by and name musicians came to listen. Because if T-Bone was a born showman, he was a born musician, too.

"Later, when he broke into records, that said it all. Till then the blues singers used mostly piano for accompaniment, or piano with guitar and drums. But T-Bone hired Bumps Myers, Jack Trainor, Teddy Buckner, Jack McVea, Al Killian, Lloyd Glenn—instrumentalists like that. He couldn't read well yet, but there was nothing wrong with his ear! And what they laid down was jazz. They were trailblazing, really, because the stuff that came later, that electric guitar, it all came from him.

"I only wish he'd been as smart about money." Marili shook her head. "I wanted him to lay some bucks to one side. But that wasn't

T-Bone. He was the partying kind. Worse, he would gamble. Prover-
bially, blues singers like women, and whiskey, too. Please believe,
T-Bone liked dice better than either! He couldn't hold onto money.
Week after week, it came and it went. He would stay up all night
and half through the day. Drinking some, too, I believe, although it
didn't show. But they told me he had ulcers real bad and shouldn't
have been drinking at all.

"'You'll never retire with your present life-style,' I told him next
time he came in to buy records. 'You want to get retired for good?'

"He smiled and, spreading his hand out on the counter, loosened
a diamond ring. 'Take this for me, and my watch, too,' he said.
'Hang on to them tight. There's a big game tonight.'

"T-Bone probably couldn't have been happy leading a circum-
scribed life. He attracted all kinds of people. Audiences went wild
over his performances, of course, but that was only part of it. Guys
were in his corner for a whole lot of reasons.

"He was a sport and a dresser with a trunk full of clothes. And
from the first car he owned, he'd drive a Caddy or Buick and nothin'
else. He loved spending. It went with feeling good. He'd buy rounds
of drinks all night, swapping stories, with everybody laughing at
his sharp wit. He hadn't height or weight, but rough company never
fazed him. There was always a chance he'd get hurt, but he was
safeguarded by his gang, which was really funny, because he had
more energy than the lot and was twice as cool.

"'Hey,' he told me, smiling, 'I'm the one keeps *them* out of
trouble.' I doubt he carried a knife or gun. He simply established a
reputation and could make it on any level. He didn't mind trouble
and got a kick out of it, I think. I remember a Saturday night at
Little Harlem when, as usual, we had a table near the stand. At
ringside a man and woman started to brawl. The minute they began
yelling everything quieted down. Bouncer Jesse walked over, but
not fast enough, because the woman grabbed a beer bottle as she
got to her feet. She smashed it on the table and into her partner's
face. Though all hell broke loose, we didn't see what happened, because Jesse gave us a couple of discreet shoves. We waited out the
action from underneath the table! T-Bone came on the stand grinning and sang better than ever that night.

"He wasn't bigheaded. It didn't get to him, the fuss people made. He was a great crowd pleaser, and I guess he saw nothing unnatural in that. But it was frustrating when there was business to discuss. He'd have friends to see, a date to keep, someone to call, a game up the street. Just maybe, maybe, his program allowed for a few hours' sleep.

"Thank God for rehearsals. That was a matter he was serious about. The guitar was the one thing made him forget everything else. I only saw him angry when someone he'd hired was playing the fool. 'Keep your mind on my business,' he'd snap.

"He never went into a recording studio unprepared, and he'd rather pay to rehearse, something you didn't often see then. When he was hiring, he was painstaking. He only called the best. He'd get a blues guy on piano sometimes, but always jazzmen for the band. They got equal footing with him and played turn and turn about.

" 'Well, we do better if everyone gets a chance to blow,' he told a surprised recording supervisor. Though it was primarily a blues-loving public that bought his records, T-Bone was the swingingest man on those dates. He never played better than in those early days back when."

Seven

Still in Love with You

On the streets back home in Dallas, the talk hinged on a local boy making good. "Ain't he sent for you *yet?*" wiseacres asked Vi. But he had, many times. He was tired of urging her to come.

"Long as you're gambling, we can't make it," she said. It was a no-win situation. He wanted M'Dear to persuade her, but when M'Dear married Lem Randall, Vi had thought it best to move. She had accepted an invitation from her brother and his wife to come to them instead.

"Junior was upset," she said, "but I saw him quite often. I was waitressing full-time because the depression was still on, and my hours at the Track were from 8 P.M. to 5 A.M. That was the best I could do for a while. Well, sometimes Junior would slip out from the house at night to see a picture show, and on the way back he'd stop at work asking for me. Unless I walked him home and let him get to bed while I visited M'Dear, he'd get a whipping for being out late.

"After my husband and I had been apart four years, he phoned to say Les Hite had hired him to go out on the road with the band.[1] So my brother and my sister Cleo, who lived in Dallas, too, got excited, because that was big-time, you know. The orchestra would be touring, and T-Bone wanted me to go along! But I didn't know anything about the road, and they were headed for New York. I was scared. This time I got a calling down from my family. They said my place was at my husband's side. 'If something goes wrong,' Cleo told me, 'call for the money, and we'll bring you on home.'

"Finally when I told T-Bone yes, he said, 'Phew!' and started to laugh. 'We just picked up again on the end of the line,' he said. 'This was the last time I was gonna ask!'

"The family helped me pack, and next day I was on the train to Nashville. Some of the boys in the band—Gene Fowler, Fred Tressler, and Floyd Tenor, I think—had brought their wives as well. So we traveled by car, because wives were not allowed to ride the bus.

1. For several years Les Hite led the band at Sebastian's Cotton Club in Los Angeles. It included such famous musicians as Lionel Hampton and trombonist Lawrence Brown and came to national prominence through its recordings with Louis Armstrong.

That was strictly for the fellows. We liked it better this way, driving to all the one-nighters, the whole way to New York.

"The Golden Gate Ballroom was our first engagement there, and the Apollo Theater came next. The band was in the East for the first time and was getting a name, so everyone was excited, and T-Bone went over great. Though he was booked to sing and not to play, his guitar was featured on "T-Bone Blues," and he sang duets as well with the girl singer in the band.

"All the time on the road he was backstage practicing and experimenting with the electric guitar. He had it in the dressing room, and it got so he could do just about what he liked with it. It was more exciting than when he played acoustic, and the sound was so new that people started talking.

"The pace in New York suited T-Bone just fine. Everywhere he went, he made friends, just like at home. He even got to make a record when Les Hite did "T-Bone Blues" with the band.[2] It was released in 1940 on the Varsity label, I think. There was only one thing—we didn't always get paid, and in Chicago on the return trip everything fell apart. The orchestra was to play Joe Louis' Hurricane Club, but Les Hite's girlfriend, Fluffy, who was managing the band, got into an argument with the club, and they tore the contract up. So we were laid off, and to keep everyone going, Fluffy was handing out twenty dollars a week. After paying for your room, there was nothing left for food. We were staying at the Ritz Hotel on South Parkway, so we tried sleeping all day and at night we went to a hamburger stand where T-Bone talked the man into letting us charge. We'd go round there and have pork-chop sandwiches, maybe, and sometimes squeezed out enough to go to a picture show.

"Then my husband knew a fellow who ran a beer joint and kept a little band working there, and because T-Bone walked in and jammed, the man fell in love with him.

"'Come in here and play, and I'll slip you something each night,'

---

2. He did not record again until 1942, when he made "Mean Old World" and "I Got a Break, Baby" with Freddie Slack's trio for Capitol.

he said. We'd walk over to the place together, three or four blocks, and it was winter, and cold. I had on a real pretty coat T-Bone got me in New York. That was one I never forgot—kelly green, and I had on white boots, a white cap over my ears, and a muff, so I did get to keep warm.[3] Then whenever T-Bone got through, the man stuck a ten-dollar bill in his shoe.

"After a while, I told my husband: 'I'm going to get a job. I can wait on table. I've been waiting table all my life.' There was a man T-Bone knew who looked so much like him they nicknamed him 'T-Bone's brother,' and this fellow had a girlfriend working in a restaurant nearby.

" 'I'll take you there,' he promised me. 'She might get you a job.' It was walking distance, and when he fetched me from the hotel, we were there right away. The boss was satisfied because I was tiny in those days and could wear a uniform he already had. So he hired me straight off.

" 'Start tomorrow at eleven,' he said, and I was so elated. Getting a job in a city like Chicago! At least we would eat. I couldn't wait to tell T-Bone, but when I got back to the hotel, he was packing.

" 'What's the matter? We don't have to move,' I told him, 'because I've got a job!'

"He was sitting on top of my bags, trying to strap them up. When he'd finished, he said, 'Hurry! We're going back to L.A.'

"He'd telephoned the Brown sisters and offered to return to Little Harlem, so they'd sent him the fare. They must have wired the money, because he had the tickets in his pocket. We jumped into one of those jitneys on the Parkway and got to the station in time for the bus to L.A. We were the only blacks, but we sat up near the driver and everything was okay. We were young and enjoyed the ride, and it didn't seem to take that long. When I got tired, we'd get down at the stops and maybe find something to eat.

"When we got to L.A., boy, there was a big surprise! Mattie and Robert waited on us at the depot! Mattie had got a job at Little Harlem, and the sisters had told her we were on our way. They were

3. Zutty Singleton recalled Vi Walker as that "real cute little dresser."

living at Standford Street and Twenty-third, so they loaded up our things, and we drove straight to their place.

" 'You have a home with us,' my sister said. Then we went out to Little Harlem. T-Bone had told them about me, showed them my picture and all. I was treated real nice, and I couldn't believe the way people crowded round my husband. He got to the bandstand, and oh, he played that night! He was so glad to be back.

"The Brown sisters found me a job, too. Next day I was at the door selling tickets. It was like a family thing, one of our happiest times ever," she said.

"T-Bone had no car, but there was a boy on hand who had. He was sweet on my niece Mildred, who stayed at Mattie's, too, and he visited her every night.[4] So till T-Bone got wheels, we rode to the club together.

"Then he was doing so good that the Plantation wanted him, and right away he was making a hundred dollars a week. In those days we thought that was the end! But it was a beginning instead. The new clientele was different, more white than black, I guess, and had more money to spend. T-Bone was now a star, and I had to share him with his fans.

" 'It's a living, that's all,' he said. 'You got to look at it that way.' He didn't want me to be jealous or anything like that. 'Too many women don't know how to handle themselves, so their marriage goes down the drain. You be smart,' he advised.

"What he taught me that year stayed in my mind, and I learned to recognize that there are people who like to make trouble. Best close your eyes, I decided. Your ears, too, at times.

"T-Bone loved me, like I did him. That was the thing everyone knew. I had no call to feel bad. Anytime the money was there, anything I wanted was mine."

4. Eventually settling in Chicago, Mildred married tenor saxophonist Gene Ammons. Boogie pianist Albert Ammons was his father. Gene composed the jazz classic "Red Top," which was inspired by his wife.

Eight

The Rhumboogie

T-Bone felt certain that 1942 would be a lively year. There is a sixth sense about these things that performers develop after a time. The break at the Trocadero had come as a complete surprise, but the tour with Les Hite he recognized as a sequel. Already crowds had followed him from the Plantation to the Club Alabam, and now he anticipated another step up. It happened early that year when Charlie Glenn reserved a table to catch the late show. Glenn operated Chicago's Rhumboogie Club at Fifty-fifth Street and Garfield Boulevard, known in the thirties as Dave's Place. Heavyweight champion Joe Louis was the club's major backer and accompanied Glenn in the constant search for new talent.

"Milly Monroe had let me know they'd be in," T-Bone told me. "She was a classy gal, a big fan of mine. When they came into the place, everybody looked over, because Joe Louis was boss man, you know."

The way T-Bone had things figured, it was now or never. He had to come on like gangbusters that night! In the wings he beat the tempo out loud and clear so the band would get it just right. When he came onto the floor playing "T-Bone Shuffle," he was met by a sustained wave of applause. With Johnny Otis on drums, the band swung out behind him. He went to "Jealous Woman" and then to "Mean Old World." The audience was clapping with the beat, urging him on. He saw Charlie Glenn nod when Milly called for "Stormy Monday Blues." After that he tried going off, singing "Sail On Boogie," but he was called back to encore again and again.

When he was free, Milly waved, and he crossed over, intent on shaking hands with Joe Louis, scarcely aware of Charlie Glenn.

"Here's a man we could hire," Joe Louis said.

"He means that," Glenn told him. "You can come work for us at the Rhumboogie anytime you say."

Within a month contracts had been delivered to Mattie Lee's house, where T-Bone and Vi were still staying, and soon afterward T-Bone was headed for Chicago and a full week of rehearsals. Ziggy Joe Johnson, who had a big reputation in the East, had been hired to produce a show on a lavish scale. Glenn hoped to establish the Rhumboogie as a big-league contender in a class with New York's

Cotton Club and the South Side's Grand Terrace. Too short of capital to hire an Ellington or a Hines, he intended to build, not buy. He was betting T-Bone would prove an effective attraction.

T-Bone wasn't troubled. He liked the challenge. He had been waiting for this chance—a setup with a choreographer, designer, stagehands, lighting men, lyricists, and prompters. And besides the second-line acts, there was an eye-catching line of kickers, and Johnson himself.

His sense of euphoria was complete when he sighted Milt Larkin on the premises, surrounded by a group of musicians T-Bone had worked with in the past. His mind went back to the amateur show at the Majestic in Houston at which he had been awarded first place and Larkin's Wheatley High School band had been runner-up.

"My lucky day!" T-Bone called out as Larkin hurried to embrace him.

"We're all getting the breaks this year," Larkin told him, exulting. "Let me bring you up to date, man, how things been going for us. You remember I had fine guys from the start. Cleanhead Vinson and Arnett Cobb were with us when we played with you, OK? Then Illinois Jacquet came in, and we pretty well stayed together after you left. We'd go out on the road three or four months at a time. Some of the spots I would book myself. One time we were in L.A., and we heard you with Floyd Ray, battling the blues with Wynonie. Illinois left us after that, joined Hampton and went east.[1] But we still had his brother Russell and Eddie Vinson, and we'd gotten Arnett Cobb back.[2] We had Wild Bill Davis as well. Cedric Haywood

1. Illinois Jacquet's tenor saxophone solo on "Flying Home," which he recorded with Lionel Hampton, attracted wide attention and became the model for a new school of big-toned, extrovert tenor-sax stylists. Russell Jacquet played trumpet in his brother's band and led a group of his own for a time in the Cotton Club in Los Angeles. An outstanding alto saxophonist, Eddie "Cleanhead" Vinson attained prominence when he was featured in Cootie Williams' orchestra, where he also made his debut as a blues singer. He has since traveled extensively with his own group and made many records.

2. Throughout much of his life Cobb suffered from ill health, and for a time, in his teens, he was not strong enough to travel with Larkin's band. Eventually he joined Lionel Hampton and remained with him for five years before forming a group of his own. Ill health forced him to stop in 1948, but in 1951 he again fronted a

was playing piano, so Bill was playing guitar.[3] Then we went out with Lil Green. Well, you know how it goes. You keep on, one thing and another, trying to elevate the attraction. After a month in Kansas City we came on here. We were booked in for two weeks, and we're here six months already!"

"Wonderful!" T-Bone told him. "You bet I'll wail with these cats behind me!" As Larkin walked over to the stand, Arnett Cobb stopped him. He had been appointed spokesman for the band.

"Are we tickled to see Bone!" he said. "He'll hear it when we get up there." A show band fills a secondary role as a rule. At times it lays out altogether when a star who prefers piano accompaniment comes on. Dance acts are more rewarding if they look for the musicians to swing out behind them, but few bands get a chance to star on their own. Maybe this time it would be different. Here the band would be part of T-Bone's act, and everyone had the same thought: this was the break they had been chasing. T-Bone would be swinging in the wings before ever he walked on, setting a tempo for them to groove on. The club might be on to something big.

"Boy, oh, boy!" Ziggy told Charlie Glenn when rehearsal came to a close. "We've landed a star, and we've got *music*. I'll open a spot in the show for the ensemble to be featured."

"I'll get a musical director," Glenn rejoined. "Let's try Marl Young."[4]

"The boss wants a hit show," Young told T-Bone, "you know, like Broadway. And Ziggy knows how to produce, but we don't have all that bread, for scenery and settings. Everything will hinge on the

group. In 1956 he was seriously injured in an automobile crash. Although having to rely on crutches, he made a remarkable and enduring comeback in the 1970s and 1980s, playing concerts throughout Europe as well as in the United States.

3. Wild Bill Davis was the first musician to bring the Hammond organ to prominence in jazz. An expert arranger, he was responsible for Count Basie's successful "April in Paris (One More Time)." During the 1970s he played with Duke Ellington's orchestra for a number of years. Cedric Haywood, a highly respected pianist and an accomplished arranger, never received the recognition he deserved.

4. Leaving Chicago later on, Marl Young, a brilliant all-around musician, made his name in Hollywood when he was hired to write music for television and films. Lucille Ball engaged him as musical director for the Desi Arnaz–Lucille Ball television series "I Love Lucy," a role he filled for fifteen years.

talent. The dance team's OK, because the Edwards Sisters have a
following, and we have some real good lookers in the line. You've
dug that, I know. You're not blind. So the rest is up to you."

Young planned to write three special-effects numbers for T-Bone
and to pace the music so it continued to build up behind him until
a finale was reached.

"He's a natural," he told Ziggy Joe.

"The boss is already figuring on a follow-up in the spring," the
producer replied.

The upcoming show caused so much talk on the street that the
dress rehearsal was like a preview. Ringside tables were crowded
with entertainers from other locations and with local big names.
The opening number featured the chorus in elaborate headdresses
and sequined tights. For T-Bone it was a walk-on part that introduced him to the crowd. The magnetism that was a part of his stage
presence made itself felt at once, and his smile brought correspond-
ing smiles all around. The early dance routines got a friendly reception, and when the Edwards Sisters came on, they reestablished a
hold on their fans. Then Milt Larkin and the band unleashed a performance that evoked a storm of applause.

As the coda faded, the sound of T-Bone's guitar vibrated in the
wings. He moved out on the floor swinging "T-Bone Boogie," and
the audience of pros let him know they had been waiting for this.
"Too Lazy to Work," which followed, was the kind of show number
he knew how to present, and the crowd laughed as he kidded and
mimed. From then on, his every appearance brought increasingly
abandoned applause.

To wind up the production, Ziggy Joe had devised an impressive
finale built around "Evenin'," the hit song of the show. In the wings
a fringe of moonlit palms suggested a tropical setting. The company, in carnival attire, dimly seen behind a scrim, swayed to faint
music. Down front on the darkened stage a bright spotlight focused
on T-Bone in top hat, white tie, and tails. Very softly he intoned the
opening stanzas of a song meant to evoke nostalgia and grief. Weav-
ing through verse after verse was a leitmotiv inspired by the mys-
tery and magic of night.

Reaching the finale, he addressed himself to the guitar and

allowed his voice to sink to a whisper again. With a dynamic sequence of chords, he commenced an arresting cadenza. Electrified,
an enchanted audience rose to its feet to applaud.

So the Rhumboogie had a hit, and for the first time T-Bone saw
his name up in lights. Night after night people lined the sidewalks,
and a queue snaked its way around the block. With the start of a
three-month run, T-Bone established his usual routine. There were
plenty of after-hours spots on the South and West Sides, and when
he finished at night, he would join friends to make the rounds. He
met musicians he had wanted to hear for some time, and he would
sit in and jam until it was daylight outside, always paying for the
last round of drinks.

There was a price for all that, for going without food and short-
changing his sleep. His ulcer returned, and more than once he was
out of circulation for twenty-four hours at a time. This was often
the sequel to a high-powered, after-hours game at the club. Ziggy
Johnson was a big-time gambler, and Chicago was a gambling town.
Although Milt Larkin tried to discourage him, when he was beckoned to the main table, T-Bone could never resist.

Once the grapevine reached Vi, she gave up her job to go join
him. Though he had called her every day, she wasn't fooled for long.

"Easy come, easy go," she said, beside him once more. "You're
doing good now, but you can be broke tomorrow. And even you can't
support every one of your friends."

"Right, as usual," he told her. "I need you around. While there's
a few bucks left, how about making Detroit next month? We'll buy
a car, and you be chauffeur while I play the Flame Show Bar."

By the time the Rhumboogie engagement was nearly over, Vi had
him back on his feet. Friends on the West Side had booked them
into Chicago's Vienna Baths, a hotel run like a spa, and while
T-Bone refused the treatments, it amused him to watch Vi try to
reform his friends. Leo Blevins was her only conquest. He was a
teenage guitarist who never let T-Bone out of his sight except at
night when he fronted a small group of schoolmates who carried
their horns over to Maxwell Street looking for a place to play. T-
Bone never acted big-time, especially with kids, and not being se-
cretive the way some musicians are, he let Leo in on some of his

tricks. At the Rhumboogie he sneaked the boys into his dressing room so they could hear the big band stretch out. A year later he was able to talk Charlie Glenn into hiring them to play Mondays, Larkin's night off.[5]

"Leo will be underfoot all your life," Vi told her husband.

"Better him than some others I might mention," T-Bone countered, smiling. And Vi knew she was wasting her breath.

5. Subsequently three members of this group, Gene Ammons and Johnny Griffin, tenors, and Harold Jones, drums, acquired national reputations, and Blevins, after a stint with Louis Jordan, formed a trio with his brother in Los Angeles.

Nona takes a bow.

Nine

A Natural Ball

Photograph by Henry Grayson. Courtesy Bernita Walker Moss

On my next visit, T-Bone and I went down to 217 West Forty-third Place, where Vi's sister Mattie and her husband, Robert Gooden, lived. "We'll rake over the past," T-Bone said. "Mattie's got scrapbooks, the lot." Vi's sister was a churchgoer who frowned on the blues, but T-Bone in print was something she could not resist. She was particularly proud of a piece by Ralph Gleason.[1]

"T-Bone didn't confine himself to the blues," Gleason had written in the San Francisco *Examiner and Chronicle* of April 6, 1974. "He sang songs like *Stardust* as well, in that sweet, warm, beautiful voice. His great torch song, *I'm Still in Love with You*, is a blues ballad of the first rank."

"I dedicated that to Vi," T-Bone said, "after one of our tiffs."

At the coffee table Mattie leafed through photographs in boxes and folders. "I'm looking for those glossies of your mare with the foal," she told T-Bone. She handed him a bunch, and he crossed over to me. I saw Vi was right. He liked talking about horses, and in Dallas he had daydreamed of having his own some day.

"Riding was fashionable here in the forties," he said. "Everybody who had some cash bought a horse. Professional people—doctors, lawyers. There were different horse places where you could buy. My first choice was Nona. She was an army mare, a jumper, very knowing. So I had her trained, and it cost me a grand.

"Here's a picture," he said. "She's playing dead and I'm beside her. She would lie down on command and then roll over dead. She'd bend her knees in a curtsy, and stop and go behind me, without me even looking around. She was somethin' else. Then there was the small mare, the one I got for Vi, plus all the stuff I kept in the garage. I owned more than nine hundred dollars' worth of boots, big Stetsons, cowboy saddles, and all that. Ready for the rodeo, dig?" He grinned.

"Tell about the shows you put on for the children," Mattie prompted. His passion for riding was something she understood.

"Yeah, we used to do that, too," he said, "because I had a little colt besides. He'd cost me nothing. A friend of mine owned a stal-

1. The late Ralph Gleason was a widely read jazz critic, based in San Francisco and popular with musicians of all persuasions.

lion, and he serviced my mare. That little palomino pony was so pretty! When I was playing in Oakland, I'd get Vi to come with me, and we'd go riding those trails. There were miles and miles of them in Richmond. You could ride way up into the hills. I bought a trailer and used it to transfer my mounts up and down from L.A.

"I can't remember when I wasn't crazy about horses. Trouble was, mine ate their heads off most of the time, and as soon as Vi had got pregnant, there was no one to ride. I stabled them in an academy in Watts, and it was like ninety dollars a month for keep, and half my days I was out on the road. I had to let them go in the end." He pulled a wry face.

"That hurt him," Mattie said, holding up another picture. The mare was curtsying, head lowered, forefeet straight out in front, and T-Bone was smiling alongside.

"When it comes to animals, I'm soft," he confessed.

"We know," Mattie said. "Only a sucker would hang on to that mutt you've got at home."

"Blondie?" T-Bone looked at her, affronted. "She's not dumb. She's crazy about me!"

"And good-looking, too, I suppose," Mattie smiled.

"There you got me." He grinned again, "Forget it. Let's see what that glossy is under your hand. One gorgeous chick, right?" As the girl he had been partnering had sprung into the air from behind, T-Bone had gone down in the splits. The dancer was spreadeagled above him, and both flashed exuberant smiles.

"Lottie the Body," he said, "from the Frolic Show Bar in Detroit. For four or five years I played locations like that. I traveled all over, even back east. Because by then I'd broken into the TOBA. You know what that is—the Theater Owners' Booking Agency. But that's not what *we* call it! 'Tough on Black Asses'—that's really more like it! Begging your pardon, Mattie. We all played the Toby theaters in the big eastern cities, the Apollo in New York, the Earle in Philly, the Howard in Washington, the Royal in Baltimore, the Paradise in Detroit, and the Regal in Chicago.

"When I was due to play the Majestic in Houston, I was in bed a week instead. We had to forgo pay when stomach pains grabbed me and I couldn't finish the gig. In Chicago, too, I got slung into bed—

---

in 1945, a week after I'd finished recording for the Rhumboogie label. Marl had written the arrangements for the band he fronted at the club. The titles were 'Sail On Boogie,' 'I'm Still in Love with You,' 'You Don't Love Me Blues,' 'T-Bone Boogie,' 'Mean Old World Blues,' and 'Evenin'.' But those sides were not so hot, not as good as the ones in L.A. later. They were big band numbers, more like what I recorded with Hite, but they were things the audiences requested a lot.

"During World War II, the USO sent me out regularly to play army camps. I'd been called up earlier, but the service turned me down." He smiled. "You'll never guess why. They got me for flat feet! Of all the ailments that have laid me low at times, they picked flat feet! When I stared, the sergeant told me, 'So long, Buddy. You don't think we're into rehabilitation, do you?' I have to confess these feet have traipsed more than a few miles!

"So the USO decided I should entertain instead, and it meant I had to come up with a band. I couldn't support a bunch of guys based on those army camps, so I got Jim Wynn to come with me, because he could bring fellows who worked weekends with him. The rest of the time I was booked as a single, like at the DeLisa in Chicago, the Flame Show Bar, the Frolic in Detroit, Don Robey's Peacock in Houston, and a lot of spots here in L.A." Glancing at his watch, he broke off.

"Gotta get home a minute. Joe Turner has a record date scheduled for 6 P.M. He wants me on hand. Pee Wee Crayton will pick me up, so he may come by here first. Leaves you plenty of time, Mattie. Don't pull a face."

Mattie grimaced. "He won't ever stay put long. Something is always cooking with Bone. Robert and I have been watching him for years. After we had moved to Forty-second, by Wrigley Field, they stayed with us, him and Vi. He was working Little Harlem at first. Vi and I took turns in the box office, and though we might put up STANDING ROOM ONLY, the people still crowded in. When he got through for the night, T-Bone had shoeboxes of nickles, dimes, quarters, and halves. When they got home, he and Vi would stick them under the bed!

"By then, you know, Robert and I had changed our minds. About

T-Bone, I mean. He was a problem all right, but he was crazy about Vi, no two ways about that. A money-maker besides. The thing of it was you had to live with it, that's all—the gambling, I mean. Vi never knew where they were at.

"Colleen, in Oakland, another of us girls, won't hear a word against him. She's got a big family and a husband with no luck. T-Bone brings gifts for the lot. Every time he plays Oakland he invites the kids out for a meal and ends buying them shoes.

"Vi takes things hard at times. I don't blame her. I'd have left him, more than likely. But she never lets on. They go places, and she won't be seeing him again until they're ready to go home, women pulling on him all the time, and him emptying out all his change. 'People love him—that's how it is,' Vi told me once. I don't know where he'd be without her, that's for sure. She's seen him through many a bad time. He never changes. We don't look for that no more. Long as he keeps going, that's all. God only knows how he does, sick like he is, stomach, heart, lungs, and what have you.

"But you don't hear him complain. He just kids. But not about his act. It upsets him when he can't go all out. Like at the Apollo when Honi Coles warned him: 'Don't go down in those splits no more.'[2] He was afraid of his heart, I guess. So T-Bone would put the box back of his head instead and dance clear across the stage, some of the stuff Chuck Berry learned from him how to do. He can't hold himself back—that's how he is.

"But the dice robbed him of a fortune." Mattie shook her head. "Except one time. He won a few thousand dollars, a whole lot, in fact. Vi was upstate with Colleen, who was expecting again.

"'T-Bone's had a windfall. Get down here fast,' I told her on the phone. Just three doors from us, No. 197, was for sale. Arthur Adams had it. His son Joe manages Ray Charles. There was a home in the back for M'Dear, and T-Bone liked that. By time Bernita was born, T-Bone was able to go to Dallas to fetch them here, his mother and Uncle Dink and Junior besides.

"I don't know when M'Dear, Movelia that is, married Lem Ran-

2. Another of the founders of the Copasetics, the dancers' club, Honi Coles was stage manager in the Apollo Theater at the time. In the 1980s he remains an attraction on Broadway.

dall—a good time ago, I guess—but long as any of us knew him, we called him Uncle Dink, and her M'Dear. When T-Bone was on the road, Dink was caretaker for the place. He mowed lawns for the neighbors, cut hedges, and fixed their tools. M'Dear and Vi were happy because they get along fine. And Junior was all smiles, four-teen and back at school.

"Hard to believe about Junior. How he's grown! He's a supervisor in the payroll department for the school system in L.A. Claims he owes everything to his dad. But T-Bone was a tiger if Junior stayed out late. Vi had to tell, and he'd get walloped, like as not. If he went to a movie in the week, he'd get a caning from his dad. Junior was always crazy about Vi. Anytime he heard her tell someone he was a stepson, he'd get mad as heck. 'She's kidding. She's my mother,' he told folks who would ask. But it was his dad made him toe the line. And T-Bone still likes to say, 'Big as he is, I could whip him today.'"

"He could, too," Pee Wee Crayton confirmed from the far side of the screen door.[3]

"It ain't locked," Mattie told him. "Come on in. T-Bone got tired of waiting on you."

"I talked with him already. Hoppy is with him, and driving." Hoppy, Lightnin' Hopkins' cousin Willie, was a blues harpist in the area who liked to chauffeur T-Bone and Joe Turner around. "Joe's on his way over, Mattie, if that is OK. Them two will pick us up here."

Mattie nodded, and Pee Wee turned my way. "I'd like to tell you how and when I met Bone. I was living in Berkeley, in the Bay area, about 1944. I'd bought records by Benny Goodman, to hear Charlie Christian, that's all. I was crazy about guitar but couldn't play it. I don't know how it happened, but one day I got so worked up I went to a secondhand music store and bought me an old beat-up box. I started in my own way, which was all wrong, of course. Then I found out T-Bone Walker was in Oakland, at a place called the Swing Club. I knew Slim Jenkins there, so down I went, and T-Bone

3. Pee Wee Crayton, one of T-Bone's close friends, was a guitar player whose composition "Blues After Hours" was a hit in the 1940s. He commanded a following into the 1980s. He died in 1985.

Rance Walker (*left*), T-Bone's father, as a World War I soldier

Movelia Walker Randall, T-Bone's mother

Vida Lee at age two

Vida Lee, Bernita, and T-Bone

Publicity photograph

Marguerite Seymour

Clarence Seymour

The Three Rockets. Phace Roberts
is at left.

Rhumboogie poster

Joe Turner, Scatman Crothers, and T-Bone

Bernita and T-Bone (*left*) at the Celebrity Club in Providence, Rhode Island

T-Bone with a comedian on the "Duffy's Tavern" radio show, *ca.* 1945

T-Bone and Bernita backstage with Sugar Ray Robinson

T-Bone and Lottie the Body

was at the bar. I'd never met him, but I walked up and said, 'Are you Mr. Walker?'

"'Yes, I am,' he said.

"So I told him, 'My name's Pee Wee Crayton, and I'm trying to learn to play guitar.' I don't know what he thought, but all he said was, 'Good for you.' I'm not the retiring type, so I asked, 'Would you help me sometime?'

Pee Wee looked Mattie in the face and laughed. "He didn't throw me out on my ear. You know him better than that. 'If you can catch me when I'm not busy,' he told me, 'I'll do what I can.' Then he said, 'But I'm going riding now.' I figured I knew where he was going, because a fellow called Smitty, who was a good friend of his, kept a bunch of horses out at the edge of town, near Albany, I think.

"'Well, I don't have a horse,' I replied, 'but I'm going with you. OK?'

"Would you believe that when we got there he jived me into *buying* a horse? I paid $125. Afterwards he let me know he'd listen to me play. Well, it was terrible. I tried and tried, but I couldn't play in time. 'No, man. You're not playing in *time*,' he said, kind of fierce. 'Music is played in time. You have to feel it.' I couldn't get it into my head how he meant I had to *feel* it. T-Bone plays bass, and piano too, so he said, 'Come on. You got a piano at home?' and with that we went back to my house, and he sat at the piano, and there I am, strumming away.

"'You're supposed to change here,' he said, 'and here.' He thought for a moment and then decided what to do. 'I'm at a hotel,' he told me. 'I'm going to move in with you instead. My wife is coming, but I'll bring her over, too.' That's exactly what we did. Vi came, and every day T-Bone would play piano, and I'd play that guitar. At least I could play chords, because a good guitar player called Eddie Young had started me out on that. First off, T-Bone taught me how to tune the guitar to where I could get the blues sound.

"Then he'd say, 'Do this here, and after that, this.' But he had to work with me, because I couldn't stay with the time. Then I started trying to play his records "Bobby Sox Baby" and "Mean Old World."

"After a while it got so when I'd go to hear him play in a band or a show he'd say: 'Ladies and Gentlemen, there's a friend of mine in the house. He's going to be a good guitar player. You have a chance now to hear him.' Phew! Was I scared! He'd start playing a number and tell me to go get my guitar. I'd be jumping the time, and the band would get mad. They'd quit back of me, and T-Bone would raise sand. " '*Play* with him,' he'd say. He stayed in Oakland a month, and we came to be the best of friends. Finally I got to where I could do pretty good. I would be out there, and people would throw money for me having had the nerve to get up and play.

" 'All right!' T-Bone would say. 'You gotta split fifty-fifty.' And we'd laugh. After a while I began to understand and get the feel of the blues. He told me, 'Feel your changes, understand?' and in time it began to unfold. Seems I was popular, for I started to work at the New Orleans Swing Club in San Francisco. Tony Valerio, who distributed Melody Sales, was a good friend of mine, and one night he brought Jules Bihari in to hear me.[4] I was fronting a little trio, and he had us do T-Bone's "Still in Love with You." Then he flew us to L.A. to record it.

"There was a little number, like a theme, that I'd been working on at the club. I wanted to play it, so I started it off. He told me, 'Wait, we're going to record.'

"Well, you know, that baby didn't have a bridge! No middle. So I said, 'I don't know what I'm going to play after that.'

"He told me, 'Play anything.' It was like that then, because no one ever knew what was going to be a hit. So I started playing and ideas just came. I was making T-Bone's stuff into what little I knew. That turned out to be one of the biggest records I ever had—'Blues After Hours.' It was backed with 'Still in Love,' and that made it a hit all around. But because T-Bone had the number copyrighted with a publisher, he got more royalties on his tune than I got with all three of mine!

"I told T-Bone, 'Give me some of that money!'

4. Jules Bihari was one of four brothers responsible for the Modern record catalog, whose subsidiary labels included RPM, Kent, Crown, and Flair.

"And he told me, 'Give me that tune. It should have been mine. Why didn't *I* write that thing?'"

Joe Turner, who had come in by the back door, interrupted Pee Wee's story. "You probably had stole it anyhow," he said. "And you didn't know I'd snuck in while you was holding forth, did you?" he asked, making Pee Wee laugh. An invincible blues man throughout his career, Joe Turner no longer resembled the lanky bartender who sang with Pete Johnson in the 1930s at the Sunset in Kansas City. Although he weighed some three hundred pounds now and was bothered by gout, his spirits had suffered no ill effects.[5]

Once Mattie had introduced us, he took over the floor. "Wanna hear what we pulled on Bone one time? We were playing a big auditorium, and the place was packed and jammed. It was a blues session, I guess, because there were a lot of us guys. T-Bone was supposed to come on fifth, but he didn't show till the last half was going strong. Then he strolled in. Some of us kids said: 'We'll fix him for coming late. We'll pull the plug on him!'

"Where you plugged in your guitar was way back of the stage. T-Bone, you know, had that long cable, so they showed him where to hook up. He walked onstage, tuned and everything, and started into his act. All of a sudden he was strumming and no sound was coming out. He kept looking back, wondering. He didn't know what was going on. We were in the wings, laughing. Then we plugged him in again, and wheeee! That was some kind of noise! A couple of times we did him like that, and he cut his songs real short!

"Another day he was on a big show in Texas, his own part of the world. So about half an hour passes, and he's still up there playing. Men were pulling their hair, but he wouldn't get off the stage. Everyone out front is shouting, 'Play, T-Bone, play!' so he don't want to quit. He's goin' to take over the show. How do you get him off? I was supposed to go on next, so I just walked up onstage and started singing along.

"'What's goin' on?' T-Bone said.

"'We're singing this together,' I told him. 'You been up here long

5. Joe Turner died in 1985 at age seventy-four.

enough.' We laughed, and because he still didn't know what had
happened at the auditorium the other night, we let him in on that,
too.

"'That's how you did me?' he asked us. 'Y'all dirty sons of a gun!'

"'Yeah. And we started to do it this time,' we said, 'but we figured your fans would tear up the joint.'"

"Hold it, man," Pee Wee interrupted. "You hear Hoppy leaning on
that horn outside?"

"Well, Bone will tell you," Joe advised me. "We laughed about
that many a time. You can have fun with Bone. And he don't never
get mad."

Ten

Petrillo Strikes Out

Black and White began the regular release of 78 rpm singles by T-Bone in mid-1946, and many sides became classics. Among them were "I'm in an Awful Mood," "I Know Your Wig is Gone," "Plain Old Down Home Blues," "On Your Way Blues," "Too Much Trouble," "Prison Blues," and "It's a Lowdown Dirty Deal." With each successive hit his popularity increased and soon three or even four of his numbers would be listed at one time on the R and B charts among the top ten. Since blues were very big in the Southwest, on one-nighters he drew enthusiastic crowds, conditioning audiences for other artists in the same field, blues men like Wynonie Harris, Jimmy Witherspoon, Joe Turner, and Lowell Fulson.

The first recordings T-Bone had made under his own name were for Capitol Records in July, 1942. They featured Freddie Slack on piano, Jud De Vaut on bass, and Dave Coleman on drums, and two sides, "Mean Old World" and "I Got a Break, Baby," were released.

Later that year, James Petrillo, president of the American Federation of Musicians, initiated a recording ban to force the three major record manufacturers to pay increased royalties. But Petrillo's timing was bad. With the outbreak of World War II, shipments of shellac were halted, and the record companies were content to sit things out, merely releasing sides made in advance of the ban. Production was geared to whatever reserves of shellac were on hand, and the companies were prepared for a ban of a year or longer.

Although events had seemed to favor the position they adopted, early in 1945 a wave of independent producers, many of them operating on a shoestring, signed new royalty agreements and hustled into a wide-open field, hoping to parlay a few hundred dollars into hits that might result in huge profits. The character of the industry underwent a change. While sales had always been the main factor governing a company's roster of talent, lip service, at least, had been paid to the quality of music being marketed. By the end of 1945, however, when the three major companies had finally negotiated and signed the union agreement, Petrillo had already licensed a remarkable number of independents—some 350—and this noticeably altered the nature of the market. Now, in a do-it-yourself age, everything pointed to generally lowered standards.

In the popular field, rhythm and blues was at first almost indistinguishable from what the majors had been accustomed to identify as race music. This was now being transformed into an eminently salable product, with titles like Jack McVea's "Open the Door, Richard," Louis Jordan's "Swinging on a Rusty Gate," and Mike Riley's "The Music Goes Round and Round" grossing hundreds of thousands of dollars for producers who seldom knew much about music. Many operators made a practice of buying original material outright to avoid royalty payments. The fine print in their contracts tricked most musicians, and over the years a kind of legal larceny proliferated. Yet, knowledgeable people with specialized tastes in jazz and blues occasionally produced material that surpassed the efforts of the major labels.

But bluesmen like T-Bone, Lowell Fulson, Joe Turner, Jimmy Witherspoon, Wynonie Harris, Pee Wee Crayton, Muddy Waters, Johnny "Guitar" Watson and many others, found it difficult to size up the companies extending them contracts. "I was pretty lucky," T-Bone said, "because Ralph Bass was A and R man at Black and White, and he took care of our early releases."[1] People in charge of sessions were referred to as artists and repertoire men, and occasionally, but not often, they could relate to the musicians and accordingly get good results. Ralph Bass was, as he himself put it, a "jazz fanatic" who early on had recorded for Comet's Black and White jazz label, using musicians such as Dexter Gordon, Wardell Gray, and Dizzy Gillespie. A good many of T-Bone's sessions, some of the best he ever made, were earmarked for Comet instead of being marketed as R and B. "But there was never any talk of royalties," T-Bone stated, "which is why Capitol was a better break."

"Capitol was a tiny company in those days, the early forties," Dave Dexter recalled.[2] "T-Bone was one of the company's first art-

1. Still in the business of recording the blues, Ralph Bass was with T. K. Productions in Chicago in the late 1970s.
2. In later years copy editor and feature writer for *Billboard* magazine, early on Dexter was a newspaperman with the Kansas City *Journal-Post* and a contributor to *Down Beat* and other jazz periodicals before he joined Capitol Records on the West Coast.

ists. We had him under contract before the recording ban, and Capitol was three months old when that went into effect in July, '42. We couldn't get any more masters until around November of '43. That was a long haul for a small company just beginning. So we couldn't hold T-Bone to our original contract.

"I joined the company sometime during the ban, and when it was lifted, I was red hot to make jazz and blues, and somehow—I don't quite remember how it came about—we bought at least fifty T-Bone masters from Paul Reiner, who owned Black and White. Ralph Bass A and R'ed many, but I believe T-Bone made 'Stormy Monday' for us early on. He'd cut four sides before the ban, though only the two with Freddie Slack were released. However, another 'Stormy Monday,' different altogether, recorded by Billy Eckstine and Earl Hines, came out in '42. Still, it's my recollection that T-Bone's was made first; only we couldn't release it because of shellac and the ban. But later we did especially well with one title, and that was it, I am sure.

"Around 1947 we put out several singles, and eventually a shellac 78 rpm album, and we got pretty good mileage out of some of those masters. A while later I did an LP of what I thought were the twelve best T-Bone masters. The twelve-inch LP didn't really take over until about '52, because originally they were all little ten-inchers. Afterwards they all became what the Europeans called thirty-centimeter LPs. So I think it must have been around 1955 that we brought our last T-Bone out. Those old masters had just been down in the vault all that time. And I would say probably twenty-five of the fifty we bought were never issued at all!

"T-Bone had quite a career, but I don't think he got the credit that he deserved. He was playing electric guitar ten or fifteen years before most. He was playing it before Christian, I believe."

Between the time Capitol let T-Bone's contract lapse and re-signed him in 1946, he recorded in Chicago for Charlie Glenn's Rhumboogie label. Although these sides featured some of his best compositions—"Sail On Boogie," "Still in Love with You," "You Don't Love Me Blues," "T-Bone Boogie," "Mean Old World Blues," "Evenin'," "My Baby Left Me," and "Come Back to Me, Baby"—Marl Young's big-band arrangements were more effective as production numbers than as a setting for a swinging guitar, and they never accounted for much in the way of sales. But when booker Harold Oxley signed him with Black and White, T-Bone could select his material and hire the musicians of his choice. In retrospect, blues authorities and historians agree that at this point one of the most fruitful stages of his recording career commenced.[3]

"About his contract . . . that was funny," Ralph Bass said. "There was a man in town called himself T-Bone's manager, a Sammy Goldberg, I think, a con artist for sure. Other record companies were dickering with him for T-Bone. They were talking contract, but behind everyone's back I discovered T-Bone was handled by Harold Oxley. So I remember coming up to his office on the Strip, introducing myself and telling him who I was with and why I was there.

"'We got a deal,' Harold said.

"'That fast?' I came back.

"'You know why? Everyone else has been messing with Goldberg, but I'm his manager and you came to me.'

"Well, it was a coup for us. The backers of the other companies, whom I knew personally, were taken by surprise. At that time Modern Records, owned by the Bihari brothers, Specialty Records, owned by Art Rupe, and Aladdin Records, owned by the Messners, were the principal independents on the West Coast. They were the pioneers in the entire R and B industry, really, along with Black and White. Imperial wasn't in business yet. Well, they found out I'd done a little homework and had got T-Bone signed up.

"Another thing which was funny was later when I was sent out to pick up an option and get his signature on it. He was very big in Texas, and I went down to the club where he was playing—in Houston, maybe, or Dallas. I don't remember, but wherever it was the audience surprised me. It was a very old audience, you might say, much older people than I would normally have thought he might attract. Also, they were very straight. I couldn't understand what was happening, so I asked the promoter.

"'Well,' he said, 'the last time T-Bone played here, the day he

3. See Appendix A.

left town, the preacher's wife went along.' So all the church members had come to see what he was putting down! T-Bone had an unusual way of performing. He had a long cord plugged into his amplifier, and it went clang, clang, clang across the boards. For about the first eight bars you wouldn't see T-Bone, only hear him, and then he would come on stage with the spot on him, very handsome, you know. He used something to make his eyes glisten, I guess. Before it was over he had all those sisters in the palm of his hand! He was the easiest man in the world to record, always genial. His first hit, which I did with him, was 'Bobby Sox Baby.' It was his first release for us."

At that time, after having recorded Parker, Gillespie, Dodo Marmarosa, and Slim Gaillard, Bass was about to discover, quite by accident, that rhythm and blues would outsell anything else on the market. With Jack McVea's "Open the Door, Richard," he produced one of the biggest pop hits in the country. McVea was a versatile musician who played in Eddie Barefield's big band in 1936 and for a number of other West Coast leaders. In 1940 he joined Lionel Hampton's band, and in 1943 he went to Snub Mosely, and then he appeared with Jazz at the Philharmonic. "Open the Door, Richard," his most successful record, was made in 1946.

"So with that," Bass said, "I got more interested in R and B, and in T-Bone especially, because he had a good format and the musicians he used were just great. In those days jazz musicians, especially out on the coast, were often out of work. They couldn't get a job playing their kind of music, because few people understood it. As far as the public was concerned, jazz was noncommercial. So they had a hard time, and it was easy to get the best. That's how come I got Gillespie. The guys were playing Billy Berg's, where the people wouldn't accept them, so they were glad to pick up a couple of bucks from me.

"We never had a chart making our R and B things. That wasn't the day to make charts. We had to keep everything loose, everything was created right then and there. Oh, T-Bone might have called a rehearsal beforehand. But reading off the music? It was never a question of that. Read the blues? Blues can't be read—that's a feel. And I'm going to put myself on the line right here: T-Bone was the daddy of all the guitar players today.

"Everybody thinks of B. B. King as the man today. It was T-Bone. B. B. got his style from him. Everybody did. B. B. is a sweetheart, and he'll tell you the same. T-Bone was an influence on jazz musicians as well, and this goes for latecomers, too. Some of them may not know him, but he changed the whole thing around. He was the first to play fills, and the sound of guitar today, and everything that has happened to it since, came from T-Bone, that's all."

Eleven

Bernita on Tour

"Guitar players get big money now, and Bone should take the credit," Lowell Fulson told me one night in the Parisian Room. "He made blues guitar famous and was the first to reach the top. He was older than me and had more experience, but he was always friendly."

Fulson was born in Tulsa and brought up on the Choctaw Strip, where his grandfather was an administrator. Prior to World War II, he had little experience on the road. "All I'd ever done," he said, "was partner Texas Alexander, a little man with a great big voice.[1] A terrible voice, but he could make plenty of noise. I used to accompany him on guitar, and he didn't need no mike. We'd go to different spots, honky-tonks and backwoods places. He could play a little piano, but since nobody ever had one, he'd just walk in and sing. He'd been doing it a long time, and he used to tell me about all the things he went through. Like he got into some trouble in Texas and went to the Huntsville penitentiary, where they sentenced him to life. But he sung his way out of there! I think he stayed three months and twenty-one days. They run him off, telling him, 'Come back down here again, and we'll kill you.'

"He said what happened was that they couldn't stop him singing. He sang all that old mourning-type stuff. Nobody wanted to be in the place where he was. He just got next to them all, so they let him go. They run him out of there."

Fulson was smiling as he hoisted his guitar and readied himself for the next set. It was a Tuesday night, a little bit slow, and he was subbing for T-Bone, who had had to return to the hospital for tests. Fulson sang two of T-Bone's numbers and closed with two of his own recorded hits, "River Blues" and "Cryin' Blues." After a round of applause he returned to me at the bar.

"My family quit Tulsa when my father was killed in a sawmill there," he went on after I had bought him a drink. "My mother moved to Choctaw Strip, where my dad came from. Somehow when Oklahoma became a state, the Choctaw Indians and the

[1]. Alger "Texas" Alexander represented an older generation of Texas blues singers, who followed migrant cotton workers from camp to camp in the 1920s and 1930s.

freedmen were given land. My grandfather had enough kids to get a whole section for himself, for his sons—including my father—and his daughters, brothers, sisters, nieces, and nephews. Grandfather was in charge and had like a little town of his own. They had their own mission, their own doctors—mostly herb doctors—and we raised everything ourselves. I even learned to butcher and cut meat.

"But music was drawing me, and I mastered chords in high school and left to go out with a boy named James. He had only one hand. He was catching a freight train once, and it cut off his right leg and hand, too. So he had a wooden leg and a big old pick he put onto this hand. That boy knew such beautiful chords, you wouldn't believe, so I stayed with him till I got all I could, and then I met Texas Alexander."

Fulson was called up by the navy when World War II broke out. Three years later, before being shipped to Guam in 1945, he was sent to the Alameda Air Station near Oakland, California. "Alameda suited me fine. I'd get through Friday evening around twelve and not be needed till Monday A.M. I'd go to Oakland and be out playing somewhere, maybe at a house party or even on the street. Then I got lucky. There was a guy showed up who had me make some records for him. The label was Swing Time, I think. And that's when I sang up that last verse for Memphis Slim's 'Every Day': 'I'm gonna pack my suitcase and move on down the line.' It caught on like wildfire, and there I am, working in the navy shipyard and don't know I've got a hit!" Fulson laughed.

"But I noticed the houses I played would be packed. So I said, 'I must be playing pretty good!' Suddenly on weekends I was making a hundred dollars and more, and finally some guy hipped me to my sales. That's what I mean when I say we owe T-Bone a lot. He regularized the thing. Like when I was making records for Aladdin—they paid me outright for the session. No talk of royalties or nothing. They told me the band on the session took up all the money. But I'd get mine someday, they said. If you acted like you were going to balk, they'd run out and buy you a car or somethin'. And by me being a kid, never having had no pretty cars and no more than a few dollars in my pocket—well, first thing you know you've sold out.

But after T-Bone and Wynonie became so big, those companies got to being careful. Wanting to re-sign you, you know.

"When I first heard T-Bone play, I stood spellbound. I'd been out on tour where I thought I was raising sand, but when I got a look at him, how he worked the audience, I said, 'That's what you call professional!' I'd just go out there playing and singing and didn't entertain my audience. I just played and sang. But he's entertaining *his* house. The man's a genius. We'd taken a liking to one another, and when the agents found out we got along great, they had what they called the Big Three Battle of Blues—Lowell Fulson, Big Joe Turner, and T-Bone Walker. They ran it on and off for five years. Because by the time you'd go 'round the horn and back, like Texas, Oklahoma, Arkansas, and part of Louisiana, you'd be ready to start again. So by the fall of the year we'd be back together one more time.

"In Texas an agent named Howard Lewis booked us. He's dead now—a suicide, I heard. Bone went out for him with Ray Charles a good while back. And later, because Ray and I were both recording for the Swing Time label, he sent us out together, too. I had about eight pieces, and one of my saxophonists, Stanley Turrentine, would write charts for the band and Ray brailled them out. He was conservatory-trained, you know.

"After a while Lewis said, 'I'm goin' to put on the best blues package you can get!' And that was Wynonie Harris, Jimmy Witherspoon, T-Bone Walker, and myself. So they're all arguing about who's going to close the show!

"I'm going to. You know who I am!"

"No, I've gotta. I'm so and so!"

"Well, who's going to open the show?"

"I said, 'Me! So I can get out of the way! T-Bone and myself are the only ones can play guitar. So I'll do my little solo, open the band, get things cooking, and then be through!'

"After a time Spoon dropped out, but it was still crazy. When Joe Turner came in, he'd get up and sing, and then Wynonie would say he'd stayed on too long, and he'd get up and butt in. But T-Bone always closed. He was playing guitar and crossing the stage on his knees, doing the splits. Yeah, he always closed! We had things just

right! Bone had his Cadillac, Joe had his Cadillac, and I traveled
with my boys on the bus. We all had a ball!"

T-Bone was finishing up in San Francisco before starting out on one
of those second Lewis tours, when he had a call from Vi.

"I wanted to tell him he was in for a surprise," Vi explained.
"Because the doctor had said I was pregnant.

" 'You mean you're going to have a baby?' my husband said. 'After
eleven years of marriage!' He was so astonished I laughed.

" 'You heard right,' I told him, and let him know the doctor had
said we'd lose out if I went on riding a horse on those trails.

" 'Don't ride no more,' T-Bone came back at me. And from there
on he didn't want me doing anything at all. 'Don't let her fool
around,' he warned Junior. So after that, his son cleaned house and
did all kinds of stuff for me.

"Junior always called me Mom. When he was small and we used
to go to parties, he'd never tell kids, 'Yeah, she's my stepmother.'
He'd say, 'She's my *mom*.' When the time was coming for me to go
to the hospital and T-Bone was on the road, Junior called him and
said, 'Dad, you better come on home, because the baby is near due.'

" 'Don't let it come till I get there!' my husband said, and went to
inform Mr. Lewis he must quit. He had to work one more night,
and then he set off and went through Dallas. After talking M'Dear
into coming to L.A., he piled her into the car. She said he didn't
stop for nothin' all the way home.

"So when he arrived, they booked him into the Lincoln Theater,
because it turned out I had more than a week to go. He took me
somewhere and had the prettiest suit made so I could go to the
theater with him. That Sunday night he was guesting at the Plantation, and when it was almost time for him to go to work, I realized
the hospital was where I should be. That same niece of mine, Mildred, had come in from Chicago, and once he'd gone, we jumped in
the car and went off right away.

"In the morning the nurses told me, 'We have had a time with
your husband!'

" 'What did he do?' I asked.

" 'He was going to whip us,' they said, 'because we wouldn't let him get to you.'

"And he sent me all kinds of beautiful flowers, roses and lilies and Lord knows what. I was in a florist shop! About midday they let him see me and the baby. Well, my husband just loved that child to death. When I brought her home and she'd cry at night, he would rock her to sleep. The clubs were closing by 12 P.M. right then, and he'd be back shortly after, so he'd take her on his arm and do her like this. She would settle right down, and he'd put her in bed, saying, 'There's nothing wrong with that child.'

"Junior had wanted a baby brother, but when Bernita was born and he came to the hospital, he kissed me and said, 'You couldn't help it, Mom, so don't feel bad!'

"After a while T-Bone had to leave and go back east, but when he returned to San Francisco, he sent for us, and with the baby just three months old I caught the Daylight Express and joined him where he was staying, at Pee Wee Crayton's. Then when she was eight months old, he had us fly to Texas, and from there on we traveled right along with Daddy in the car. Except that one time when he took her by himself. He was booked in Texas, and she was little more than a year, but I'd had a miscarriage and couldn't make it.

" 'What are you going to do?' I said.

" 'Take her with me,' he told me. And then when she was two years old, he did the same, because Bernita was crazy about her daddy and always wanted to go. A boy called Sleepy was working for us then, and he always traveled with my husband. That way he had a valet along who could carry the bags when they were taking a plane, and my husband could sling Bernita over his shoulder like a knapsack." As she pictured it, Vi smiled.

"In San Antonio he roomed in a private home and paid the landlady to comb the baby's hair, dress her, everything. Then when he went to work, and everyone was hollering, 'We want T-Bone!' he would appear with that baby riding on his hip! We managed pretty well till Bernita was four and ready for school. By then M'Dear and Uncle Dink were living in the house back of us, so they told me:

'You go with T-Bone if you want. The baby will be fine.' But I'd get lonesome, so in the summer she came with us till she got that old that she wanted to stay home. Looked like I was always torn."

When T-Bone eventually toured with his own group, Vi was needed because she helped with the driving, though Sleepy did a lot of it, and T-Bone himself liked getting behind the wheel, especially if he was driving a Cadillac or a Buick he hadn't had very long. Five-hundred-mile one-nighter jumps were not unusual. Sleepy was never any more rested than the others, because he doubled as band boy, so Vi sometimes took a room and slept during the act. Then if they set out again right after the job, she drove while they dozed.

"I hated to quit them," Vi said, "because I was useful. But I wanted to be with Bernita, and of course after she got to be a teen-ager, I had to be home. But earlier on, one summer my sister called on me because she was sick, so I had to let Bernita go to her daddy on her own. She was only nine years old, but I put her on the train, and Mildred met her in Chicago. From there they flew to Washington, D.C., where T-Bone was. She stayed with her daddy all summer, traveling every place.

"One time in New York City when he was working at the Baby Grand, he let her go to Jones Beach with the chorus girls. When they got back, he'd already left for work. She was in his room alone when a storm blew up and there was a power cut. She was frightened, so she called and told me, 'Mama, the lights have gone out.'

"When she was away, I always had my fare laid by me in case of trouble, but first I told her: 'Telephone Daddy. Ask him to come get you.' So he sent Sleepy around after her, I learned later, and the chorus girls said she was the only nine-year-old-somebody they had ever seen up at 4 A.M.—taking a bow at the Baby Grand!

"One time before that I'd been with them in Providence, Rhode Island, when T-Bone introduced her at his club because it was her birthday, and she was eight. They'd baked her a big cake, and there were soldiers who kept begging for her to be allowed to dance. The soldiers were crazy about her and threw money on the stage. She really enjoyed that.

"Another thing she liked was eating at the little cafe where the jukebox played her daddy's records. When they saw us coming, the waitresses and the cook would pretend to be mad.

" 'We're going to have to hear those records again!' they would say."

Twelve

The Wrong End of a Mule

Booker Harold Oxley, by this time in his fifties, was a stocky, heavy-set man with a florid complexion that belied an equable temperament. When he signed T-Bone in 1946, he was taking on a new attraction, the first in many years. He had started out as a musician, but by the 1930s he was handling the Jimmie Lunceford band, which was playing dance tours in and around Ohio, eastern Pennsylvania, and northern New York State. He took them to New York City, onto the stage of the old Lafayette Theater. He negotiated a contract with Decca, and soon Lunceford records were being played coast to coast. An engagement at the Cotton Club followed, and later the band was a success at a celebrated roadhouse in Westchester County.

A piece by editor Ned Williams, dated March 7, 1952, in *Down Beat*, recalled Oxley as "one of the few remaining band managers of the old school, a group that left an indelible imprint upon the music business as we know it today. Such managers not only booked the band and negotiated contracts for all its work but frequently advised the leader on personnel, helped select and buy the arrangements, had a voice in styling, arranged transportation, purchased uniforms and other equipment, collected money and made up the payroll, and even found time to institute and supervise promotion and publicity. Band biz has since become big biz, and instead of a single manager most name bands employ a personal manager, an attorney, an arranger, a road manager, a booking office, an auditor, a press agent, and several secretaries: in short, a dozen individuals performing duties once lumped in a single package upon the stooped shoulders of one man."

In the early 1940s Lunceford's star sidemen began to drop out. Sy Oliver moved to Tommy Dorsey, Willie Smith to Charlie Spivak, Trummy Young to Charlie Barnet. Lunceford, eventually tiring of profitable but tedious semiannual one-nighter tours, decided to break his association with Oxley and sign with a major booking agency. (Ironically, the Lunceford band never again enjoyed its former popularity.) So in the mid-1940s Oxley, honest but also shrewd, was on the lookout for an artist who could profit from the kind of

104

single-minded expertise and concentration he knew how to provide. T-Bone was his choice.

"Harold was the greatest," T-Bone recalled. "That guy could have taken me right to the top—only he didn't live to see the day. We don't forget him, because he was a *friend*, the only man in the business the musicians could trust."

In the spring of 1946 on a cold, wet day in Chicago, Oxley was backstage in the Tivoli Theater, where Lionel Hampton was headlining and T-Bone was advertised as a coming attraction. On the desk in the manager's office, Oxley deposited T-Bone's black-and-white glossies and a caricature to be used as a newspaper mat. Ned Williams, stopping by the theater after the show, stepped through the door, looked over his shoulder, and commented: "You're a thief. That was *my* brain wave, the caricature."

Oxley started to laugh. He knew the only person who could make that claim was one who had commissioned the familiar Ellington and Calloway cartoons. He turned to embrace the man he had worked with for some years in the Mills-Rockwell office. Williams, impeccably turned out, as always, and sporting a boutonniere, slapped Oxley on the back.

"Did you think I wouldn't spot that, in my own territory?"

"Even us dogs rate crumbs from the master's table," Oxley replied, grinning.

Williams had introduced Oxley to Irving Mills in the 1930s when he was publicizing Mills's stable of talent, which, besides Duke Ellington and Cab Calloway, included the Mills Blue Rhythm Band, Ina Ray Hutton's All-Girl Band, and the Eddie DeLange–Will Hudson group. Since he was one of the top PR men in the business, Irving Mills set store by his judgment, so when Oxley came east with Lunceford in tow, he went uptown with Williams to hear the band. A takeover of Lunceford's bookings was discussed, and it was Williams who insisted Oxley retain personal control.

"No mean feat," Williams said subsequently, "and it called for daily celebration in a bar across the street. In later years, when I was waiting for Glenn Burrs and Carl Cons to settle their differences in court so I could join *Down Beat*, Harold took me into *his* office. There I wrote and mimeographed a complete advertising manual for the Lunceford band. When I ran into him that time in Chicago, he hadn't changed one bit. He started right off selling me a bill of goods.

" 'Wait till you hear T-Bone Walker,' he said. 'I'm touting another surefire bet. He's a sweetheart, besides.' That surprised me, because I knew T-Bone had a name for gambling and booze. But Harold read my mind.

" 'You wait,' he said. 'He's some musician, believe me.' And he returned to it when we parted. 'Go pick up his records. He's got four on the charts!' "

In the fall, deciding the record hits had created a sizable audience in the Southwest, Oxley arranged to send T-Bone out with a band. And T-Bone asked Jim Wynn if he wanted to go with him, because he himself planned to front the group.

Wynn's friendship with T-Bone dated back to T-Bone's first engagement at Little Harlem. Jim had been in charge of the music at the time. Born in El Paso in 1912, he had decided to become a musician some years before his family moved to Los Angeles. Once there, he took up a paper route to pay for a new saxophone. In time he developed a talent for management and by the early thirties could keep a group working with few layoffs.

"When Oxley approached me," he said, "I was using seven pieces, with Zell Kindred on piano and Henry 'Shifty' Ivory on bass. Robert 'Snake' Sims was my drummer—Snake stayed with me fifteen years—and Freddie Simon, Maurice's brother, was on tenor. I had someone on alto I can't remember, making three reeds, which included me on baritone. When we went out with Bone, we hired a trumpet as well. We used practically nothing but 'heads.'[1] Oxley was experienced and booked us in spots where the money was right. The jumps were okay, and we seldom covered more than four hundred miles.

"It got going so good, it was soon obvious we were a growing

1. Improvised arrangements created by a band during a performance.

attraction. Bone's hits went over big, and Black and White kept them coming. This went on for two or three years, and as the crowds got bigger and bigger, so the money increased. Everyone was happy. Wherever we played, things were laid on just right—pictures, stories, everything like that. The only drag was when we had to cancel a date. T-Bone's digestion gave him trouble. He was supposed to drink nothing but milk, and goat's milk at that. That was more than he could take. He claimed he could spot a goat a half mile away.

"For a long while we kept going, and then after our second year on the road he ended up in the hospital again. In Houston, I think, and we lost out on that gig. But when Oxley promised we'd be back in the spring, the booker was prepared to play ball. The trouble was that after the job, T-Bone would get to playing cards with the locals who waited around for him, and he'd stay up half the night. The next day he'd feel bad, but he wouldn't say much. He'd keep going, keep going, until suddenly the pain would be worse. Then Oxley would be down and spirit him away. That happened two or three times—like where he'd stay in the hospital a week.

"It didn't do us much good, and any other office would have dropped us long ago. But we kept on, until finally we were sued. Because anytime we were playing a week's engagement, a club owner stood to lose thousands of dollars. Still it continued like that until after Oxley died and T-Bone had to quit the road altogether. He had to face up to the operation he'd been putting off for so long. It knocked him out for a good time. But he was lucky," Wynn added, "like they told him at Freddie Simon's wake the other day."

T-Bone had found the conversation in the funeral parlor depressing, and at home he complained, "People ought to watch what they say."

"They didn't intend to drag you," Lester Skaggs told him, as he and Patty Jack passed him on their way into the kitchen, where they had a bottle of vodka stashed.

T-Bone accepted a Coke from Vi and settled back on the couch, and his thoughts returned to the road. "After Oxley went," he recalled, "it was bad. Harold was so great. I never met a guy like him.

The others are all the time stealing your money. But he banked
mine and watched over it for me. If I needed anything but didn't
have the cash, he went into his pocket and put it on the line—like
when I had the panel truck built. After 1949 we were on the road
so much I figured it was the only thing to do, and it cost me four
thousand dollars even back then! I had lockers put in and all kind
of stuff—so the guys could store their uniforms and gear and lock
up their horns. I carried my own PA system, and the truck had a
big picture of me fixed on one side: T-BONE WALKER AND HIS OR-
CHESTRA. It carried five of the fellows, and I had a driver for them.
Sleepy and I rode in the Cadillac, or sometimes he drove the station
wagon that I had as well. It had the truck hitched on behind. With
Vi along, and Jennard, Vi's niece, who did the payroll, there would
be like ten, sometimes twelve of us in those three vehicles I had.
Harold financed all that. I never had to worry.

"But I got sued one time for something that happened on the
road. Remember, Vi, when the trailer got hit and came loose? It was
a Sunday, in Mississippi, and the guys were on their way to Merid-
ian. I wasn't along. There was plenty of time, and I had stayed over
in Baton Rouge. So then I got a call! When the trailer had broken
free, it pulled to the left and started out across the street. People
were coming that way, and it ran into different ones."

"It was all horrible," Vi said. "And we got sued for a lot of money.
I think Mr. Oxley settled out of court, but it cost us nine thousand
dollars." T-Bone began to laugh, and she glanced in his direction,
surprised.

"Don't you know where my mind is at?" he asked, leaning over
to pat her hand. "I'm remembering that mule." He turned to me.
"You won't believe this, but that was another time I nearly got
killed. We were on our way to Opelousas, and this time my piano
player was driving the car I was in. That year we had a Buick, and
it was Zell Kindred, I think, behind the wheel, while I sat in front
alongside, my head resting against the passenger door. I was tired
and pretty well asleep. If I hadn't been, I'd sure as hell have been a
dead man today!

"A mule came up on the highway, one of them big old sawmill
mules. He'd slipped off a bank and into a ditch. Then he just clam-

bered out and came walking. Out of nowhere. And because it was
dark, you couldn't see him any kind of way. All at once, ke-boom! I
was lucky! His whole leg came through the windshield where I was
at. When I woke up, this mule's hoof had landed upside my head!
You should have seen the car, crumpled like an accordion. It was a
mess. It was totaled, really, and here the man talked about how I
was going to pay for his mule!

" 'I ain't gonna pay for no *mule!*' I told him. 'I don't believe this,
you letting a mule run around here in the dark. You are gonna pay
for my car!'

"Well, Oxley got after him. But you can bet he had no money.
All the same, I think Oxley got something. I remember, because
he came off his honeymoon especially for that! He'd met a real
pretty girl when he'd crossed the Mexican border one time. Later
he brought her back and carried her before a justice of the peace."

"Such a sad thing," Vi recalled, "because they hadn't been married very long, and Harold was crazy about his wife. Then he died,
just like that. Likely it was his heart, they said, because he was
always overweight."

"It was terrible. We had no warning at all," T-Bone went on.
"He'd just booked me into the Apollo Theater in New York. I'd
taken a plane and stopped off in Chicago first. And he was all right
when I left. Then it was my opening night, and here comes word he
was gone."

After a time, Vi added: "If he'd lived, things would have been
different, because we'd never had to worry. Harold took care of all
our business."

"Afterwards," T-Bone grumbled, "I had to go back to the Shaw
office where I'd been booked before. But this time the agency was
being run by his son. Even Billy Shaw, Sr., had died. The best I got
was a runaround by comparison." The phone rang, and he reached
over to the coffee table, holding the receiver up so that Vi, too,
could hear.

"I *know* who it is." He smiled. "Ana Louise. Back from Japan.
Hang on a minute. Vida Lee wants to talk."

"Come on over, sugar," Vi said. "Daddy needs cheering up."

Thirteen

Ana Louise

"Remember me? Do I need a passport like last time?" Ana Louise asked. T-Bone saw her framed in the doorway, as pretty as when she used to sing with the band, and recovered his spirits. He welcomed her with a kiss and explained, "She means Chuck Berry isn't alongside her this time.[1] Wait your turn, guys," he said, seeing Lester and Stymie lined up behind him. Vi forestalled them and pulled Ana Louise down on the couch.

"It was you we wanted to see. Forget Chuck," she said. "Now tell us about Japan."

In the twenty years since T-Bone gave her her first chance, taking her out on the road with the band, Ana Louise had covered a lot of ground. She had made a name for herself in Europe and married there, settling down for a time. In 1973 she returned home after two successful tours of Japan.

"Tokyo is great," she said. "Maybe that's where I'll end up. If they like you, you've got it made."

"Listen, Babe, you had it made years ago," Lester assured her, angling for a smile.

"You're looking at the wrong person," she said. "Let T-Bone take the bow. He took me on after Hot Ashes broke me in. Ashes worked as a comedian. Remember, Vi? Maybe before your time? Anyway, he persuaded my grandmother to let me appear at a little club near here. It was called the Brass Rail, at Broadway and Vernon. Mom and Pop Davis ran it, and for a while there was a white-only clientele. Then Ashes sold them a bill of goods about the shows he could produce. He turned the place into a black-and-tan, and people in the area began to come in. I was a dancer then. Kind of," she laughed. "I had an act on skates! Something different.

"I wanted to be a star so bad, like T-Bone and the artists that played the Lincoln Theater. My grandmother was a concert singer, so I figured I could sing, but my family had me study international dancing—Polynesian, Hawaiian, Russian, and all that. They wanted me to *entertain*. So when Hot Ashes came to the house, I showed

1. Chuck Berry was said to be indebted to T-Bone for much of the material that had made him famous in the field of rock music.

him my act on roller skates. I was just out of school, about sixteen, I guess.

" 'Let me book her at the Rail. I'll have her home early each night,' he told my folks. 'I'll see she doesn't smoke or drink, or do anything wrong.' "

Seeing T-Bone signal to Lester Skaggs and get to his feet, Ana stopped. She laughed as Blondie, T-Bone's scatterbrained dog, always looking for a ride, beat the two of them to the door.

"Carry on, doll," T-Bone said. "Skaggs and I have to pick up R. S. We'll be back."

Ana was interested at once. "That boy Junior you mean?" She remembered breaking in on the road with Rance Rankin.

"You've just about got it," T-Bone said. "My nephew, my step-sister's boy, named for my dad. He ain't no baby no more!"

But she would know him right away, he thought. R. S. had been married nineteen years but still looked like a kid.

"He was cute," Ana remembered, "sitting by himself in the back of the car while Vi and I did the talking."

"I'll hip him you're back," T-Bone called out as he left. Holding open the door, he added: "The Brass Rail, remember? We cut you off."

"Well, that was in the fifties," Ana went on, "and sometimes T-Bone would grace us with his presence. There came one weekend when he discovered I wasn't working. There on the stage I'd gone clean through the boards, broken my ankle. I used to do a leap in the air, and this night when I'd landed, the floor caved in and I heard some bones crack. After that, I couldn't work, and Pop Davis wouldn't pay me, even what he owed!

"Then T-Bone came by the house, asking for my dad. He was mad that the Rail hadn't paid me. He told my father that as soon as I was better, he'd take me out on the road with his show. He'd let me start in rehearsing to see if I could sing with the band. Dad got all excited, figuring Bone might make me a star. Or at least do like he did for Baby Davis, the girl Lester here married and who had sounded so good with the band. She duetted with T-Bone on some of the records they made. At that moment he was giving Al Gode-low a break, and people thought he was crazy, because Al sang like

B. B. King, and here Bone would be selling him to the audience when the fans had paid to hear *him* sing.

"But you have to understand how Bone was—he loved kids. He always had a lot of feeling for what was happening around him. Like sometimes when he was gambling, he wouldn't play to win. He had all kinds of friends in the South, and most were family men whose paychecks were small. So even if he ended up out of pocket, he never sent them home broke. He knew what went through their heads. They wanted a taste of the big time, that's all—to sit down with T-Bone Walker. And T-Bone didn't intend taking their money when the brothers didn't make much and had only just got paid. Rather than send them away busted, he'd take chances that boomeranged if there was a cardsharp in the crowd. Al and I could spot those sharks, and we'd be fussing to get him away and out to the car. 'I'll be right there, kids,' he'd say, waving. But mostly he'd keep right on. 'Mama's on the phone,' we'd tell him, because that worked sometimes."

Ana knew Vi was paying close attention, so she looked over and smiled. "You never let us down, did you? Vi never forsook us," she said, turning to me. "If she was along, she would hold money from him. If she was back here, we would phone, and she'd wire enough to get us to our next stop or bring us on home. There were no hotel bills, nothing like that. All the towns we played, everyone roundabout came to meet us, and there were always folks waiting to take us home. When we pulled in, all we had to do to find a place was go by one of the cafes or the club we were to play. T-Bone made out like every one of us was a star, so the people were glad to take the band as well.

"He always stayed good-humored. If he got mad and used cusswords, it was behind my back! He was never too hurried either. He handled himself kind of relaxed. Wherever he was due, he wasn't going to let it be one of those frantic things. Remember driving through that storm with the lightning bolt hitting the road a few feet from us, Vi? T-Bone just kept driving. Drove around it, and we went on. 'Don't worry about stuff like that,' he told us.

"He was lucky, too. Like the time a hurricane was headed for the town we were to play. It took a switch instead and tore up a place

behind us. And then waited till we got through to wreck our loca-
tion!" She laughed. "Oh, you *know* T-Bone liked it out there on the
road. It was a kick the way people got excited when we arrived. He
was never fussing to eat and go to bed—even when he'd driven all
those miles. He'd always find time to talk and kid around. People
closed up their businesses when they learned he was coming to
town. He went all over, and the crowds tagged along, because back
then people weren't scared to go up to a star, not like today. He was
family, talking to everybody, even the kids.

"The whole town partied and drank before the music came on.
But they came to the club all dressed up, and that kept them together for a time. The band went on first and would start riffing
away. A little later when T-Bone walked out, you couldn't hear a
word for the sudden uproar. There would be times when he really
felt like playing, and that's when the people got into those fights.
They just hauled off and started hitting on each other. They felt so
good, they fought to prove it!" Ana paused, laughing along with Vi.

"That's like when he played Lubbock, Texas," Stymie added. "We
still die about that. We were on our way into town when the sheriff
met us. We couldn't play there that night, he said.

"'Why not?' T-Bone wanted to know. 'We gotta play. We've got a
contract.'

"'Y'all broke up the town last time you was here,' the sheriff
said, sounding mean.

T-Bone got him calmed down after a while, and he let us through.
But as we started up the car, we saw him scratching his head.

"'What kind of music do you play,' he called out, 'that makes
niggers *fight* every time you show your face?'"

Stymie grinned. "Bone and I fell out!" he said. "Bone near
cracked a rib."

Ana heard T-Bone's step on the porch and went to the door.
"Where is he?" she asked, looking for R. S. R. S. got his arms
around her, kissing her before he stepped inside.

"You're right, Bone." She laughed. "He's not a boy no more." But
despite everything, she saw the boyish look had persisted. He was
heavier than T-Bone, taller and bigger-boned, but she could see the
resemblance. It was the adventuresome look in his eye.

"You're something else, Ana," he remarked. "She's twice as foxy now, ain't she, Bone?"

T-Bone laughed. He saw that inside of the hour R. S. would take over from Stymie and Skaggs.

"I never caught *your* act," he heard Ana say, as R. S. sat down beside her.

"Well, I wasn't much help, really," he said. "You know Bone. He don't need no one else."

"So he's being modest now." T-Bone decided to rib him. "If he weren't a Jekyll and Hyde, he'd be with me still. But he's King Kong, you know, when he hits the bottle."

"I'm not all that bad." R. S. looked aggrieved. "But I got started wrong, with T-Bone scaring me to death. He took me out of them fields when I was still a kid. And he said he'd whup me if I didn't do right."

T-Bone smiled again. "He was picking cotton when I got him. Not fifteen years old."

"That Christmas, 1948, T-Bone bought me a guitar," R. S. went on. "I was playing the devil out of it, too, when he came back six months later. But ass-backwards, because I had it tuned all wrong. Afterwards, when he'd fixed it for me, he got me up on stage. I sure did look ridiculous, man—just a kid, roarin' and stompin' away. But I was doing my best, trying to listen to the band. Then somehow I hit a note that sounded so bad, I called out. 'What *happened*, Bone?' He just laughed, but I damn near cried.

"So then he took me on the road as valet—you know, taking care of his clothes and all that. And I was driving a little. Remember, Ana, when we first met? But the thing was, it looked like Bone's suits kept disappearing. Mostly his white ones, it seemed. They just walked. I never knew what happened—I swear I didn't. But after three or four times he got mad. Every time we played Detroit, he'd come up with a suit missing, or a pair of shoes, something like that, and he would get on my back.

"Later, when he took me to Dallas, he bought me a suit, a beige outfit, real pretty. Well, I messed up that thing. You remember zoot suits? That's what I wanted. So I tried to make mine over! Bone must have done some thinking, then, because he took me downtown to the music store. He bought me some picks, and a music book from Montgomery Ward. That's how I got started—getting it all together, the different keys, the notes, and so on. Then when he went back on the road, he entered me at Jethro High in L.A. and let me live here at the house."

"But you ran out on us." T-Bone's expression hardened. "Because you had no faith in yourself."

"I didn't, that's a fact. I was scared all the time. Scared of that stage, and figuring if I didn't do right, you'd beat me up. So I cut out. You know how a boy does?" This time he turned to me. "The way a bad boy messes 'round? That's what I did. I went back to Bakersfield and started picking cotton again. No, I was setting out onions. In them doggone rows, long, like from here to Watts! Couldn't do but two a day.

"The money wouldn't buy nothin'. And I had a girl friend but couldn't take her out. Then there was the lawman, as well. The sheriff was known as W. J. and man, he was mean! T-Bone remembers. He tried to jump Bone one time. Bakersfield was having a party Friday, Saturday, and Sunday. It was a local celebration, and even my father was there because he hadn't to go into the fields till Monday. We were stoned, everyone, and then that sheriff walked up. You could have heard a pin drop. Everybody hushed, all of us black dudes. We were *scared.*"

"Not me," T-Bone retorted. "I walked up there and told him, 'I'm Rance Walker's son.' I shoved my face in his . . ."

Because everyone broke out laughing, T-Bone let Stymie finish.

"The man was so surprised," Stymie said, "his jaw went all slack. And boy, was he unhappy to see what T-Bone was driving! It made him so mad to see him cross the road and climb behind the wheel of that torpedo-blue Caddy—two-tone, with skirts. Outta sight!"

"You're wrong, man," T-Bone objected. "It was the Buick Special, the solid green. We went everywhere in that four-door, remember? When I bought it in '47, I'd paid *cash!*"

"Back to my story," R. S. said. "After the ruckus, I figured I'd had me just enough. So I turned right 'round and went home and pulled out my guitar. After that I played different places. In a couple of years I was in Fresno, working for a musician called Little Jimmy.

Our gig was the Elks Club, and we played fashion shows and things like that. Afterwards I jumped up and went north and worked with guys like Al Simmons. That's when T-Bone called me back. In 1955, remember, Stymie? Y'all heard me playing in Denver, Colorado, where Woody Woodson was."

"You had a guy playing bass, all hunched up. We remember," Stymie replied.

"That's because his pants were busted." R. S. grinned.

"Well, he couldn't play no bass, besides," T-Bone remarked.

"But you didn't dig it, Bone," Stymie explained. "His pants were showing his you-know-what!"

"So that's what it was," T-Bone smiled.

"Yeah. And afterwards you carried me back with you to the Flame Show Bar in Detroit," R. S. said.

"And billed you T-Bone, Jr. For the first time, I guess." T-Bone nodded.

"We went to the Crown Propeller from there," R. S. continued. "And after that you were robbed."

"Chicago. Right." T-Bone grimaced. "A gangsters' town. I lost plenty there at different times. Like once I ordered five silk suits—made of shantung, you know, when that stuff first came out. I bought five—three for Junior, two for me. Well, I was upstairs shootin' dice, and when I returned to the room—nothin'! No sign nor trace. What to do, since maybe the stage manager who was staying there was in on it, too?

"Later on I lived at the Pershing, and one morning when I came down and went out on the street, my Cadillac was hoisted on Coca Cola cases. They'd taken the tires! Chicago, South Side! They would clean us right out."

"The way they were after Bone, it was like white on ice," R. S. said. "I guess they figured on getting it the best they knew how. They could have even been his friends!"

Fourteen

Into the Heat

"I finished my time in the navy in 1952," T-Bone's son, Aaron, Jr., told me. "Then it was out of the navy and into the heat. That's when I started traveling with my dad, and I stuck with it almost two years. But I didn't like it at all. I'm much happier where I am now." When he elected to remain at home in preference to going on the road, he was hired by the payroll department of the Los Angeles school system. At first T-Bone was surprised. Afterward he was impressed, because it was evident Junior was going to get ahead.

"That's one of the things you give Dad credit for," Junior said. "He's a family man. He's proud of his daughter and proud of me. In fact, he overdoes it. You would think I was superintendent of schools. Maybe what pleased him was his feeling it had paid off, the way he had brought us up. Because he was strict. When I was a teenager, I had a curfew. I had to be in bed by 10:30. One night I remember I went to the movies and decided to stay and see the show a second time. It was 11:30 when I got in. My mother said, 'You know what time your daddy wanted you in!' So when he called— he'd telephone every other day when he was on the road—my mother put me on, and he told me, 'Junior, I'm gonna have to whip your ass.'

"It was a couple of months before he was back again, but once he'd walked in and said hi to my mother, he headed for the kitchen, where I was washing up. Straightway he started lambasting me! He was strict. But, you know, I'm glad he was, because I don't drink or even smoke. Regardless of what type of life *he* was living, he would tell me, '*You* are not gonna be a bum!'

"He gave a lot of good advice. In boot camp one time I was having some problems. A lot of fellows were from the South, and I told my father, 'First time one of them says something to me, I'm gonna pop him one.'

"'Let me tell you something,' my dad said. 'Those kids are going through the same thing as you. Like you're not used to being around them, they're not used to being around you. So judge each one as a person. Don't make snap judgments; don't group people in a bunch. You never know. Until you got reason, treat everyone OK.'

"Well, he was right. I found out on board the *Seminole*. One time

I'd taken an automatic dislike to a guy. He was from Mississippi, and the speech and all that meant Bilbo to me. Another fellow who was from the North I thought seemed pretty straight, but it so happened he was the one to make an ugly remark. I grant you the black guy he insulted was an asshole, all right, but the Mississippi man wouldn't buy it, and after telling the other man to shut up, he ended by knocking him down. For that he was transferred, and I felt real bad.

"But Dad's funny," Junior said, remembering his first leave after boot camp. For a moment, as he smiled, he resembled his father. "Since I had a week off, he sent me the fare to come out to him in Detroit, where he was working the Frolic Bar. When I got to the airport, without thinking it out, I took a cab instead of the limousine. I was tired, and when the cabbie said he knew where to go, I fell asleep and never realized what a long trip it was. When my father came outside to get me and settle the bill, he just about died. 'Well, my God,' he said, 'did you ride this cab all the way from L.A.?' And then, just to show he wasn't mad, when we got inside, he stopped a lady he knew. 'This is my son,' he said, 'he's in the navy. Here from California, first day of furlough. So will you take him upstairs and go to bed with him, please?' I was flabbergasted, and he took one look at my face and fell out."

R. S., Junior's cousin, brought T-Bone to mind in an undefinable way, but not much about Junior showed any similarity to his father. He was more reserved and surprisingly mature. Taller and rather more solidly built, his passion was sports—bowling in the winter, hiking and fishing in the summer, when he took girl friends along.

"But don't think because we're that different that we're not close," he said. "I know some people think so because we don't hang out together. They're all wrong. My father has a kind of magnetism that's hard to resist. He acts tough, but he's real warm. He'd do anything for you if you're in trouble, you know." For a moment Junior hesitated. "I don't want to keep tapping his bell, but it's like he feels responsible for anyone who is down and out. Look at the guys he hires—people other musicians won't touch. This fellow Sleepy—Dad made him his valet because there was nothing else he could do. One thing I know: he never turned anyone away from the door. Many times he made my grandmother mad inviting half a dozen friends to sit down to a meal.

"And it isn't like everyone treats him so great. I've quite often watched hustlers set him up for a killing in the kind of illegal gambling joint you encounter on tour. Because they knew he liked to gamble, the local pimps would take over, steering him into those places. They didn't try to rob him or anything like that. They'd just gang up and lay crooked dice on him. Of course, after his name got big, he started making money so fast it seemed there was always a helluva lot coming in. He felt he could blow it, I guess. He never thought about tomorrow. I wouldn't want to be like him, but I wouldn't want to say he was wrong, because regardless of setbacks with managers and agents—and there are all kinds of people who rip you off one way or the other—regardless of the lot, he always enjoyed himself. He *always* enjoyed himself.

"But I couldn't hack that life on the road. At first for me it had a kind of glorified sound, because when I got my discharge and joined my father, I was only twenty-one. But I never got used to it, and what shook me the most were the one-nighters. Sometimes you had to cover almost a thousand miles in a day. And back then in most places you had to find a black neighborhood right away. Some of the places you stayed in were ridiculous, believe me. I was road manager, and I got to thinking, 'How in the world could anyone like living like this?'

"Then there was one engagement I messed up good and proper. We were working out of Chicago and had two dates set up—one of which was a 9 P.M. gig in Michigan City, Indiana, and the other in South Bend began at midnight because we couldn't get the ballroom until after the whites. I got the details reversed, and when we arrived in Michigan City, we found the people had tired of waiting and wrecked the man's place. My father had to pay out in every direction: return his deposit, reimburse the damage, and take care of the band. It must have cost five thousand dollars. All he said was, 'These things happen.' But by then, after more than a year on the road, I had got so nervous I couldn't think straight, couldn't even drive, and I talked defiant, which went over like lead pellets with him. So we had a helluva row. 'Fire me, and let me go home,' I said. 'I don't know how long I can stand this.' But I felt bad, because he was never a really well man, and it was a lot worse for him.

"But he hated to let on how mean those ulcers could be. People thought he drank, but he told me that once he'd left Dallas, he'd quit drinking altogether. But after the operation it was different, because when more than two-thirds of his stomach went, it meant he couldn't take in much. But it also meant what he takes doesn't hurt him so bad. For a while at home we were mighty scared of what that knife might reveal. However, my mother's so great—if she worries, she never lets on. She's a wonderful person. Even my real mother, who lives in Louisiana, thinks there's no one like her! Over the years they've had a rapport you wouldn't believe. Even *her* mother looks on Vi as one of her own. We all owe her a lot, because sometimes my dad is away six months at a time. She never allows that to throw her, even if there happen to be women trying to call the house. She is able to cope with it, where many wives can't. One thing about Dad: whatever he does on the outside, he never involves us at home. He feels he can count on my mother. He knows she won't get excited.

"I remember her that way in Dallas, from when I was eight years old and had moved to my grandmother's house. Vi wasn't with us there. She was staying with her brother in Oak Cliff, cut off by the Trinity River from where we lived in North Dallas. They have freeways now, but it was viaducts then, with one set aside for streetcars to cross. The levees were anywhere from one and a half to two miles apart, and the river was more or less centered there, with room for spread if a heavy rain came and water flowed down from other spots. Oak Cliff was a wide-open kind of place, where you had clusters of little shotgun-type houses, but in North Dallas, which you would consider closer to downtown, the houses were crowded side by side. We lived on Allen Street, and you could walk to town in less than ten minutes. When you went down to the viaducts and the levees, you headed for the Bottoms. H Street was a sort of main thoroughfare, and anything past that was called the Heights. You had East and West Dallas besides, and scattered around were sections like Queen City, Bellum, and Pickett, more or less black areas at the time, with West Dallas considered the worst.

"Central Avenue wasn't really an avenue at all. It was where the railroad tracks ran, and not for passenger trains but for freight and things like that. Things were always jumping down there, with restaurants open all night and cafes full of people. In daytime the pawnshops and barbers took most of the trade. The movie house was there, and the cafe where my mother worked was a few doors down. My grandmother let me go to the movies on Mondays, especially during the summer, but I always managed to overstay my time. Then I had to get hold of Vi to save myself a licking. She knew that if I was on my own, I would get it from my gran, so she would walk me home. Otherwise," he added, smiling, "I would be sent out to get a cane from the chinaberry tree.

"One thing I learned about my dad while I was on the road is that where music is concerned, he is another man altogether. When it came down to the band, he was serious 100 percent. Guitar wasn't his only instrument, you know. He played piano, too, good piano, and he played bass and could get about on the drums. He played more than enough to keep on top of any groups he had, and he wanted perfection, in the rhythm section especially. He wasn't a great reader, I believe, not in the beginning. He probably never got that much practice, but he had a terrific ear, and after a while he made out pretty well. He always knew what was going on, and he liked the new progressions, the augmented chords. That's how he took up with jazz.

"One memorable night in Chicago," Junior recalled with pride, "he and Lester Young got together and played till dawn after Basie's gig. No one else, just the two of them downstairs in the basement of the Ritz Hotel.

"Though he doesn't always give an even performance, Dad's got the ability to get the best out of any group he is with. On an occasional night the audience may be flat, but other times there's been so much emotion directed at the stage that my father couldn't help working like a tiger. Not being a performer, I can't say exactly what causes this, but if I liken it to sport, I think I understand. When I was playing baseball, there were certain audiences I *worked* for because they brought out a lot in me. Another time you might think you were putting out, but you weren't, and it could be that deep down in your heart you knew you weren't being appreciated.

"At home we didn't understand what it was all about, what it meant to him. I didn't catch on till I heard him playing every night. That was his passion. Not the money-making or even building his name. He wasn't sophisticated enough to keep trying for hits. Making music was basic. He was no businessman, and I think he felt guilty about that where the family was concerned, but I feel it was a very fine thing. It was probably not the right way to be, but I admired him for it. He didn't put on the kind of show a lot of attractions work out, where each performance features hits from recordings, from albums you want people to talk about and keep buying. The band soon gets bored playing that kind of show every night. What they're doing becomes automatic, and it's seldom that anything gets called that is fresh and unrehearsed. Where you concentrate on audience reaction, that gets to be more important than what the band can do and what you yourself want to play. My father was opposed to all that. 'Where's the fun?' he'd say. And believe me, he was serious about his fun. When he came on stage playing, that's when he was most himself. And that's why he was strict with the guys. He didn't say much, but if anyone was kidding around, he'd get burned up right away.

"Younger musicians liked to hang out with him, you know, for that reason. Their heads were into music, same as his. You wouldn't believe the adrenalin he could put into a bunch of guys, even with a mediocre band. One white group that I remember played their fool heads off after he'd run down the show for them. As I said before, color was no issue where he was concerned. If you were an OK guy, you were dandy with him, black or white. He was aware of the inequalities we coped with all the time, but it would have to be *bad* before he let it get him down. He never let that part linger or make him bitter. He'd always look for the good side, and hated talking race. But that's not to say anyone could deliberately step on his toes. I've seen times when he scared me so bad . . .

"Back in the days when we were denied a lot of our rights, he would sometimes get angry to a point where he was ready to fight, no matter who or what. Two things in particular he was uncontrollable about: when a promoter was trying to use him, or contractors were false. And next in line, when he called a rehearsal, he wanted everyone there! It was never dull on the road with my dad. And he taught me a lot about race that I use in my job today.[1] It's not always a black-and-white thing. It's something more personal that we probably can't help—English, Irish, whatever we are. For instance, if you're watching someone your own kind, you want them to do well. That's automatic. When you see a black footballer, fighter, or ballplayer, deep down in your heart you want him to be the best because he's part of something dear to you. There's the other side of the picture, too. When something bad happens, like a robbery or a killing, if it involves blacks you feel especially bad and say, 'Jeez, I hate for him to have done that.' It sets *everyone* back when that kind of thing happens. Years ago I'd think we were never going to get anywhere at all, but it's different today, thank God. People are finally learning not to lump all blacks together, beginning to see that where dimwits are concerned, we have our share, like everyone else. It's got to the point now where you can discuss these things, actually crack jokes. Not so long ago you couldn't put on a TV show like 'Sanford and Son' or 'The Jeffersons,' where the comments would once have been very offensive. And jokes blacks make about *themselves!* At one time we were too sensitive about the whole thing, but I think Dad knew how it should be. He was always very cool.

"Too cool sometimes. He was notorious for hanging around too long when by rights he should have headed for the next engagement. On one occasion the band had left earlier in the day, but we didn't leave until late that night, so he was trying to make up time. We were going through the town of Waco, Texas, and of course he was speeding. I was lying in the back seat, attempting to sleep. The next thing I knew, the cops had stopped us. I kept my eyes closed and listened to the tale my father concocted.

1. Aaron Walker, Jr., has been a superintendent in the Los Angeles school system's payroll department for a number of years.

"'My son is very sick,' he said. 'Look there in the back. I'm getting him to the hospital fast as I can.' I about died when the sheriff said, 'Well, in that case, follow us.' So we race to the hospital in Waco, and I have to trump up some lie. I swallow some badass medicine to get him out of this, because otherwise it would have cost him a ticket. And in those days, in those little towns your ticket could cost you from one dollar to a hundred. One other time he didn't make out so good. He ran into a ruckus when the band was on the way to a gig in Santa Fe, New Mexico. His biggest mistake was paying to stay out of jail! Because he had to end up going anyway. This car the police stopped was registered in his name, though he wasn't riding in it that day. But the marijuana they found—they wanted to pin that on him. He might have got out of it with a lesser term, but he figured if he spent the right kind of money, he might not have to stay.

"It didn't work like that. He pulled some strings in San Antonio, and it saved him for a while, but eventually he had to go. And was it ever weird? Here's a man the police are picking up—and they send a private plane for him! After they'd let him finish his engagement, he was borne away, taken to that prison in Hobbs. And in three weeks' time he was a trusty, he said." Junior smiled and shook his head. "He stayed about nine months and worked in the hospital, I believe. He told me later, 'If I'd been in a while longer, I'd have had more pot there than I could have got my hands on outside!'"

Fifteen

Michigan Idyll

In the summer of 1956 T-Bone starred in the Idlewild Revue. It was the first of many times he was booked at this island resort two hundred miles north of Detroit. After the summer season the show went on the road and toured for three months, as did Larry Steele's Smart Affairs out of Chicago. At Idlewild, T-Bone's friendship with stand-up comic Bill Murray began.

"I had met him casually before," Bill Murray said, "while I was working for the Chrysler Corporation and was one of those life-of-the-party-type guys on the side. After a time I was laid off in a recession and decided to try my luck in an amateur show staged in a theater where T-Bone used to headline. They had got him to appear to make sure of a crowd, and that night he dug the fact that after winning the most votes, I got the judge to part with fifty dollars instead of a watch. Next time we met was at the Vogue, a little nightclub on the outskirts of the city where we were both on the bill. I think it was my first engagement, and I was doing slapstick comedy, with the baggy pants, the wine bottle, and the big floppy hat. I was tagged 'Winehead Willie,' after the song 'Winehead Willie, Put the Bottle Down.'

"After the first show, Bone wanted to go down the street for a bottle. He said the whiskey at the club was too high. When he reached the car, he'd either lost the keys or left them inside, so he got the trunk open and found a hammer in there.

" 'What are you going to do with that?' I asked.

" 'Hit the damn car,' he replied, 'because I've locked my keys inside.'

" 'Wait a minute,' I said, and felt in my pocket. He was driving a Chrysler, and I had an old '48 Plymouth made by the same company. 'Let me try,' I told him, and for the hell of it stuck my key in the door. Sure enough, it opened. And that's when he and I first got to be close. After that, when I eventually got going good, I'd run into T-Bone two or three times a year, but Idlewild was the first long stint we worked together. People flocked to the island from all over. This was when blacks congregated in their own locales, before things opened up. New Yorkers not booked at the Sir John Hotel in Miami came over to us, and a lot of the clientele hailed from Indiana, Ohio, and Illinois. Not all the artists presented were well-known names. There were unknowns as well, many on the verge of fame, people like Della Reese or the Ravens or the Four Tops, who made a name for themselves when they signed up with Motown. A lot of performers got a start in our show.

"We operated two clubs, and I was comic, MC, and show director for the one they called 'budget,' and over where T-Bone was working was the heavy show. Both opened at the same time, and those who couldn't get in to hear T-Bone came across to us. After the first performance we'd allow a half hour so people could switch, and then begin again. The following year I was there once more, and T-Bone was back, but R. S. was with him this time, and Bone was breaking him in to his act. Here was a youngster in an environment way over his head, but he had that southern background and was scared of Bone, so he got on OK. In fact, the older ladies found him real cute, and T-Bone had to keep his eyes peeled.

"The Revue was a show-girl type of thing, like you have in Vegas. Each year a different choreographer was engaged in order to have something new. This time our producer brought back a Mexican ballet company he had seen in Acapulco, and we invested thousands of dollars in costumes and recruited six tall, light-skinned girls for show. The hoofers were less regal, and there you had several pigmentations, so when the Mexicans were alongside our dancers it was a sight to see. A *beautiful* melting pot. As well as the parade girls and the ponies, we had chorus boys, too, and everyone lined up for the opener. Two supporting acts came after that, and by then the audience was geared for the production number, the *Watusi Wedding Ritual*, which was allotted thirty minutes. The show lasted two hours, with the star appearing just ahead of the finale, and the audience sat spellbound.

"We always allowed T-Bone as much time as he wanted. How he handled the people depended on how he sized the audience up. No two occasions were ever the same. If he thought the reception warranted it, he was the kind of pro who would break the format to do a *vibration*. Today when you refer to a guy's *vibes* you mean the same thing—a 'happening,' I guess, at a decisive moment in the show. T-Bone would start to ad-lib, then elaborate, and often ended having the audience entertain itself. He'd cater to the ladies at ring-

side, who always went ape. They considered it a black heritage
thing, and he was the blues man supreme. If he could have held on
to the momentum he'd established at that time, no one could have
topped him, not even Presley, who, everybody knows, stole his act.

"But he was on the scene too early, ahead of his time. A lot of artists who followed picked up on him and cashed in when the blues
became hot stuff. In some ways, though, he was inimitable. Like
how he handled his guitar, holding it near horizontal, wrist bent
way over. Instead of strumming at the bottom like the rest, he
picked closer to the neck and would get a thing going where, at certain tempos, he'd strut. Later he'd lift the guitar off his neck, letting it drag behind, fretting it with one hand. Try it for a minute,
and you'll find your fingers lock. Then he'd raise it to his shoulders,
put it back of his head, and play from there. Since he had records
out all the time, often on the charts, he had plenty of hits: 'Bobby
Sox Baby,' 'Cold, Cold Feeling,' 'Mean Old World,' 'Strolling with
Bone.' He'd keep the lyrics coming and finally start up the number
that climaxed the show. The people would be waiting for this and
would go haywire before he was through. Playing and singing, keeping the guitar back of his head, he'd go down slow in a long side-
ways split. Without losing a beat he'd first twist around and face
front, then inch all the way up. He always closed that way so that
no act could follow.

"I learned a lot from Bone. 'Until you know how to come on and
get off, you have shit,' he said. 'Come on like gangbusters, and go
off the same way. Leave 'em hungry, you know.'

"The way he handled the audience was another thing I admired.
Occasionally a lady got unruly, and though he showed her no dis-
respect, he could embarrass her. A remarkable thing was how much
he could take in stride. He fooled around quite a bit, and this has
been the undoing of a number of artists, but he'd skirt what was
real bad. When he indulged himself, it was with style and grace,
proving the thing can be done. The way he partied, for instance. I've
seen where there were so many people around him at times he had
to hire an extra suite. He knew how to win, but he could lose, too.
If somebody had cleaned him out and he had a job to go to, he'd
find a way to borrow. He'd either make it to the gig or return to the

game and win his money back. That was his style. He was always
cool, always sharp. And he had friends to turn to when his luck ran
out. He would call Ziggy Johnson in Detroit at the Gotham Hotel
or Sonny Wilson at the Mark Twain. Wherever he happened to be,
he could always get on the phone to these men. He might be drunk
and call them mothers, which would lead to them cussing him out,
but after arguing awhile, he'd get what he wanted. They would wire
money, and he would be on top again. Because he never did a snow
job. He always paid back, even if he turned around and borrowed
again!

"He was a determined man, and if you made him mad, he'd let
you know it. He didn't get salty over trifles, but if you wanted to en-
croach on his manhood, he'd be hard to handle. And if you were
doing something he didn't approve of, he'd get so forceful at times—
so domineering, really—in his attempts to dissuade you, that to
avoid a confrontation, you'd be forced to give in. 'You so-and-so,'
he'd say. 'You're young. Shut up and listen.' That's when he'd show
some ego.

"You'd see a negative side sometimes, where there was no getting
round him. The people in his crowd, used to his ways, knew they
could only get away with so much. If any indulged in vices, they
had to go behind his back. Although T-Bone didn't get depressed
very often, when he did, he would drink. Pot he reserved for a better frame of mind. I always got along with him fine. He treated me
like a son more or less and would look out for me if things threatened to get rough. Like in a hotel room one time when some of his
friends were telling jokes and the lady present was a stripper. He
sent me off for something as soon as the language got crude, and I
knew enough not to come back. He had respect for me—for everyone, in fact, according to the level they were at.

"Now the women around him—that was a whole other world. In
and out of his dressing room you met all kinds. One of those good-
time Charlies, maybe—a lady who had something going for her,
like selling bootleg whiskey, perhaps. Or who was into nightlife or
had a thing for performers. This never amounted to intimacy, but
for T-Bone and the rest such a lady held some attraction, and a
buddy-buddy situation could develop.

"Another type would be a lady with stars in her eyes and hopes of getting next to the man. If T-Bone took a notion to spend time with this kind of woman, she'd have to cater to him. He'd act arrogant at times, but likely she'd dig him enough and be ready to live with that. Once in a while there'd be a woman in some other category who might be attracted by him but would freeze when he was crude. This kind of lady he would view differently and might even divorce himself from his surroundings for her. For a while he'd act real good, as long as she was all right with him.

"Of course, every now and then he'd come across a high-stepper, a show girl with looks, used to things going her way. For a time you might see a reverse situation. But I never saw a woman who could be domineering with him. Some guys are like that, you know. If a lady latches on for prestige or whatever, they figure she knows what to expect. They say, 'If I tell you move, you *move*. Or else.'"

Occasionally T-Bone met someone who held his interest for a longer time, such as the lady in San Antonio whom I will call Beulah Banks. When they met, she had been a hostess at a nightclub there for a number of years.

"Same as Bill Murray said," Beulah confirmed. "Women buzzed around T-Bone like flies. He had to shoo them away. But my case was different. There was competition he had to fight off. Life was hectic in San Antone, and my neighborhood was Spanish, French, and German. We never had real race trouble, like Dallas or Houston, but things got hot once in a while, because this was a booming town. At the club I was the first black hostess to entertain whites. We drew an integrated crowd, and I pretty near ran the club for the owner. Our money was fantastic because besides gambling, we sold bootleg whiskey. Monday nights the greenbacks would be stacked so high I could hardly see over. Since we were going together, with me in his corner, the boss became a rich man. He'd go off for a weekend sometimes, but every penny waited for him whenever he got back. I was in love, that's why.

"I came to the club straight out of school, and he was the first man I knew. Besides the grill, he operated five cabs, and while he was away, I'd collect his money, put it in an oatmeal box, and bury it in the sand. I let no one get at it, I was so mad about the man. But out of the blue one day he got married on me! Just took him somebody else, and that broke my heart. I left the job and went off to St. Louis with a railroad fellow who was crazy about me. I had two daughters by him. But later I saw there was another woman on his mind, so I took the children and came home. I went back to the same club, and a year or two passed before T-Bone played there. T-Bone was a fascinating man. My old boss was after me again, but by then that meant nothing. I would have been a fool to pass up Bone. He gave me lots of money and at first won me that way. Later I got more involved, and seems like he did too.

"'When I'm playin' upstate, how about payin' a visit?' he said. I liked that fine and began to accompany him when he was on tours close by. They called me Lady Bones and made a fuss of my children because T-Bone treated them so nice. He had a thing for kids. By 1956 we'd been together, here and there, for nearly ten years, and then my boy was born. T-Bone was playing the auditorium in Houston at the time, and they told me that when my telegram arrived, he nearly took a fit, he was so pleased, and acknowledged him right away.

"He didn't do like he did about his daughter born out of wedlock, same as my child but early on. I've known her mother all my life. She was a pretty little thing, and fellows were wild about her. When she first met T-Bone, years ahead of me, she was waiting table in a Chinese restaurant. She was only a kid, and she came up pregnant after she'd been with T-Bone no more than twice. He didn't recognize the baby for the longest time, but he admitted to me that at first he'd fallen head over heels in love. Still, men do like that if it suits, you know.

"After my own baby got bigger, I sensed he had others besides myself. I spotted them on tour, hovering around. Though we stayed friends, we broke up because we were getting nowhere, really. T-Bone knew how to give, but he wouldn't give quite enough."

When the fall bookings ended for the Idlewild Revue and T-Bone went back to the West Coast, Bill Murray said he didn't see him for a while. "I was working around Detroit," he explained. "Berry

Gordy and I used to gang-bang up and down Hasting Street long before Gordy got into Motown. So of course when the company started, I made my first recording for them. Though Timmie Rogers and I made 'The Last of the Bigtime Spenders' for Motown, I got discontented with the company, since they had no interest in comics. And soon they were experiencing growing pains that were so disturbing I pulled out.

"This was the rock 'n' roll age, during the first Dick Clark era, and I moved over to Henry Wynn's Supersonic Attractions. We traveled everywhere and at the end of each tour returned to base, which for us was the Royal Peacock in Atlanta. I began seeing T-Bone again, because for a while he was often the star of our show. Since I'd gained experience on the road, I was promoted to management, and it fell to me to hire and routine the acts.

"In the late fifties, after T-Bone had been ill, he'd started drinking again, and a lot of times he wasn't really up to par. By now he wasn't drawing so good. But he never acted big shot with me or anyone else I know of, never came on with 'I am a star.' The guitar said it for him, and anyone coming after still had to scuffle like mad. 'Hey, Scoop Nose,' he'd say, because that was our name for each other, 'when am I on?' He never made me worry about his place in the show, like some who had to be farther down on the bill. 'Hey, long as you don't forget me when payday comes around!' was all he'd say.

"He got plenty of respect for that, and more than once it paid off. In the early sixties, at the Tivoli Theater in Chicago, the lead we'd hired was a young lady featured in 'Star Trek.' T-Bone we had dropped, since he'd been with us all season, but he was still in Chicago. Now the kind of ego trip this young lady was on had her insisting on heavy roles. Since it wasn't that kind of a show, right away she and the producer got into a fight. He fired her on the spot and said, 'Get Bone on the phone.' He came back just like that, and for the rest of the week, you are right, it was Standing Room Only!"

Sixteen

Rhythm and Blues, U.S.A.

"When you look back on your career, it's like a chain," T-Bone told me. "With some years—a string of them, I guess—ending one part of your life and sending you in another direction. Parts of what you remember make you feel pretty good. Others are a drag. That first period in my life when I was fooling around in Dallas was great. The future never crossed my mind. The way Seymour remembers it, we were just having a good time and figured we knew all the answers. We had the world on a string. Even the racial bit didn't bother us because we didn't let it intrude.

"Some memories stay with you because they mean a lot at the time. Like my friendship with Clyde Barrow. After I left Dallas, I never saw him again, so I didn't know him during the years he was supposed to be Public Enemy Number One. But for a long time we boys hung out together. Color didn't bother him. I slept over at his place, or he slept at mine. It was OK with his folks and my mother, too. She said that later on people in Dallas called him Robin Hood. They were sorry to see him captured and see him die, and me, I'm sorry to this day.

"A thing I enjoy is thinking back to L.A. when I first landed in town. Those must have been maybe ten years all told that were exciting as hell, and they never faded that much. Maybe you enjoy your first successes most. I get a kick out of remembering my reign at Little Harlem, my name in lights at the Troc, and entertaining at the Rhumboogie in Chicago in the star's dressing room. I appeared with Ed Sullivan on 'The Toast of the Town,' my first time on TV, and after my records got going, I had quite a few hits. Once I had four all at one time on the charts. You remember these things because of what they signified right then. For a dozen years you're still climbing, and then all of a sudden—boom! You're taken by surprise. You find out you have a name to maintain. Guys in the band are dependent on you, so you can't fool around anymore. For a while that was great, but not for long, because when you have to think ahead all the time, you've tied a stone round your neck.

"That's why Harold Oxley meant so much. Harold brings another period to mind. The best, maybe, depending on your point of view." He smiled, remembering his arguments about not wanting so much to make money as to have a good time. "For a long while we made

plenty, as long as Harold was on the job. But then he died. Afterwards it seemed like I got sick more often." He was silent a moment, recalling. "In the end I had to quit dodging," he said. "I was
down to ninety-three pounds. Then the doctors took over and finally cut me up. Robbed me of my stomach pretty near. But I came
round all right. It was a real load off my mind, although I didn't
snap back that fast and had to let the band go. What a drag! Still,
the bookings were too hard to handle, so that's when I broke in
R. S.

"He played great, you know—better'n me, I would say. But you
had to build his confidence up. He wasn't much more than a kid,
and the only bad thing about him . . . he couldn't drink either.
Some people are like that, you know, crazy when drunk." Again he
smiled. "It was the blind leading the blind, because after the operation I liked to indulge a little myself. But we played a whole lot of
spots for a good number of years, places like the Bronze Peacock in
Houston, the Celebrity Club in Providence, the Showboat in Philly,
the Sportstown Club in Buffalo, the Flame Show Bar in Detroit,
the Chatterbox in Cleveland, the Blue Mirror and the Sugar Hill in
San Francisco, the Five-Four Ballroom in L.A., the Savoy Club in
Richmond, California, and the Longhorn Club in Dallas. Then one
night in San Francisco—we were at the Blue Mirror, I think—that
boy got so high he ran up a tab at the bar that took me all week to
cover. After he'd treated every barfly in sight, he got fired outright!
That put period to another phase in my life.

"Things hadn't exactly slowed at that time, because guys like
Muddy Waters and John Lee Hooker were doing OK, and B. B. was
climbing fast. But for me the situation wasn't so hot. Word got
around my condition was poor. One time when I was laid up, I
know people said it was heart, but the only thing the doctors said
was to take it easy awhile. Then in 1960 I got me a break. And blew
it to hell!" He shook his head, still mad. "I have never yet figured
myself out. The deal was a big-time package show built round Count
Basie and the band, and there were other stars like George Shearing
and Ruth Brown. Jimmy Rushing was long gone from Basie, and Joe
Williams had split, too, so I was being hired to appear with the
band. We were getting together in New Orleans and going to work

our way back to the Coast. Don't get me wrong. I wasn't drinking any more than the rest, but somehow I felt my act had fallen kind of flat. That's what *I* thought. I got to feeling real bad. It wasn't how I was handled, because Basie treated me great. And it wasn't the money either, because I'd have paid my own salary just to hear those cats blow. I can't account for what I did then. I quit halfway and went home. 'Now, Bone, don't do like this,' Basie said. 'It's gonna be hard to live down.' I knew he was right. Nothing came between us, but my mind was made up.[1]

"The Basie band went to Europe the following year, and because I ought to have been with them, I was griping. But in '62 I got my chance, with a package called "Rhythm and Blues U.S.A." It was a tour booked by Lippman and Rau, and what made it great was that Horst Lippman had hired a whole bunch of people who were friends: Memphis Slim, Shakey Jake, Willie Dixon, John Lee Hooker, Helen Humes, the drummer Jump Jackson, plus Sonny Terry and Brownie McGhee. We had a ball, start to finish, and couldn't believe the kind of audiences we had. People there *listen*. You've got to be a showman back here. Over there first time I did the splits the fans booed! That was hard to credit, but it was all right with me. They came to hear the music. From there on, I *played*, wherever we were. The Concert Bureau had us booked for concerts in France, Italy, Germany, Denmark, Sweden, Switzerland, and England as well. Then when we got to Hamburg, Memphis and the rest of us recorded."

Released in the United States by Decca as the Original American Folk Blues Festival, the album was a success. The session took place October 18, 1962, after a concert that was presented at Hamburg University's ultramodern Auditorium Maximum. Although the affair, held in Deutsche Grammophon's studio in Rahlstedt, did not begin till after midnight and did not end till 5 A.M., the musicians were keyed up and responded to an audience that materialized like magic. Side 1 opened with Memphis Slim at the piano and

---

1. "I think what happened," Count Basie said later, "he didn't feel at home in our groove. We have our own thing, maybe a little different from his, and he felt a breeze, somehow. Sad, because we could have got along just fine."

T-Bone on guitar, backed by Willie Dixon on bass and Jump Jackson on drums. During the next two numbers, which T-Bone sang, the group remained the same. Then Memphis followed Sonny Terry and Brownie McGhee, this time without T-Bone, to deliver his original version of a song about a racing mare called Stewball who stumbled at the track and left Memphis behind.

"Let's Make It Baby" featured not only John Lee Hooker's voice and guitar but a rhythm section that was built around T-Bone at the keyboard. He produced his same driving style on piano, and this inspired the rest of the band. He enjoyed being a sideman in company like this. It was not his nature to squeeze-play anyone, so he was happy back of Hooker in a Kansas City style that gave John Lee a lift. Hooker can be heard shouting, "Mighty eighty-eight man, T-Bone Walker," as the audience begins cheering as T-Bone's solo concluded.[2] Carried over onto Side 2 as "Shake It Baby," this number was the most successful recorded.

"Back home," T-Bone continued, "I saw Vi wanted to go abroad next time, so I took her along in '65 when I went to England again. I was teamed with an English blues group that John Mayall had rounded up.[3] The fellows knew my records well, so we hardly needed to rehearse. We got along fine, and by the time we'd played a few towns, I'd gotten kind of used to their English ways. We ended up at the Flamingo in London, and because the blues were all the rage, the reviews were real great. Vi got a kick out of that."

T-Bone had expected to return home after he closed at the Flamingo, but instead he and Vi crossed the Channel to play four concerts in France. The occasion was vividly described by Jacques Morgantini, vice-president of the Hot Club de France, in the *H.C.F. Bulletin* for December, 1965.

For a long time T-Bone Walker was one of my favorite musicians, and for a number of years I was committed to obtaining every one of his records. But though I was familiar with so much of his work I could

2. Hooker meant that T-Bone was a great keyboard man, accomplished on all eighty-eight keys.
3. A versatile harpist, Mayall was an innovator in the field of English blues.

hardly believe how great he sounded when he appeared in Paris in
1962. From that moment on, I never stopped wanting to see and hear
him again. Once we learned, my friends and I, that he was going to be
in England three weeks, it was unthinkable to allow him to return
home without trying to move heaven and earth to bring him to Pau
first. Aided by Hugues Panassié, we contacted his English manager
and were able to arrange for four concerts.[4]

On November 3rd, we awaited T-Bone at the airport. But was he on
the plane? Was his guitar aboard? Had it been sent on elsewhere? *Non,
il est bien la!* With him was his sweet and charming wife, and his
guitar as well. But . . . no amplifier! His manager had forgotten to
advise us about this. But eventually we find a young guitarist who
will lend us his. *Ouf!*

Because T-Bone was always accompanied by an orchestra, or at least
a rhythm section, we had to find accompanists familiar with the blues
and capable of providing workmanlike, lively *swinging* support.
Therefore we had sent for one of the best guitarists in Europe, Jean-
Pierre Sasson, a man who has often accompanied Memphis Slim, Hal
Singer, and Stuff Smith, and who *knows* the blues. Also present were
Jacques "Popoff" Medveko, a solid bassist, and our old friend Teddy
Martin on drums. Here was a closely-knit trio which permitted T-Bone
to feel at home right away. This was clearly established during a brief
rehearsal, and we were wholly reassured about the quality of the mu-
sic we would hear at the concert that night.

Everybody was astonished by the way T-Bone conducted. His relaxed manner and the driving beat he introduced with his feet showed
he knew how to stimulate his partners and set them to swinging as
hard as they could. Of all the musicians I've had the good fortune to
see and hear in person, T-Bone, along with Louis Armstrong and
Lionel Hampton, has the greatest dynamism. And like them, with a
single brief phrase at the start of a chorus, he transports his listeners
into another musical world.

*On reçoit alors un véritable coup dans l'estomac tellement l'im-
pression de swing augmente en une fraction de seconde.*

---

4. Late author and critic Hugues Panassié, president of the Hot Club de France,
was Europe's best-known authority on jazz.

Often T-Bone would play an electrifying phrase like that and follow this with a rest (itself charged with the beat) to allow his audience to recover. I think it useless to try to describe T-Bone Walker's guitar style and attempt to define the incredible influence he has had on other guitarists since 1942. His records speak for themselves. But I *must* refer to his marvellous *sound*, to the way his improvisations abound with subtle contrasts, and to his sense of rhythm which results in quite devastating swing. How to depict the way he makes his guitar "talk?" Intense inflections, glissandos and elongated notes each in their turn create the most beautiful kind of speech in the world. It is impossible, at least for me, to find fitting words to describe a T-Bone Walker concert. One is enchanted, because not only is his music wonderful but his demeanor gives it a new dimension.

One word about his "show." I am always astonished to hear certain fans express distaste when musicians play-act and dance during the course of a performance. Hugues Panassié has already addressed himself to this point better than I ever could. Nevertheless I would like to emphasize that in T-Bone's case we have the kind of jazz musician who, in addition to music, gives us dancing, miming, humor—*bref, la vie en scene.* A magnificent show which enchants the eye as well as the ear.

A final concert at Bordeaux concluded these remarkable days and heralded T-Bone's departure. How sad we felt. Because T-Bone is not only an admirable musician, *mais un homme d'une gentillesse, d'une droiture, d'une intelligence, d'une sensibilité très rare.*

Seventeen

Les Trois Mailletz

"Going abroad was an education for me," T-Bone explained. "I dig the way those people live. They consider you an artist and treat you that way. That's why a lot of the fellows stay over there. It's not just the women. It's something more than that. For the first time us guys could hold our heads high. Maybe there's no place like home, but in the U.S. when you feel less than a man, something is really wrong. That's how we felt, anyway—guys like Ben Webster, Stuff Smith, Don Byas, Kenny Clarke, Hal Singer, Memphis Slim, Bill Coleman, and a whole lot besides.

"I think I was received better in France than anywhere else. Maybe it was because alongside the blues I played jazz, and that pleased them. It worked out different in England. In 1966 when Norman Granz hired me to appear with Jazz at the Philharmonic there was a little outcry in London because people were saying they didn't want R and B. But Norman paid it no mind.[1] He was always in my corner because of the jazz I played. I had been in on some of his earliest jam sessions and in 1943 was featured in JATP alongside Billie Holiday, King Cole, Woody Herman, and a lot of other names. So when the reporters talked to me about mixing R and B and jazz, I told them, 'Better come and hear for yourself. Ask the guys. I want no R and B. I like nothing better than playing with Dizzy, Clark Terry, Teddy Wilson, Zoot, Flip, and the rest.'"

This musical experience made up for the setback with Basie, and T-Bone was well pleased. "Once we arrived on the Continent," he said, "there were no more gripes. And later Milt Buckner, Jo Jones, and I did a tour of our own."

Shortly afterward, Kenny "Klook" Clarke renewed his acquaintance with T-Bone. Playing with Dizzy Gillespie in 1939, Clarke was credited by Gillespie with inventing a bop style of drumming that evolved from the old sock-cymbal routine into a subtler approach. Using the top cymbal for the beat, he featured the bass drum for punctuations, completing the phraseology of artists like Charlie Parker, Thelonious Monk, and Howard McGhee. In

1. In *Melody Maker* (December 16, 1966) Max Jones reported that impresario Norman Granz drew him out to the stage to hear "some of the best playing of the evening," making it clear that T-Bone was a forceful influence.

Harlem, as the contractor for the house band at Minton's, he engineered sessions where fledgling bop musicians were welcomed, and introduced a new role for drummers. Clarke-inspired percussionists were identified by varied interpolations of the "klook-a-mop" genre. Celebrated, but disillusioned and frustrated after a decade of expectations, Clarke eventually settled in Paris among expatriates of that era.

"When Bone showed up here," Clarke said, "we got together for a drink because it had been a long time since we'd met. Bone liked to try you sometimes. He said, 'How you doin', nappy-haired boy? Making any money at all?' Keeping my cool, and my hands where they belonged, the next thing I knew we were laughing. We stayed good friends from that time on. He was OK that year, but in '67 his health was poor. Tuberculosis or something was what the guys said. But you know they like to talk, so I'd ask, 'How you feel?' 'Well, I don't know,' he'd say. If I pressed him, he'd be offhand. 'I must be fine, I guess,' he'd throw out and in a minute would be kidding so you'd forget for a while.

"One thing I remember was the way Wynonie Harris back home was jealous of Bone. 'You know T-Bone?' I'd ask, and he'd holler back, 'Don't talk no T-Bone to me!' But Bone and Memphis Slim got along fine, and that's how he moved to Les Trois Mailletz when Slim went on tour.[2] This was a nightclub on the Left Bank, a *cave* that had been a torture chamber in the seventeenth century. The torture instruments are still there—the leg-irons, spike boards, and the thing for your neck where they can hang you or reverse it and string you up by your feet. Madame Denise kept all the stuff because it went over big with the tourists. There was a small floor where people could get out and dance, although when Memphis was booked, he'd have them wheel his piano out and do his show from there. The place seated a couple of hundred, I guess, and the bandstand was big enough for seven or eight guys. The clientele went for T-Bone in a very big way, and Madame was well pleased. She brought him back often, whenever Slim took off. They hit

---

2. A well-known pianist and blues singer, Memphis Slim (Peter Chapman) was an expatriate living in Paris.

around 10 and kept on till 3 A.M., when Bone might just be persuaded to quit. He stayed with Hal Singer if he was in town any length of time."

Singer was an American tenor saxophonist whose R and B hit "Cornbread" remained some months on the charts in 1949. Born in Tulsa, Oklahoma, he played with Nat Towles's orchestra in 1939 and for the next twenty years worked with groups fronted by Jay McShann, Lips Page, Roy Eldridge, Don Byas, Red Allen, and Sid Catlett. Before emigrating to Paris, he played briefly with Lucky Millinder and Duke Ellington.

"I didn't know Hal well then, but I'd heard about 'Cornbread,'" Kenny Clarke said, smiling. "Once upon a time I made that kind of record, too. Bob Stevens at Decca would say, 'Why don't you pick up on the race record bit?' So in order to keep the bread coming in, I'd record with Marie Knight, Sister Tharpe, and Sammy Price. But at Decca I had to sneak in! They had the main studio on the second floor, so you felt you had to come up those stairs. But then you'd go out through another door and downstairs—that's where the race records were made. I would come in like I was going to make a jazz date, and the cats would say, 'Klook, who you makin' it with today?' Those bebop cats. So I'd walk in and down those stairs and wouldn't let the guys know so they couldn't put me down! Then one of my best friends, Russell Morris—we were raised up together—married Rosetta Tharpe, and the three of us became real tight. When she would hit Paris, she'd put on a home-cooked dinner and call me straight away."

"Well," Hal Singer recalled, "people don't feel the need to put you down over here. That's one of the reasons T-Bone was happy. He and I liked to talk over old times. I met him first years ago, playing at a dance in Houston where he was already showing drawing power, and after that we saw each other on the road in different places. Then in '68 we had a tour in France set up by Jean-Marie Monestier, who founded the Black and Blue label. He had us make a session in Bordeaux in November. The album was called *Feeling the Blues*, and Delmark released it at home later on as *I Want a Little Girl*. We used Muddy's drummer, S. P. Leary, and George Arvanitas on piano and Jacky Samson on bass. Then before T-Bone opened up at Les Trois Mailletz, we went out on the road with Ram Ramirez, the composer of 'Lover Man,' on piano, Wally Bishop on drums, and a French boy called François Biensen, who played trumpet like Louis. We played in France, Switzerland, and Belgium, and somewhere near Bordeaux is where T-Bone lost his guitar.

"He'd been playing it fifteen years, so you know how he felt. Later on Ram said: 'T-Bone thought maybe the stage manager had let the wrong person backstage, but we knew better. It was those hippie chicks hanging round him all the time, those Scandinavian blondes who were up to no good. But you couldn't convince *him*. They had him blindfolded, I guess. They stole the big white guitar from him, the Gibson 400 that they don't make anymore.'

"Well, anyway, it walked," Hal Singer went on, "and never returned. It was a terrible drag, but *he* could reach the public with any guitar, so our tour was OK. At that time my wife and I had a little girl four or five months old. We were living near the Tour Eiffel. We had a living room, bedroom, hallway, and kitchen, and T-Bone was staying with us, sleeping in the front room. He was generous, too generous, with my family and me. Each day he would play the piano, and with my little baby on his arm he'd sing the blues. He indoctrinated her, my wife said. And spoiled her, no doubt of that.

"Since he was not much of a sightseer, he liked to stay home. Unless Memphis was in town. Then they might hang out together. All kinds of people came to our apartment to see him, writers and people from radio and television. T-Bone was just happy being T-Bone and having a few little drinks, so he made no effort to learn French. But still, most everyone who saw him either spoke English, or my wife or somebody's friend would translate.

"While he stayed with us, we wanted for nothing, and at Les Trois Mailletz he picked up all the tabs his musicians or friends ran up. At this time he was drinking a bottle of gin a day, and one each night at the club. The problem was how to feed him. After several days of our begging, he might let my wife fix him some bacon and eggs, but it was hard to get him to take anything else.

Maybe half a sandwich before he left for work. The sets at the club were not difficult. With him in the band were Dominic Chance on tenor; Michel Sardaby, piano; Henri Touchet, bass; Michel Denis, drums; and Claude Guy, vibraphone. They were on the stand forty minutes at a time, and the last set was 1:30 A.M., but it regularly went over because T-Bone would be feeling good, and the public as well! It would be hard sometimes to get him down from there!

"Later on he made two more sessions for Black and Blue, one with Jay McShann and myself, another with Eddie 'Cleanhead' Vinson.[3] He stayed with us twice, but on this third trip to Paris my mother was with me, and we'd had our Nina, a second little girl. We were in a new apartment, and it wasn't big enough for five, but he still visited us when he could and talked with my mother, whom he loved.

"By 1970 it was rumored Polydor was interested in signing him up. When I heard it discussed, it embarrassed me because I didn't care for some of the company T-Bone was keeping and preferred not to make a session with him at that time. Since he was a heavy spender, there was always a bunch of no-goods hanging around him that you wouldn't want to call friends. But such guys know how to make themselves useful—like getting you home when you're drunk. And the way Bone was made, he thought well of everybody except real *evil* cats. But now I could see he was hooked up with people who were very bad news. Memphis, too, could have told him, but figured he'd turn a deaf ear. I guess T-Bone was impressed by what looked like a cool life-style, because it seems that right away he considered having these cats handle his affairs. He'd wanted to rid himself of that burden ever since Oxley died. 'I'm sitting pretty now,' he told me. 'These guys can just take over. Why didn't I run into them a few years back?'

Singer hesitated a moment and then asked me: "Do you dig? A year ago these fellows got their name onto my music somehow, and in order to unload them as part composer, I had to appear before

3. Titles of albums: *Confessin' the Blues* by Jay McShann, and *Wee Baby Blues* by Eddie Vinson. A fine alto saxophonist and popular blues singer, Vinson often performed with T-Bone.

SACEM and file a complaint. But how could I tell Bone, after what he'd just said? So because these guys were in charge of the date, I had to find some excuse. Then, as luck would have it, when the album was released, it won an award at home, and after that no one could bad-mouth his sponsors any kind of way."

Eighteen

Super Black Blues

The drinking T-Bone was doing in the 1960s began to be more noticeable. The old passion for gambling had finally subsided, but it had been gradually superseded by a kind of alcoholism. "It was gradual, I grant that," Junior told me, "because the first time I saw Dad inebriated must have been at least two years after the operation was over. By then I'd gotten away from home and wasn't in contact as much as before, so I was really surprised the first time I saw him . . . well, drunk. He'd called my home and told me to come and get him. I said, 'Well, where are you?' and it turned out he'd parked his car in the parking lot of a taco stand because he knew he couldn't drive. This was on Vermont, near Jefferson and the USC campus, and I remember I was just so surprised to see him like that I was flabbergasted. After hearing what he was drinking, I said, 'It's a wonder you didn't take off, downing stuff like that.' Because it was the weirdest concoction of gin and Coca-Cola.

"It more or less began to take shape from there. He was becoming a problem drinker. Well, it's a hard life, and you have to be a very strong person, I feel, not to let it get you to the point where you're into alcohol or maybe drugs. I tried to talk to him, tell him it was nothing to be ashamed of, just something that ought to be treated like any other illness. I told him, 'If we find it's turning out to be a problem, we should just deal with it that way.' But he only nodded, and I think he deluded himself, because as long as he could play, he thought he was doing all right.

"His constitution, though, couldn't take all that battering, and he had setbacks time and again. I think it was in 1959 that the doctors treated him for a heart attack. He took it a little easier for a while, but not too long. For a few years there he was happier, traveling abroad and all. But later on, even over there he started drinking more, and when he came back in 1970, he was the worst we'd ever seen. We didn't know it, but he was sick by then a different way and had been for some time. At home after that mess-up with his car, he'd started hemorrhaging from the lungs. On account of all the damage the doctor found, they kept him in the hospital for a real long period this time. We'd been thinking of the problem as drink, and that's probably what he'd thought, too. But now he had double trouble."

In live performance it was not always easy for a listener to discern T-Bone's condition, but on records it was. This was serious, because throughout his career it was mainly his records that had guaranteed and preserved his success. In 1950, after Capitol released the last of his Black and White recordings, he signed a contract with Imperial, and in the next five years he recorded sixty titles, many of which turned out to be popular R and B hits. Imperial eventually released three long-playing albums of the best-selling titles.[1] When his contract was up, Nesuhi Ertegun invited him to sign with Atlantic, but this was the period of the long aftermath of the 1955 operation, and by 1958 he had made only three sessions for them, which were marketed in a long-playing album in 1959. The first session was made in Chicago, and the effect was foreign to him, since the back-up band played Chicago style. On one track, "Play On, Little Girl," Junior Wells was featured on harmonica, producing a blues effect from an earlier time. But T-Bone did not mind, because, like everyone else, he admired Junior's model, the harpist Little Walter, whom Junior had eventually replaced in Muddy Waters' band.

The second session, made in Los Angeles, had a more typical format, with Lloyd Glenn on piano, Billy Hadnott on bass, and Oscar Lee Bradley on drums. The third provided something new. With the recruitment of guitarist Barney Kessel, an alumnus of the Charlie Barnet and Artie Shaw bands, as well as R. S., who was by then regularly featured with T-Bone, it showcased three guitars, and the album came out with the title *Two Bones and a Pick*. Although the quality was not consistent throughout, it received favorable reviews. Then, for the first time in his career there followed a period when T-Bone had no releases at all.

For the next three years he was in a comparative slump. It ended with the American Blues Festival session in Hamburg in 1962. By 1970, besides having resumed recording at home, he had made five

---

1. Shortly after T-Bone's death in 1975, United Artists issued a two-record set from this source, in the Blue Note Reissue Series, entitled *T-Bone Walker: Classics of Modern Blues*. It contains much of T-Bone's finest work. For an extract from its liner notes, see the Introduction to this book.

albums abroad, three featuring him on piano as well as guitar.[2] Besides the tracks for Polydor, Black and Blue had released two albums in addition to *Feeling the Blues*—one with Jay McShann and one with Eddie Vinson. All the albums made in Europe were of reasonably high standard, but this was not always true of those recorded in the United States during the 1960s. In the intervals between his performances abroad, T-Bone continued to appear in the usual round of nightclubs and theaters. In Los Angeles he played the Ash Grove and the Sportsman Club; in Buffalo he played Soul City; in New York he was billed at the Apollo more than once and was featured at Fillmore East. By 1967 he was appearing in festivals at home. At Monterey, California, B. B. King was featured along with T-Bone, and they were nationally televised. Later he was at Watts in Los Angeles and then at Ann Arbor, Michigan, for a festival dedicated to the blues.

In 1963 he began recording again. He appeared on the Prestige label accompanying Jimmy Witherspoon, and in 1965 he made some titles for Modern in Chicago that were probably unissued since no trace of them was ever found. Around the same time, in Pasadena, Texas, he made several sides for a label called Jet Stream. These sessions were produced by Huey Meaux, who eventually compiled an album entitled *The Truth* and sold it to Decca. Although the selections were less pretentious than those on Atlantic, T-Bone was saddled with uninspired backing, and his performances lacked luster.[3] But, reviewing *The Truth* in *Jazz Hot*, in March, 1969, Jacques Demetre wrote: "Here is the T-Bone we are accustomed to hearing and we can see that he has in no way become outmoded. Although he is fifteen years older than his disciple, B. B. King, it is clear events have not passed him by, and he is still *l'un des chefs du monde blues.*"

Then in 1966 T-Bone joined Norman Granz again on the West

2. On Black and Blue's *Feeling the Blues*, T-Bone plays piano on "Ain't That Cold, Baby." "A really good pianist, in an authentic low-down mood," commented Jacques Morgantini in the liner notes.

3. Some years later, using the same type of accompaniment, Meaux recorded another album, entitled *Stormy Monday Blues*, again featuring T-Bone originals, as had its predecessor. This, no better than the first, was distributed by SSS International Records.

Coast, and once more he was in a jazz context that included stars from the Duke Ellington orchestra and even Ellington himself. In liner notes to a three-record album entitled *The Greatest Jazz Concert in the World*, released later, Benny Green wrote, "T-Bone carries off consorting with Oscar Peterson with such aplomb that it is the rest of the group which finds itself adjusting to him."

The following year T-Bone signed a contract with BluesWay, for ABC Paramount Records, and made two albums under the supervision of Bob Thiele, *Stormy Monday Blues* and *Funky Town*. The title *Stormy Monday Blues* reintroduced the issue of performing rights, something that plagued T-Bone throughout his career. An ironic twist of fate decreed he must often forfeit royalties accrued from his most enduring hit. His "Stormy Monday Blues," recorded many times and by a variety of artists, became a standard that is still featured in many repertoires. But because of a recording ban that held up T-Bone's early version, another blues bearing this title was marketed first. His number was then retitled "Call It Stormy Monday," but this difference in copyright was seldom noted, and his royalties often went elsewhere.[4]

The *Stormy Monday* sessions took place in Los Angeles at the Western Recording Studios, and the contractor was a Basie alumnus, alto saxophonist Preston Love, who had been Earle Warren's replacement. "Mel 'Bubber' Brown, the guitarist on the date, was a great pal of mine," Preston said. "We'd worked together for Gene Connors' band—Gene the Mighty Flea. And we were racetrack buddies besides, and very close friends. Since I was the contractor on this date and Bone had only requested two or three guys, everyone else was there at my suggestion. Tenor saxophonist Mel 'Tank' Jernigan did the charts. Tank and I were associated with the Motown band and we'd made some big dates together, with Billy Preston and all that. At this time he wasn't all that experienced, but I think these were some of the best arrangements he ever made.

"The idea behind the session was to pinpoint T-Bone in an up-to-

4. As late as July, 1978, another album entitled *Stormy Monday* featured a version of T-Bone's hit played by guitarist Kenny Burrell. It was released by Fantasy Records and was credited to Eckstine, Crowder and Hines, with Warner Brothers Music as publishers.

date context. Thiele wanted a new audience for him, and the whole thing was R and B slanted. But the way it worked out, those disco formats in the rhythm section—the heavy guitar and drums that had the beat all boxed up—didn't suit T-Bone at all. Everything he represented was wrecked. His imaginative patterns, his flexibility—all that was drowned out. If the accompaniment had only stuck with the fine riffs in the brass, which highlighted Mel Moore, everything would have been all right, because starting way back with Les Hite, T-Bone had a big-band background. And years ago when I was playing with Lucky Millinder at the Los Angeles Plantation, with Billie Holiday and all the rest, when he got off work, T-Bone would come by and sit in, just to play. That's how much he loved working with a band.

"The second reason why the R and B sound was pronounced was T-Bone's own fault. I hate to say it, but what I think is that as he got older, T-Bone deferred miserably to younger guys—musically, I mean. He was always generous, especially if anyone knew how to play. He knew the younger guys wanted to be doing their own thing, and he just invited them in! He pushed Bubber Brown up to the front all through that album! He's featured on the guitar in 'Cold-Hearted Woman,' 'Little Girl,' 'Don't You Know,' and T-Bone's *own* ballad 'I'm Still in Love with You.' But what really determined the music on the date was the fact that Tank Jernigan did the arrangements and wanted *his* direction, to show how modern and up-to-date and hip he was. That's how it happened, simple as that. T-Bone was so busy deferring, he never questioned the fact that the direction wasn't his, although the producer had given him the right to his way."

"But it was my feeling," Bob Thiele said, "that T-Bone should be presented in a more professional setting. I don't want to sound like a put-down of anyone else, because his records were always great, but times had changed. After I'd discovered Mel Brown playing someplace in L.A., I'd recorded him on Impulse. So I said, 'Hey, why don't we get you with T-Bone and let you make some great stuff together?' On *Funky Town*, which was a sequel to *Stormy Monday Blues*, the same personnel was used, and after that I left ABC to form my own company.

"*Every Day I Have the Blues,* the album I made with T-Bone later, was one of Flying Dutchman's first releases on its BluesTime label, and Tom Scott, who became very big out on the West Coast with his L.A. Express group, was hired to arrange. He was a jazz guy at the time, who had got into the blues, but afterwards he arranged a lot, for Joni Mitchell and people like that. At the time I thought he was right for T-Bone, so I engaged other rock names, like Louie Shelton on guitar, Paul Humphrey on drums, and Arthur Wright on bass. I think T-Bone liked the idea that I wanted to give him a background that was up-to-date. I feel that in addition to their fine basic roots and rough street sound, T-Bone and Cleanhead and even Otis Spann—as opposed to Muddy Waters, for instance— are great musicians who will cook a little more if you surround them with good guys.

"And T-Bone . . . well, it gets repetitious after a while. To me he took the blues guitar and turned it around. The early guys hadn't the technique, but T-Bone—he opened up a road for everyone that came after. B. B. King himself told me, 'Without T-Bone there'd have been no B. B.' He took the electric guitar and modernized things. The one big difference between him and Christian was that T-Bone more or less confined himself to the blues structure.

"Out in L.A. in 1969 I made the first *Super Black Blues* album, and this was strictly blues, start to finish. The intent was to add Cleanhead to Bone, Turner, and Spann. But instead of a plane ticket I'd forwarded cash, and Cleanhead never arrived, so I used George 'Harmonica' Smith instead. I'd been going to record these guys separately, but when I found them repeatedly dropping in on one another's dates, the idea of a summit meeting occurred to me. But I provided a contemporary setting, with Ernie Watts on tenor and the rhythm section as before."

The ABC-Paramount BluesWay albums had been reasonably well received, but *Every Day I Have the Blues,* the first album made for Thiele's own label, was not great. It was followed by Volumes I and II of *Super Black Blues,* which according to some critics were far from successful and certainly not up to T-Bone's standards. Although the opening number of the first, "Paris Blues," came alive when Joe Turner was at the mike, the momentum died when

T-Bone took over. He was obviously striving for effect. The lyrics eluded him, and none of the spark and excitement Thiele was after materialized. Despite Otis Spann, the rock-oriented rhythm section unsettled the group, and the relaxed groove so essential to the blues was never achieved. Perhaps for the first time an easy interchange between the two blues singers was missing, marred by overemphasis on T-Bone's part. This deterioration, though not yet pronounced, resulted in part from the ill health that was dogging him.

The second album was made a year later when a concert at Carnegie Hall, advertised as "B. B. King and His Friends," was recorded live. The rhythm section, considerably improved, consisted of Elvin Jones on drums, Wynton Kelly on piano, Al Hall on bass, and Lawrence Lucie on guitar. Cleanhead was present this time, along with Joe Turner, and the first side of the album heralded their contributions. Unfortunately the second side featured a lengthy performance by a Flying Dutchman artist, Leon Thomas, who was accompanied by his own group. Although Thiele showed respect for T-Bone by programming him to follow and close the first half, this precluded the support of a surefire rhythm section that later demonstrated its capabilities behind B. B. King in the remainder of the show, which was recorded separately by ABC.

Joe Turner had been drinking, but came across well, and his following, primed to the blues, shouted encouragement. Cleanhead, while less renowned, sparked the audience even more with "Person to Person" and "Cleanhead Blues." But with the advent of Leon Thomas, a new trend was set. The high-spirited blues fans found his topical, semisoul songs acceptable, but obviously T-Bone was more to their taste. His appearance onstage at the close of "Damn Nam" signaled a vociferous round of applause, and the first stanzas of "Stormy Monday" were hailed with delight.

But the band had set a tempo that dragged, and the gin T-Bone had consumed during the long wait backstage now affected his fingers and gait. The audience, however, sensed nothing wrong, and the number, when it was concluded, met with an uproarious ovation. Picking up the tempo, T-Bone segued into "Sail On, Little Girl," always a hit. Standing back from the mike, he bent over the guitar, but the band accompaniment was overpowering and nothing carried out front. He resorted to singing again, and on the other side of the footlights they applauded, unaware that recalling the lyrics was almost beyond him. After two more choruses, he knew he had to wind up the show. Still strutting and strumming, leaving the band to play on, he set out for the wings. A bewildered audience continued to scream for more, but T-Bone had disappeared, and finally it was Joe Turner and Cleanhead who had to acknowledge the applause.

"T-Bone had stayed with us the night before the concert," Lois Badsen explained to me later in her New York apartment.[5] "After rehearsal he'd taken a nap. 'OK, how did it go?' he'd asked me when he woke, meaning the show! I couldn't believe it for a minute—that he thought it was all over. I should have realized then he was real sick. Harold and Jimmy Cross had said he didn't look good when they'd picked him up at the airport the day before. You know, I was married to Jimmy before Harold and I got together," Lois went on, "and when T-Bone would come to town the three of us, Harold, too, sometimes, would hang out in a bunch. All of us were real close." Harold Badsen and Jimmy Cross, seated together on a small couch, nodded and smiled.

"We had a fabulous friendship that started when T-Bone came east with Les Hite's band," Jimmy said.[6] "He and I stayed at the Braddock Hotel, and we were both real young and hung out together all the time. Then for a while I didn't see him again, until my partner and I went out to the coast to make pictures. There we were on the same bill with Bone, and we worked in San Francisco, Oakland, and up and down the coast. After that I'd go out to Chicago to catch him. At the Rhumboogie, for instance, where he rocked the blues so hard a lady fell off the balcony where the bar was and broke her legs!" Catching Harold's eye, Jimmy laughed. "But she ain't never sued," he said. "Wow, back then T-Bone was vibrant, a real sight to behold. He could find an after-hours joint in the Sahara Desert! On tour we'd both meet someplace, maybe in

5. Lois and her husband, Harold Badsen, were two of T-Bone's closest friends.
6. Jimmy Cross was Big Stump of Stump and Stumpy, a popular dance team that had entertained theater and nightclub audiences for years.

the lonesomest town, and after the show I'd say, 'Bone, there ain't nothin' to do.'

"Bone would say, 'Come on with me,' and somewhere out in the boondocks he'd find this beautiful joint. Soon as they saw him coming, everyone was shouting, 'Here comes Bone!'"

"He enjoyed a little mischief, too," Harold said. "You could count on him for that. One time I was in Veterans' Hospital, where on certain occasions you could get out on weekend passes. Well, this day they wouldn't give me one, although it was the night of the boat ride up the Hudson, you know—the big party of the year. They'd hired Milt Larkin and the band for the gig, so you knew T-Bone would be along." As Harold stopped to reflect, Lois took over.

"Bone and I packed your things, remember? We'd fixed it up on the phone. Once at the hospital, Bone went to the men's room. He'd brought your shorts and a dashiki in a paper bag. After you'd dressed yourself there, you put on your bathrobe and, like always on a summer evening, came out and sat in the car with us."

"So then we all took off," Harold added, smiling, "and was that a fantastic ride on that boat? The minute people knew T-Bone was there, they came crowding around from all over. Believe me, he rocked the boat that night!"

"Milton had to coax him at first," Lois said. "But when things got to going good, you couldn't tear him away. They were still at it when we tied up at the dock."

"When it comes to playing," Jimmy said, "Bone never kids."

"Right," Harold nodded. "Like there was a rehearsal on that Saturday afternoon for the Carnegie Hall concert. T-Bone was already downtown and went over on his own. When I arrived, I went backstage and up to the rehearsal hall. He was coming back with us afterwards, and we were going to return him in time for the show. He thought B. B.'s men would accompany him, but as you know they weren't on the first half so he had to use the other fellows he didn't know at all. He'd passed out his music, and they were running it down when Joe Turner walked in.

"Joe said he was getting ready to do some rehearsing himself and started moving around the room, talking. He stood there making wisecracks like a big, babbling kid. T-Bone put up with it for a while and then said: 'Joe, I'm here trying to rehearse my men. Don't interrupt.' Well, Joe persisted some more, and by then T-Bone had had it. 'Get your ass outta here, Joe!' he said. 'You know you don't have to rehearse. All *you* gotta do is stand up there and sing. You don't care what music they play. You're gonna sing what you're gonna sing anyway. But I have to rehearse these men. So get the hell out!'"

"I think he was worked up about playing Carnegie," Jimmy said. "They all were, for that matter. It's a far cry from the Apollo. And it had taken a mighty long time."

"Maybe we ought to have tried keeping T-Bone away from the bottle that night," Harold said, but Jimmy cut him short.

"He wasn't that drunk. No, it's all in the breaks. He's had plenty of good ones. Bad luck won't do him in."

"But Peggy must have been dragged," Lois said. "T-Bone's daughter," she explained, turning to me. "I didn't know her back then. He introduced us later on. Her name had never come up when we were talking with him on the phone in L.A."

"That's because Vi is not my mother," Peggy Foulkes told me afterward. "T-Bone and my mother were raised together, you might say. They went to school together and been knowing each other all their lives. Mother and I were living in Denver when T-Bone and Vi married. That was a long time ago, I'm sure, because then I was ten years old and I believe they have been married now thirty years. Once, much later on, he came to Denver with the band and got sick. It was pneumonia, and Mother nursed him and let him stay at the house. I lived in Denver for a good while longer, and then I came to New York.

"After a few years passed, in a soft moment my mother let T-Bone have my phone number here in town. When he finally called, he was in town for a Battle of Blues that was going on at the Apollo. He wanted me to catch the show. I think it was Ivory Joe Hunter and Wynonie Harris. Onstage T-Bone put the guitar behind his head, but he no longer did the splits. The stage manager, Honi Coles, had said not to after he'd had the heart attack. After I'd come backstage and seen him, we were together the whole time he was here. I had him stay at the apartment, and he was eating OK then. He's told Vi he sees me, I think he's been trying to make up for a couple of things, although it's not necessary, really. I can see life gets rough for him at times, though he doesn't let on. For instance, that show at Carnegie Hall. He probably shouldn't have been performing at all. I wasn't at rehearsal, because I knew his old friends had him in tow."

Apparently Harold and Lois had thought T-Bone seemed more like himself when they headed for the theater that night. Since they had arrived early, they went up to the rehearsal room where T-Bone saw a piano and sat down to play. The Badsens were surprised, because they had never heard him play the piano before. Big Mama Thornton was on the program, too, and after a while she stopped by with her bass player. Then B. B.'s sidemen drifted in. Everybody listened because T-Bone was turning it on off the top of his head. Finally, when B. B. showed, T-Bone got to his feet. B. B. put his hands on T-Bone's shoulders and pushed him back down.

"Stay, Bone," he said, looking around the room. "I want to tell these people something. This man here has been an inspiration to me. First time I heard him play piano, I was working as a disc jockey at station WDIA in Memphis, Tennessee. I was the same as I am today. I'd come in about ten minutes before I was to go on the air, and that's late! So when I arrived, I heard this piano in the next studio from me, and one of the announcers came over and said, 'Do you know who that gentleman is at the piano there?' I said, 'No,' because he had his back to me and I'm trying to pull out my records. So I am saying, although not in so many words, it doesn't really matter right now. Because I'm running late and I've got an armful of records. 'It's T-Bone Walker, that's who,' the announcer ended up. *Wow!* I drop the records right there! I take another look and see this fellow is sharp. T-Bone was a dresser, too. And it was T-Bone all right—my idol, next door.

"I went in and he greeted me real nice, and I'm saying to myself, 'I'm shaking hands with the man who made me get the electric guitar! Once I'd heard him for the first time, I knew I'd have to have one myself. *Had* to have one, short of stealing! Do you know, an-

other announcer had to interview him that day. I was too nervous!"
By this time T-Bone was on his way out of the room.

In the corridor he shook his head and smiled. "B. B. *never* finds
a bad word to say! What a guy!"

"I meant everything I said," B. B. commented long after, when he
and other guitarists were being interviewed about T-Bone for a
piece in the *Guitar Player* of March, 1977. "T-Bone was the first
person I ever heard on guitar who had a distinct sound, different
from everyone. It's a sound that anybody, me or anyone else, could
only come by from him. T-Bone would play any guitar, any amp,
and he would get that same sound. It was the *man.*"

"T-Bone liked to credit the Gibson," Lowell Fulson observed.
"'Try it,' he'd say, 'and you'll get your sound.' I know that after his
Gibson was stolen in France he came back and ordered another,
an ES-335. Gibson sold a lot of guitars because of that man," Fulson said.

"He was the only player I've ever seen that held his guitar out
flat," Fulson went on, "and was still able to watch his whole hand.
Flat, like he was going to play piano. That was the one thing the
other guys couldn't do. So they finally let that alone. But all his
lead playing he did like that. Then when he got ready to riff, he'd
drop it down so he could swing his box, you understand. But when
he really got to playing, he'd push it up again. And instead of a
wrapped G he used a plain one, because you couldn't bend or quiver
a G without it would unwind on you too fast. So the slick G became the thing, mostly all the blues players went to it."

Rock musicians, too, considered T-Bone a prime source. Steve
Miller, who was eleven years old when he first met T-Bone, said, "I
picked up my basic lead phrasing from him, and I still use a lot of
that type of sound. T-Bone was way ahead of his time." Boz Skaggs,
a charter member of Miller's first band, agreed: "He was my earliest
influence, a guy I learned a lot from."

"He'd give you plenty of tips," Fulson agreed. "He didn't care
who you were. Take a lot of musicians—they get famous on certain
licks and tricks and they won't tell you anything. But Bone didn't

care! He'd show you anything. He'd say, 'It goes like this.' Then he'd tell me: 'Swing the blues a little more. Put in a little life, a little pep. Rock into it, tap your foot off of what you're doing.'"

"He was the first guy I ever heard using a ninth chord playing blues," B. B. King remembered. "And his touch was so clear. I don't think he did much up-and-down strokes. I think he mostly picked down. He hit the strings with authority, almost a measured touch. You don't find too many people have that kind of control, especially in blues. You find it more in jazz.

"He was one of the greatest," B. B. concluded. "He was a teacher, and my friend."

Nineteen

Live at Montreux

Photograph courtesy Norbert Hess

For T-Bone 1970 was an eventful year. In the spring, *Good Feelin'*, the album he'd made in Paris for Polydor, was named the best blues performance of the year, and T-Bone was a National Academy of the Recording Arts and Sciences award winner.

But before his new backers succeeded in parlaying this into better bookings, T-Bone met with an accident. He was driving to a one-nighter in Watts with Eddie Vinson beside him when he slammed into a car that had pulled up short for a light. When Vinson got him clear of the steering wheel that pinned him down, T-Bone said: "I'm all right. Shook up a bit is all. Hurry up, bubber, we gotta hit by nine."

But three days later he was on his way to the hospital, hemorrhaging from the lungs. The doctors retained him this time, keeping him five months before letting him play the jazz festival in Nice.

At home, starting in the mid-1960s, blues had begun to acquire an enthusiastic following. With the advent of English groups like the Rolling Stones, the Who, Eric Clapton's band, and others, rhythm and blues had taken the younger generation by storm. Suddenly Muddy Waters, John Lee Hooker, Howlin' Wolf, and T-Bone Walker had become household names. The Allman Brothers Band, recording at the Fillmore East in New York City, released an album featuring "Stormy Monday" that went to the top of the bestseller list and introduced T-Bone to a new generation of fans. Elated, T-Bone's backers foresaw themselves cashing in on this wave of popular acclaim. They booked him into the Jazz Workshop in Boston, fronting a New England rock group that hoped to build a reputation as his backup band. The only member of the group who struck T-Bone as outstanding was the blind guitarist, Paul Pena.

"I always hated music being loud," T-Bone told me later, "and these other boys had amplifiers and all kind of stuff. You wouldn't believe the equipment they carried. Their beat was so heavy the whole place shook. But to hear my managers tell it, that's what goes down with the kids. After a while I gave up. I'd let them open ahead of me, and then I'd come on with my numbers, reining them in best as I could. But it was hard to pace the act. And I didn't like that. Still, in a couple of months the money we were making said my sponsors must be right. They got us bookings in places I'd never played before, like the Colonial in Toronto, and in 1972 we headlined at the London House in Chicago for two to three weeks. There had never been a blues band there until then. After that the American Blues Festival hired me to tour Europe with them once again."

Memphis Slim remembered those dates with regret because T-Bone, who considered himself carefree at last, was now disposed to drink whenever he pleased. "He had us worried," Memphis Slim recalled. "He performed badly in Berlin, and in Bremen fell off the stage. This was a terrible drag, since we had a very nice show. We had a wonderful lineup: Mama Thornton, Roosevelt Sykes, Bukka White, Jimmy Rodgers, Big Joe Williams, and a whole lot more. Horst Lippman had brought us over and saw to it that we recorded.[1] It came out pretty good, but Bone was juiced again. He wasn't supposed to be drinking. He knew it, but couldn't stop."

Before returning home, T-Bone appeared in a film made in Paris called *L'Aventure du Jazz,* which was later released in England as *Jazz Odyssey.* In Los Angeles, Vi tried to ration his drinking and get him to rest, but before long he had returned to Europe once more. This time it was the Montreux Jazz Festival, and with him again was the Boston-based group. Their selections were taped and released by Polydor on an album entitled *Fly Walker Airlines: Live in Montreux.* The Montreux festival is popular, and its fans are enthusiastic. T-Bone's performance not only met with acclaim but also showed that Paul Pena was the kind of challenge needed to inspire T-Bone once more.

"If I don't have a guy like that alongside," he told me later, "I might as well give up. When Pena went to the West Coast, I was lost till Junior Hansen took his place."

"But a year ago Paul was still with him," Harold Badsen told me backstage at Carnegie Hall after reminding me that T-Bone had stayed with him in 1972. "Although he was in pretty bad shape, right then T-Bone was playing some pretty nice gigs. One time when he was booked for a week in a Manhattan club, the Vanguard or Max's Kansas City, I guess, he and Pena had a ball. They were

---

1. The American Folk Blues Festival recorded in Lünen and Munich in 1972.

reversing roles, I remember. While Pena got off on guitar, T-Bone
went to the piano, and then they switched back and forth. Pena
was that good.

"Well, on a Saturday night, surprise of surprises, who walks in
but B. B. King, back from Europe in time for T-Bone's last show. So
he gets up on the stand, everyone cheers, and all three have a go.
The place had to stay open all night."

"That was the week Bone brought B. B.'s guys over to PS 123,
Mahalia Jackson School, where I teach," Lois said. "The bunch of
them played for the fifth graders. Those kids will never forget. And
the teachers had wondered if they were too young to relate! T-Bone
brought some of them onto the stage with him, and they were all
on Cloud Nine. The fellows couldn't quit, and afterwards T-Bone
came to my classroom upstairs. Grabbing himself a little chair, he
talked with them all. The following day, a Saturday, he was up visiting friends at 141st Street, and walking back to our place, he was
spied by fifth graders. 'That him? Can it be! No kidding! T-Bone
Walker!' The grapevine took over, and there by the projects, he was
suddenly surrounded by a hundred kids. Bone got a kick out of
that! Check it out, if you're going to see him after the show."

I nodded, and leaving Harold and Lois backstage where they
waited for a word with him before he went on, I made my way out
to the front of the house. It was only now I determined there could
be no further delay in getting T-Bone's story straight. The occasions
when he performed well were getting fewer and farther between.
How much his health was to blame I did not know, but watching
the show, I was concerned.

I had not yet heard the band from Boston, but I had an idea of
what to expect. The group was already onstage and into their
theme when the lights came up. In a moment Junior Hansen, who
was playing lead guitar in Paul Pena's place, introduced T-Bone, and
the rhythm section began to vamp when he appeared in the wings.
I could not recall seeing him make an entrance like this before. His
gait was unsteady; yet he did not seem to be drunk. A fascinated
audience watched in silence as he proceeded in slow motion toward
the mike.

Laughter broke out when he got his hands on it and shouted: "Don't worry. I made it all right." As he cried, "Gimme a boogie, fellas," the house came to life, and before he finished singing, people were waving and calling for more.

"Here goes. I'm gonna play you one on the box, 'Mistreatin' Mama,'" he announced, crossing over to the piano. Getting both hands going and signaling to the band to fall in behind, he opened up in the bass with a driving beat. In the gallery they were on their feet shouting again before the last chorus got under way. Then he signaled to Junior Hansen to bring the Gibson over, as he moved to center stage. Adjusting the strap, he hoisted it until he had it flat out and struck up "Mean Old World" with a flurry of chords that reverberated through the auditorium. Fired up once more, the audience let him know this was what they had come to hear.

Hansen and the band had learned how to support him, and the numbers that followed, "I'm in an Awful Mood" and "T-Bone Jumps Again," went over well. At the mike T-Bone established a routine with Hansen, swapping choruses and sharing a series of eights and fours that roused mounting excitement, but he was soon exhausting dwindling reserves, and a change of tempo was due. He called for "Stormy Monday," and there was another round of applause. But his staying power was at an end, and after two choruses he was through. He waited in the wings, hoping to get away with returning just for bows, but the audience refused to quiet down and called him back again. When the band struck up "Sail On, Little Girl," he had to return and play till it closed. But as he went off, he was smiling. From a shaky beginning, he had pulled things together once more.

Backstage I found him getting ready to leave, and it was there and then this book really began.

"I'm going to do that story about you," I said.

"You must be kidding." He stared in disbelief.

I shook my head. "No, I'm serious. I've been wasting time till now."

"I'm getting past it, you mean." He laughed.

"Don't joke, T-Bone. I'll see you in Toronto next week."

"How come?" He grabbed my arm.

"First off, Toronto is my hometown. Next, you open at the El Macombo on Monday. And my daughter is there." Terry, our eldest, was at the University of Toronto that year.

"Well," T-Bone grinned, "I'll have to cooperate then, long as Daughter's involved."

Twenty

El Macombo

Photograph courtesy Norbert Hess

The night Terry and I showed up, the El Macombo was already crowded. They had told us to come early, because business had been good all week. Obviously T-Bone was a draw. A fair-sized dance floor was jammed with frantic kids.

"I thought dancers that age were more into rock," I said.

"It's not just teenyboppers. All ages are trying to get onto that floor," Terry pointed out. "Look around a bit."

Glimpsing T-Bone at the piano, I said, "They're playing 'T-Bone Shuffle,' that's why."

By the time we had ordered, the set was about over and T-Bone was at the mike. He waved when he saw us, and we pulled up a third chair. In a moment he was threading his way through the crowd.

"Hi, there!" He was all smiles. "So Daughter is for real."

"Are you going to let the expert write the book?" Terry asked.

"Hasn't she got better things to do?" T-Bone rejoined.

Terry gave him one of her smiles. "Try being graceful about it. Any reason why not, if that's what she wants?"

T-Bone laughed and got to his feet, prepared to return to the stand. "I'll be back in forty minutes. Let me know if there's anything you want to hear."

I had not heard him play for dancers in a long time. Everyone now played theaters or concerts, venues that do not compare. T-Bone agreed with me on that.

"We prefer playing for kids like these," he said when he returned. "It's a kick to watch them. Most of them move real good. Hey," he interrupted himself, "here comes the gang." He indicated a group headed our way. "There's another party tonight," he said, "and Lady Baby says you are to come."

Later, T-Bone, Terry, and I, transported in a huge limousine, were delivered to Lady Iris Mountbatten's door.[1] We found the band there ahead of us, the focus of an admiring group. Robin, Iris Mountbat-

1. Lady Mountbatten (1920–1982), a great-granddaughter of Queen Victoria, was a jazz aficionado and a T-Bone Walker fan. A cousin to England's Queen Elizabeth II and the late Lord Mountbatten, she had elected to buy a home in Toronto where she entertained lavishly.

ten's teenage son and T-Bone's disciple, was on hand to escort us upstairs. "He's my boy," T-Bone said. "We've been pals a long time."

Before the evening was over, I managed to pull T-Bone to one side. "Will you return via New York?" I asked. Stanley wanted to set up a record session for him. We had discussed it on the phone.

"Roy likes the idea, and Buddy, naturally," my husband had confirmed. "Tyree as well."[2]

Now T-Bone hesitated, looking around the room. "I don't think my managers like the idea," he said.

"Aren't you free?"

"I don't know. They say they've got something big on the back burner. With Warner Brothers, on the West Coast. They say we're signed up already." Obviously he was not too happy about it.

"What is it you don't like?" I asked.

"Well, maybe I'm nuts, but I've seen who is supposed to accompany me on it. Dizzy, for instance, Kenny Burrell, Tom Scott, and a whole lot of others. It's to be a Lieber and Stoller production."

I was amazed that all those names could gather on the coast at one time, and T-Bone must have had a lot of questions he would have liked answered. But he probably would not pursue it. "Well, that's that," I said. "It's a shame. You could have made a session in New York like those classics of the fifties."

By then the party was subsiding, and T-Bone took Terry's hand, beckoned to me, and rounded up Robin. "We're going to my place," he said.

"Aren't you calling it a day?" Terry asked when we arrived at the Oneida Hotel, where he stayed. T-Bone shook his head.

"I promised Robin's mother I'd fix him some eggs. But if you kept us company, maybe we could talk about the book." The suggestion was mischievous and aimed at me.

"Did he mean it?" Terry asked when we left.

"You never know." I was doubtful, but it might have been worth a try.

2. Roy Eldridge, Buddy Tate, and Tyree Glenn. T-Bone was to have the backing of a small group of stars. Some were Texans; all were friends.

Three one-nighters followed the Toronto booking, and then T-Bone returned home for a routine check-up. He was to relax for six weeks, then go out on the road, and then go back into the hospital if he lost too much weight in between. So I did not expect to see him return east for a time. But before long he called. He had agreed to play a concert in Jersey. The promoters, Joe and Sylvia Mastrianni, had managed to get hold of his number and had called him direct. He had pleaded ill health at first, but Sylvia had refused to take no for an answer.

"They're just kids," T-Bone explained. "They heard us at Carnegie that time and figured the program might draw OK in Jersey as well. I'm getting a thousand dollars in advance and a pair of round-trip tickets besides so Vi can come with me. They've got Albert King, and a sister act called LaBelle. They're figuring on having us to stay at their house."

After checking with the Mastriannis, I found they had booked a Saturday night at the Palace Theater in Newark. They said sales were poor so far, but they were buying radio time. "Joe and I are in love with T-Bone after talking with him on the phone," Sylvia informed me. "To us this means more than just the chance to make money."

They scheduled a press reception for him backstage ahead of the show and asked us to come. Carrying a tape recorder with us, we set off in good time. When we arrived, the theater was still dark. The box office had not opened, and no one was around.

"I know we're early," I said, "but does this look right to you?"

"Come and see. I'm afraid I get the picture." My husband had stepped out into the street. The lights on the marquee spelled out the next attraction. Sly and the Family Stone were to play there the following night, and certainly both houses would be packed. "It probably never occurred to the Mastriannis to ask, and no one else cared to say." Stan pulled a long face. "Evidently they haven't been at this game very long. Nobody books ahead of a surefire act. Not enough people to go around." We stared at one another.

"Guess we might as well go backstage," I said.

When we got to the stage door, we found the Mastriannis pouring champagne. Peggy and her family were there, Harold and Lois, and a handful of T-Bone's fans. Two or three loners represented the local press, I supposed. There was no sign of Albert King.

In a turtleneck top and slacks, T-Bone emerged from his dressing room, a pair of toddlers at his heels. "Hey, long time no see," he said to Stan, approaching us with a smile. "Vi, look who's here," he called and, turning back to us, said, "This time you get to meet my wife."

I now met Vi for the first time, and it was clear right away she was easy to know. "We been hearing about you at home," she said, smiling, and I was relieved. If I were going to encounter a roadblock on the book, it most likely would come from T-Bone's family.

T-Bone did not seem worried about dressing for the show or dis-engaging himself from the babies, who now had hold of his arms. "Kids have him figured every time," Vi commented, unperturbed.

"We'll testify to that," Joe Mastrianni volunteered, joining us and extending his hands. "Glad you could come. But we're not happy," he said. "It's very spotty out front. We can hardly believe it. There was enough air time, I know, and we advertised . . . ."

"But they gave us no space," Sylvia Mastrianni concluded for him, coming over and linking her arm in his. "Can you believe we didn't know about Sly until a couple of hours ago?"

"Well, that's your answer," Stan said.

T-Bone patted Mastrianni on the back. "Everything's going to be all right. Take it easy. We've been through worse than this."

"But your money?" Joe interrupted him, pressing a damp hand-kerchief to his head. "And what about Albert King? He's in his caravan with his band, and his manager has yet to allow him inside."

"Lemme go see him." T-Bone made for the door. "Maybe he could cut out early if you would let him play a short set."

Nudging me, Stan took my arm. "We'd better go out front and see how bad it is."

It was bad. About a quarter of the house was filled. "They'll have to struggle through, that's all," Stan said. "It's one of those times the producer loses his shirt." But I wasn't thinking of the Mastri-annis so much. It was a letdown for T-Bone, and he would take it personally besides. Twenty to thirty of the seats close to the stage

were occupied, and upstairs in the balcony small groups threaded
their way in. Behind us we saw Vi, Harold and Lois, and farther
along Peggy was coming across with some friends.

As the curtains parted, I saw LaBelle coming on. Without waiting
for recognition, the three sisters opened up. When they had
warmed the theater for him, Albert King was introduced. By the
time he was ready to quit, the audience showed some semblance of
life and did not want him to leave.

"Wait, now, everybody," King cautioned. "We're gonna make you
real happy tonight. We've got a trailblazer coming onto the stage
right now. Let's hear it for T-Bone Walker. He's my main man!" En-
couraged, the audience sustained a round of applause until T-Bone
and the group from Boston had filed onto the stage. T-Bone smiled
and raised his hands in the air.

"Let's go, fellas," he shouted, making his way to the keyboard and
opening up with "Mean Old World." He probably figured there was
little chance he would black out on lyrics to a standard like that.
Although he hit the tempo just right, a half-empty house hollowed
the sound, and I could see he was restive. Switching to "T-Bone
Shuffle" and drumming out a series of rhythmic figures in the bass,
he got the band rocking behind him. When he left the piano and
walked to the mike, Hartley Severn, his rhythm backup for the
date, handed him his guitar. Adjusting the harness and fingering a
few chords, he slid into "Cold, Cold Feeling" and for two choruses
kept the momentum up well. The intent faces in the band and
the gyrations of the drummer behind him indicated a buildup had
begun and a climax was on the way, but suddenly, almost imper-
ceptibly, T-Bone lost control. Once his concentration collapsed,
the lyrics escaped him and he began repeating himself. I glanced
around at Vi and saw the concern in her face. T-Bone signaled to
the group that he wanted to take the number out. He turned to
Hartley, who whispered in his ear. Nodding, T-Bone raised his right
hand, and calling for a press roll on the drums, he announced "Evenin'," a number whose lyrics were engraved on his mind.

But the change in tempo was anticlimactic, and Stan fidgeted
beside me. I pinched him a moment later, pointing with relief to
Junior Hansen, who had materialized in the wings. In that instant

T-Bone spied him and, concluding with a flourish, beckoned him out onto the stage. Smiling, the two lined up together, and Junior hit the opening chords of "T-Bone Jumps Again." The lackadaisical house was suddenly transformed. Reversing roles, exchanging breaks, and driving one another, they played as though the lack of an audience no longer mattered at all. Their absorption in the music was complete. For us, a long-awaited moment had arrived at last.

When the show concluded, we were all smiles out front, and backstage T-Bone and Hansen embraced.

"How did you find us?" T-Bone asked, looking suddenly drained.

"Man, I'll always find you," Junior replied.

"My husband won't admit it, but he's ready for home," Vi whispered.

But they had to stay another twenty-four hours, because the following night there was the fabulous party hosted by the Copasetics year after year, and T-Bone was the guest of honor and MC. Vi knew this was an occasion he could not possibly postpone.

"You're coming with us," T-Bone told the Mastriannis, "as my guests."

Joe's expression was sober. "What about your money?" he asked.

T-Bone grinned. "Why not book us next year?"

Twenty-one

Not So Rare

T-Bone had not been back in Los Angeles long before I called to say I was coming out so we could talk for a while. He was pleased, but still ready to stall. "How much time will this take?" he asked doubtfully, after we had worked for two days.

"Bone don't like a lot of gab," Lester remarked, as he let himself in the front door.

"OK. If we don't get to talk too much here, we'll go places where other people will," I commented, and T-Bone grinned. "But first, I want to know about the returns on 'Stormy Monday.'"

T-Bone hesitated, looking anxious. "You mean . . . ?"

" 'Monday' is on the Allman Brothers' album, with sales close to a million. You should be in the chips. What do your royalty statements say?"

T-Bone switched the stereo off and got to his feet. Vi watched with concern as he crossed the room to the phone.

"Haven't seen any," he told me over his shoulder. "They must have gone east to my men. Let me see what Lester Sills says." After a few minutes he hung up and motioned to me.

"Let's go. Sills says come over right now."

With Skaggs driving, we headed for Sunset Boulevard and the Gregmark Music Publishing Company. As we waited for the elevator, T-Bone murmured: "Lester Sills is a nice guy. I been knowing him for years. I taught his boy some tricks on guitar, and after that he talked to his dad about me. Since I put 'Stormy Monday' with him, every now and then a little money comes in. He's really great. If times are bad, he lets me draw." His publisher waited at the door and greeted him with easy familiarity. T-Bone introduced me, and we walked into the office.

"Long time no see," Sills said. "What's on your mind?"

T-Bone's manner was unusually abrupt and the set of his jaw hard. "What's happening?" he asked. "I ain't seen no royalties. 'Stormy Monday' on the air every day and I don't hear from you."

Sills straightened up in his chair. "But you've been cashing our checks!"

T-Bone's face expressed disbelief. "Like I say: *nothing*. And you know my address all right."

182

"Wait a minute," Sills cautioned. "I have your statements right to hand." Pressing a buzzer on his desk, he spoke briefly over the phone. "My secretary is bringing in a record of the payments we've made," he went on. "Let's figure this out."

T-Bone shook his head.

"Bring the file here." Sills beckoned to one of the girls in the outer office. "Like I thought," he said turning to T-Bone, "your company has had three payments already. I'll total them for you. I know it makes better than seventeen thousand dollars."

His voice truculent, T-Bone was up on his feet. "How come you paid *them* instead of me?"

"That's how it was set up last year," Sills reminded him, "when your Warner Brothers contract was signed." Sills looked at T-Bone with concern. "This didn't get into your bank account? You're sure?"

"Those checks should have come to the house like before, like always," T-Bone countered.

Sills sighed. "For a mess like this, you're going to need legal advice," he said ruefully.

T-Bone looked despondent. "What's the use? You know well as I do that money's long gone now." Turning to me and beckoning, he said, "Come on. We might as well go home."

Sills laid a delaying hand on his arm. "You've knocked me for a loop. I'll see what we can do from this end. But there's more dollars to come, so don't worry. I'll see that it gets out to you."[1]

T-Bone managed a sick smile. "I know, I know. You're OK by me, Lester. What you did—that should have been all right, I guess."

"I'm never going to see that money no more," he said somberly as we drove back to the house. "I should have known. I had trouble in Toronto already. The money was messed up, and the boys didn't get paid. I had to take care of that four thousand dollars. God knows where it went." He shrugged. "So I've come up losers. Well, ain't no use killing anybody. Won't bring the money back."

---

1. Years later Vida Lee had nothing but praise for Lester Sills, who sees to it she still receives royalty checks.

The hardest part for him was discussing it at home. Vi said little, but Bernita, married now and newly commissioned as a deputy sheriff by the Los Angeles police, refused to let the matter drop.

"You could make a case out of this," she insisted. "Unless you signed a paper or something?"

"Maybe," T-Bone muttered. I saw that what stung most was his being had, though losing so much money when his health was poor was rough. Normally if he were short of funds, he would look for a weekend gig to make five hundred dollars. He could not do that now.

"Never thought I'd say no to Norman Granz," he told me. "He's been after me twice, and it would have been great both times. I suggested wait a month or two maybe. You want to call him for me? Tell him I'll be OK pretty soon."

Since I wanted to know what Norman had in mind, I liked the idea. "I wanted to use him on a series of half-hour Canadian television shows I've built around Oscar Peterson," Granz said on the phone. "I could use T-Bone alone or at the same time I use Joe Turner. I've had some serious discussions with him, you know, about signing with Pablo. In fact, I've sent him money. Call it an advance. I just figured he could use some right now. But first he's got to get free of Warner. I take it he wasn't happy with *Very Rare*.[2] I have plans for him to do an album on his own, then another with Joe Turner.

"My association with T-Bone goes back to 1944, to the 331 Club. I started using him in my jam sessions. He was primarily a guitar player then. Hadn't really made his mark as a singer, and funnily enough he was my guitar player when I had Nat King Cole on piano. I'd hired him to play jazz and this was one of his frustrations later, I think—that he'd gotten away from that. He liked the idea of being recognized as a great guitar player, not just as an accompanist for himself.

"But by the end of the forties he had made his big reputation. He

2. Recorded in the summer of 1973, *Very Rare* was released that fall with a lineup that included Dizzy Gillespie, Herbie Mann, Gerry Mulligan, Al Cohn, and Zoot Sims.

started traveling, and I did, too. After that I hadn't much call to use him, except for occasional things. I used him in that 1967 album that came out as *The Greatest*.[3] I simply invited him to sit in at the Hollywood Bowl. He wasn't a part of the tour, but I always liked him so much that when we played the West Coast, I took him to Oakland and to San Francisco with the show, even though it was overloaded with talent at that time. I just made him an added star. I especially liked the idea of having people from Duke Ellington's band play behind him.

"I took him to Europe in '66 on a Jazz at the Philharmonic tour, with Dizzy, Clark Terry, Benny Carter, and Coleman Hawkins. The discussion concerning whether he fit in or not came up only in London. As far as I was concerned, as far as the musicians were concerned, he was a perfect fit. On that tour he didn't play guitar with the rest. He worked as a singer with the group behind him and as usual played guitar both for interludes and behind himself. Teddy Wilson was our pianist, and for my part the curious combination of the many people I use, all from the same stock, meant there was no question about how everyone would work together. In fact, I am now sitting on a big album of that tour with T-Bone which I will release in due time. Well, that was the last time he worked for me.

"In '72 he was supposed to go out for me again, when I had decided to place a blues-shouting package with Count Basie. I recalled those blues-shouting contests they had in Los Angeles in the early forties, and I had managed to get the three best that would fit. One was Joe Turner, another was Cleanhead, and the last one was T-Bone. I thought all was in order, but apparently the agent who said he represented them, in fact didn't. He only represented Cleanhead. Cleanhead went, Joe Turner didn't, and T-Bone went on his own tour for Lippman and Rau in Germany. I substituted Joe Williams for the two of them, for the package, which I later called Kansas City Jazz, but I would have much preferred to have had T-Bone. Although I am not at all sure that Basie's band is amenable to playing behind the kind of blues singing that T-Bone does. . . . It's something different, say, from Joe Turner. Actually I think

3. *The Greatest Jazz Concert in the World* (Pablo Records).

T-Bone is more comfortable with a simple rhythm section or pre-
ferably a small group. Most blues singers are, as far as that goes."

Later that evening I told T-Bone that Norman thought he was not
too happy with *Very Rare*.

"I don't like it no kind of way," T-Bone replied. "Never made a
record like it in my life before. Up there in the studio *all by myself*. In place of a rhythm section behind me, I'm wearing headphones! They had taped some of the guys already, cats from L.A.
mainly. They'd been in and out a few times. It's a double album,
you know. A whole lot of tracks. And Dizzy and them others probably did their stuff in New York. Call that a great session? No one a
part of what anyone else is laying down? What's live about that?"

"Just a manufactured product," I agreed. "Nothing like the TV
show Johnny Otis told me about?"

Recalling the Homewood production restored T-Bone's good
humor. "Get Johnny to arrange a showing for you," he urged.

"It went out over Public Television," Johnny Otis recalled. "I'll
phone the station. They might schedule a rerun before you return
east. Here's the background: The story begins after our son Shuggie
was born. When he was three or four, I bought him a miniature
drum set. T-Bone was visiting us one day.

" 'Get him off those drums,' he said. 'There's enough drums in
the family. Find him a guitar. I'll work with him.' He never did,
because he was away when Shuggie began to develop, but he was
one of my boy's biggest influences.

"Then 1971 comes along, and the radio station contacts me to
put together a show along the lines of the revues I took out on the
road all those years. 'Get together who you want,' they said. So I
called T-Bone, Little Esther Phillips, Charles Brown, Roy Milton,
Eddie Vinson, Joe Turner—all the people we love. And in my own
band was Preston Love, and Wilton Fender on bass. The guitar was
Shuggie. Interesting, you know, because he was only sixteen years
old, but he could handle it because he would play the blues. So in
rehearsal, a very loose affair, we decided to close the performance
with T-Bone.

"When the show started up, everyone starred and we were having
a ball. Then time was running out and T-Bone was up. He played a

quick little something, and then he turned and called Shuggie out of the band. It was a surprise to all of us, and I wondered if Shuggie would even go down front—he's that shy. Well, it was one of those magic moments. They started playing the blues, sixteen and sixty, T-Bone with his licks and Shuggie answering him. It was just really good. Everyone that saw it was floored, because how many people would do that? It was T-Bone's spot, and this was a TV show. He showcased Shuggie instead of himself, and that was a selfless thing.

"Afterwards," Johnny Otis went on, "we worked together a lot in this way. My band was suddenly in demand. White guys like Mike Bloomfield, Paul Butterfield, Charlie Musselwhite, and those fellows with Canned Heat had stirred up an interest in the blues. So whenever I could, I'd include T-Bone, Joe Turner, and Cleanhead besides, the three of 'em together, like the old Battle of Blues giants, all great men, loving and respecting one another, but usually in their cups." Otis laughed. "The bullshit would start up when the competition was on. 'Look at him, up there drunk,' one would tell me. 'Better let *me* get on the stand,' another would say. And all three would be arguing about who'd best close the show. But soon as the gig was done, they'd be laughing and embracing, carrying on like mad.

"It's funny, you know, about the blues. 'Sure,' I told Bob Hite of Canned Heat, who was a very nice man, 'sure, whites mouth the blues and do a good job, but they don't *create*. The blues is created by blacks.' Why can't we quit looking for a white hope in every damned thing? Can't the black man have any single game of his own?"

T-Bone was amused when I told him what Otis said. "Johnny tells it like it is," he said. "Jumps in with both feet."

Twenty-two

That Ain't No Ray Charles

Later in the year, I went back to West Forty-third Place to be with T-Bone and the family again and spend time with some of the people who frequented the house. Besides Patty Jack and Stymie, who were always around, and Lester Skaggs, who still occupied a room in the back, I spoke with Joe Turner, Jimmy Witherspoon, Cleanhead Vinson, Lowell Fulson, and Roy Milton, and with Lloyd Glenn, T-Bone's favorite pianist, and Leo Blevins, T-Bone's protégé. There was always someone either on the way in or out any hour of the day.

"That suits Bone just fine," Jimmy Witherspoon said. "He never sits by himself. Did you know he gave me my start? At Little Harlem. Bone would call me up to sing, though I wasn't a professional or nothin'. But the fellows thought me entertaining, so I sang in a few places. Like where Tatum was playing, in the hallway at Lovejoy's.[1] Tatum thought I was entertaining, too, but he put me through my paces one time.

" 'You feel like singing one?' he asked me this night.

"I told him, 'Yeah.'

" 'What key?'

" 'Put it in B-flat,' I said. After that I didn't know what key he was in. We went through every key there was. I paid no attention to his chord structures, or nothin'. Just kept my mind on the B-flat. He laughed when I got through.

" 'Spoon,' he said, 'nobody else could do that, what you just did— singing straight through all them keys.' Tatum *loved* to do you like that," Jimmy recalled, smiling. "Hootie had warned me about his practical jokes.[2] Tatum thought the world of McShann. Used to follow him around like a puppy dog. He called him the greatest blues pianist he ever heard in his life. That was Kansas City. In L.A. T-Bone was the biggest name around. But I was too young to run with him and his gang. He was *big*. Used to do a Saturday radio show with Al Jarvis, one of the first blacks to do that. Though a

1. Blind from birth, Art Tatum, who died in 1956, is universally considered one of the all-time piano greats.
2. Pianist and bandleader Jay "Hootie" McShann, first heard in Kansas City in 1937, maintains widespread popularity in the 1980s.

lotta people recognized T-Bone, they didn't give him a chance to get going like he knew how. Not a real chance, like he deserved. And it won't never be any different, now. Not now, I guess.

"But he don't have regrets. He's lived a good life, made lots of money, had plenty hits. He gambled a lot and give away as much. I've seen guys walk in and tell him they was needin', but they were only hustlin' Bone. Still, Bone's hand would go to his pocket, and he never let on. That's one artist will never get stranded *nowhere*, because he helped everybody. Yeah. He don't know how to say no. Not even now when he's not doing too good."

"He's a beautiful man," Lester Skaggs confirmed. "The three most beautiful people in the world, as far as I'm concerned, are Ellington, Armstrong, and this man here, where I'm staying. They don't look down on a person that's not where *they* are. All the years I've known Bone, it's always been the same. You meet him playing in different groups, in different cities. It's always, 'Hey, how you doin'?' One of those kinds of things. I appreciate it because I've had kind of a checkered career. I've been all over—in Europe, Hawaii, Japan, the U.S. Been kind of a rolling stone. I came from Topeka, Kansas, but when I was seven months, my parents quit home for L.A. They separated after that, and I was sent here and there. About a mother or father I never knew nothin' at all.

"But I learnt on the drums from some of the best. Teddy Eubanks, Danny Barcelona, Noel Maxie, and Jo Jones. In 1955 Baby and I went to Honolulu with Que Martin.[3] It didn't last long for me, because Que couldn't take any deviation from a four/four beat, so Baby ended up singing with Bone, and I headed back east.

"'Take care of your job, Lester,' Baby told me every time I made a switch. She gave me the only mothering I ever knew. I used to fool around, drinking and all, and she used to worry about me. She was the one we should have worried about, because she wasn't but thirty-two when she died. After that I went to Europe again and tried to forget. Later, when I returned to the U.S., I ran into Cedric Haywood, a piano man who used to play with Bone. For a time we

3. The late Baby Davis, Lester Skaggs's wife, can be heard on records made with T-Bone at the time she sang with his band.

played gigs in Galveston and Houston, Texas, till finally I got myself together again and figured on going back home. Home, even
without Baby, was pretty much L.A. T-Bone was just in from the
road when I arrived.

"'Man, where have you *been*!' he said.

"'Lookahere, man,' I told him, 'gimme a place to stay.'

"'You got a home here,' he said right away. 'You been having a
home, you know that.' But lately we've hardly played any gigs, not
since Bone's been sick. One concert in Santa Monica one time.

"'You know what I want,' T-Bone said to me. 'I want you digging
in, like always.' So I laid the beat right on, because I know T-Bone's
style. Later he told me, 'Champ, I can't build a band again, not now.
So you gotta catch the gigs when you can.' And that's what I've
been doin', for some little time.

"Bone is supposed to quit drinking, you know. But like every
time he leaves the stand, someone wants to treat. He can't easily
refuse. So he just goes along with the program, and he and I stay
real close. The other day his mother told me, 'You shoulda been
brothers, you pair of cats.' Anyway, kind of sick the way Bone is
today, I'm not fixing on any new move. No way in the world I'd quit
Bone, that's for sure."

Early in the afternoon Seymour called Vi from Patty Jack's, where
Marguerite was paying a call. "T-Bone's not here," Vi told him, "but
you and Marguerite stop by on your way home. We've got a house-
ful of folks."

Seymour hesitated. "Well, for five minutes, I guess."

"*I* want that five minutes," I said, when I heard the pair of them
at the door.

Vi smiled. She knew I figured on Seymour's staying an hour. As
soon as they entered the room, she announced, "Here comes the
man got T-Bone to fishing, after all those years."

"Bone always swore he had no time for that. Or he had some
other excuse. Right?" Seymour winked at Vi.

"But see what you've got us into," Vi reproached him. "He and
Stymie set off for the pier early this morning, him with a brand

At the Jazz Expo in London, 1968
Courtesy Valerie Wilmer/Format

Pee Wee Crayton

Stump and Stumpy.
Jimmy Cross is at left.

Jazz Confreres

Louis Armstrong

Billie Holiday

Cootie Williams

Three generations: T-Bone with Peggy Foulkes and her baby, Clarence

Chuck Berry and T-Bone playing "Stormy Monday" at the Montreux Jazz Festival in 1972

T-Bone climaxes a concert in France
during his 1969 European tour.

T-Bone, Willie Hobbs, and Lester
Skaggs

Lester Skaggs, Patty Jack, and
T-Bone

Life at Home

Joe Turner and his wife, Pat

Kelie and M'Dear

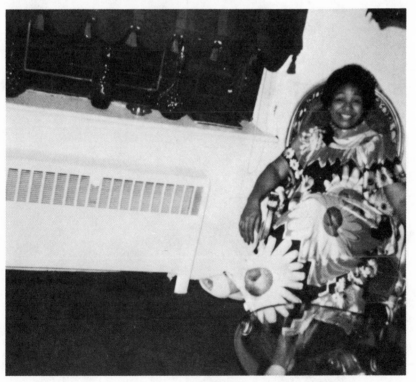

Vida Lee

Aaron Walker, Jr., and Esther Crayton
Courtesy Norbert Hess

The Memorial Concert

R. S. "T-Bone Walker, Jr." Rankin
Courtesy Norbert Hess

new pole. That's one you owe us. Anyway, how did you turn him
around?"

"Well, I always liked fishing," Seymour said, "but Bone knowed
nothin' about it. And he wouldn't listen to us guys. One time I told
him, 'Come on, I'll take you out on the ocean with me.' We had a
twin diesel boat that would sleep six. So we got up at 1 A.M. to be
on our way, me, Neil, Espero, and Roy. Up till the last minute Bone
was going. Then he changed his mind. While we were out there,
near Ensenada, one of the motors conked out. Still, that don't mean
nothin'—one's as good as two, just slower, that's all.

"But when we do get back, and with all them fish, Bone says,
'You mean to say you traveled out sixty miles and the motor quit?'
He turned to Marguerite. 'I said I was right not to go with them
SOBs. You know me, I'd 'a' been whipping their ass all the way
home.' I reckon Bone was scared at that time. He had friends came
all the way from North Dallas, and he wouldn't go out with them
either. He stayed at our place and I went instead."

"He walked the floor all night," Marguerite recalled, "waiting for
them to get back. 'What happened?' he kept repeating. Until I said:
'Will you shut up? You're making me nervous.' But he wouldn't rest
till they got in."

" 'Bone, if you'd come along once, you'd like it,' I told him later,"
Seymour continued. "But he always came back with, 'Man, I ain't
got time for that.'

" 'If I bring you a pole, will you go?'

" 'I told you. I have no time for that shit.'

"Would you believe the day I got him a pole I took him out with
me, and next time we came by *his* house he'd left for the pier? One
day his son, Junior, and I took him out on a deep-sea boat. He felt
seasick and got drunk, but the fish were biting—bam, bam, bam.
They were big ones, and this knocked him out. But after every
batch, he traveled back to the bar. 'Dad ought not to do that,' Junior
told me, but I said, 'Hell, at last he's having fun.' "

"One of them times that Seymour and Bone had fun, it cost
them something," Marguerite said. "After a gig at the Elks Club,
they went to an after-hours party and wound up at an oceanside bar

where sailors and musicians drop in to jam. They ended by eating breakfast at Jennard's in Los Angeles, and later Vi fixed them lunch. All that time they were supposed to have left the gig and come straight home.

" 'It's your turn to baby-sit,' I'd told Seymour at supper the night before. 'And see T-Bone steers clear of them fellas playing cotch.' You know what happened? They played regardless, and T-Bone lost his money and lost Seymour's as well. They never came home at all. Someone phoned me around 4 A.M. saying she'd seen them with a cop. I was too scared to call the jail. I could have tried the hospital, but I was scared to do that, too. I just walked the floor.

"Then 4 P.M. the next day they come struttin' in, ready to go back on the job. I looked them over carefully and saw nothing wrong. Time had come. I decided to *make* something go wrong. I tell you that when T-Bone went home that night he had a knot upside of his head! Good thing I had no gun—I woulda shot 'em both!"

Seymour laughed at her. "Lucky for me I don't keep a gun in the house! I carry a .25 automatic, just to keep somebody off of me, that's all. Bone and I used to wear suits we'd had made that had a pistol pocket in the double vest, just big enough for what we carried. It would be right on the inside next to your skin, so if you moved your arm or pushed your coat farther back, a person still wouldn't see it. You might have a .15 or a small .32 automatic. It's easily gotten at because it's flat.

"T-Bone had a permit to carry a gun. Working all the time and carrying money around, how could he know if someone wasn't lying in wait? But sometimes he needed it for another kind of role. Like once in San Diego he played a place on Broadway and Twelfth that held two thousand people. So many would be trying to get in, and others would be standing in the streets. That night I went along to see to the money. The guy paid all right but gave Bone a bogus check. The fellas had to be paid the next day, and I happened to have money in my pocket, so I took care of things. Bone would straighten me out later, I knew. But right till today that guy has never paid.

"We like to got into serious trouble with that, because I don't want nobody to take advantage of me, and Bone is the same. So out there one night we went gunning for him. 'I'm tired of people running all over me,' T-Bone said. 'They've run me over enough.' So he went upstairs and talked to those people in such a way I had to get us out and to home in a hurry. He scared the hell out of those people, and he scared the hell out of me."

"T-Bone would let things go on for a long time and still stay cool," Marguerite explained. "But if someone was doing real *wrong*, then he'd grab him. Climb on a chair, anything. If a guy was too tall, you'd see T-Bone jump! He can really raise hell."

"The best thing to do was get him laughing," Seymour remarked. "One time when we were in a tight spot, I got him going with a story about Ray Charles. Marguerite's cousin, Loretta, was Ray's first wife, and there was this night when we were having a party in somebody's place in L.A. If you were downstairs, you could hear a party going on, so someone might come up, thinking to crash. This particular time a big guy did us like that, and he was tall, dark, and ugly as sin. Across the room Ray Charles was singing, and the guy wanted to know who he was.

"We say, 'That's Ray Charles.'

"He say, 'Aw, that ain't no Ray Charles.'

" 'Yeah, that's Ray Charles.'

"By this time Ray said: 'Come here, man. Let me look at you.'

"The fellow said: 'If you Ray Charles, how you going to see me? You supposed to be blind!'

" 'Aw, come *here*. Bend over and let me look.' Ray put out his hands and went over his face like that, and then he told the guy: 'You know what? You the *blackest* and ugliest son of a bitch I ever seen in my whole damn life!'

"Well, the guy like to have cracked up. He just couldn't believe it, that Ray Charles had called the shots like they were. So he went to the liquor store, bought a case of whiskey, and brought it back up there. He told Ray: 'Anything you want, you just name it. I got all the money in the world. Any time a blind son of a gun can tell me how I look, he can have the lot!'" Seymour grinned.

* * *

"Damn, I missed Seymour," T-Bone said when he got back around five o'clock, obviously pleased with his catch. "That man don't believe me when I tell him my luck still holds."

"No one says you ain't lucky," Skaggs commented. "Didn't the hospital release you before the earthquake came?"

T-Bone grinned and turned to me. "Did you know about that? The hospital named Olive View in the San Fernando Valley was where some of the worst of it hit. After my car accident I'd ended up there. They released me just ahead of February, '71, after I'd been there for months. My bed was up on the third floor, and they tell me it tore away and landed two floors down. Smashed up the ambulances, and sixty or seventy people were hurt. Two or three got killed. Yeah, I was lucky all right."

"Twice lucky," Vi told him, "that they let you out of there so you could accept your award."

"She means the 1970 NARAS nomination, for *Good Feelin'*," T-Bone explained, "the best blues record for the year. So here come a day I never thought to see."

"It was *something*," Vi recalled. "We were thrilled. Bernita telephoned me at work to say: 'Come right home. You're going to the Palladium with Daddy. He's won an award.' We just couldn't believe it."

"See why my men were in so good with me?" T-Bone looked my way. "With that album they done such a great job. And the next year come to find out I'd been had."

Coming through the back door, M'Dear chimed in, "My boy is lucky, but he ain't the only one."

"Let *me* tell that," T-Bone said. "See them bars on the windows? Here's why, believe it or not. One day I was in the bathroom, and Kelie Sturgis, my granddaughter, came to get me out in a hurry. A man was walking around the house, tearing things up. He'd come across from my mother's, after he'd messed up her place. He'd come to the door and she'd let him in! Wanted to use the phone, he said. A fellow about thirty years old.

"Why you suppose I put them bars up?" he said, scolding M'Dear. "As much robbin' and stealin' and killin' as they're doin' around here, you gotta lock yourself up. They're very bad about old folks, you know that. They be looking for your Social Security checks. Old folks they will kill. You're going back to your childhood days, Mama, letting somebody in you don't even know. You see why I've got to stick around here."

M'Dear lifted her chin and sniffed. "You a fine one to talk. Been wild all your days." She turned to me. "I tried my best to break him down. Ask him. When he was a kid, I never let him have no bike. Why? Because he loved 'em. Wouldn't let him drive a car neither. Didn't want him driving. Look what happened last year."

T-Bone grinned. "OK. We'll call it quits. I'm a family boy, ain't I? I get told off sometimes. Mama won't have it no other way. That's how come it's worked out for me and Vi. Goofy as I was for a time back there, I never thought anyone would put up with me. Vi has got Mama to thank."

Smiling, Vi got up to fetch us supper, serving us on TV trays. From across the room T-Bone signaled his satisfaction. "She go along with all my programs, see? We get along just fine."

Twenty-three

One More Once

The spring came and went before I returned to Los Angeles, and it was now the third week in June, 1974. Things were much the same, though T-Bone obviously had not regained much strength. But his spirits remained good, and people, as usual, were in and out of the house all the time.

"I didn't have a chance to talk long with Stymie," I told him when we were alone for once. He gave me an odd look.

"Stymie don't do much talking," he replied, "but he's a wonderful guy.[1] I've been knowing him a long time. He spent the last seven, eight years in Synanon.[2] I visited him regularly there. He ended up heading the Synanon Gospel Family Choir, besides being in charge of the drivers responsible for the Synanon buses. He's feeling good right now," T-Bone went on, "into movies again. He was in the 'Backstairs at the White House' TV show.

"What happened to him years ago was he got busted for smoking pot while he was still a kid, and when he was doing time, the big boys let him know heroin was kicks. For cryin' out loud." T-Bone shook his head. "Me, I got no time for drugs. Still, we're great buddies. But just don't talk to him about the Little Rascals. He's ashamed of that crap."

"He didn't act that way when he was here with the Gang," M'Dear said. "I came home one day, and all the bunch was having dinner with my son, I declare."

"Could Stymie keep you company going to Pittsburgh?" I asked T-Bone.

"T-Bone's not ready," his mother stated flatly. "Right now he don't practice enough."

Irritated, T-Bone shrugged. "It's too hot," he said.

She returned his look. "You don't practice when it's cold!"

"Well, I don't think I can make Pittsburgh." T-Bone's tone was abrupt.

After a pause, Vi said, "They sent two round-trip tickets, remember?"[3]

1. Stymie Beard, Our Gang's derby-hatted little rascal, died in 1981 at age fifty-six.
2. A southern California drug treatment center.
3. An East Coast booking agency had offered T-Bone a contract for a concert in

"Maybe I could use Hooker's fellows," T-Bone mused.

From the kitchen Lester Skaggs called out, "Bone, you can't travel on no plane alone."

Walking in through the front door and crossing the floor to stand in front of her father, Bernita said, "Daddy, you can't go."

"Wow, here come the po-leece!" T-Bone said, amused. After she had earned her B.A. at California State while working days at the Bank of America, Bernita had enrolled with the Los Angeles Police Department and was now a deputy sheriff.

"How about that?" T-Bone said. "When you think of it, it's kind of comical, right? *We* have to watch ourselves around her!" He grinned, though obviously impressed. But when Bernita adopted a dictatorial tone, he was miffed.

"Well, you have to do what the doc said," she maintained.

He looked at Vi and pulled a face.

I asked, "What if I went along?"

Vi hesitated, momentarily hopeful. "Could you do that?"

"I think so. Stan doesn't expect me until the start of the week. He won't mind if I stop in Pittsburgh on the way."

"You're *on*," T-Bone told me, and I saw he was pleased.

He started getting ready for the trip three days before time to leave. "I'll be OK," he said. "I've been traveling all my life."

"Don't kid yourself," Lester muttered under his breath. But the next morning he was on hand to load up the bags and see the guitar safely aboard our rental car. Standing on the front steps, he and Vi waved good-bye. T-Bone wore a dark suit with a pinstripe and one of his favorite shirts. He turned to me, smiling. "I gotta look prosperous," he said.

I checked in the car, and we boarded an airline shuttle. "We'll be royals out here," T-Bone informed me. "Those guys know me from way back."

A couple of redcaps hurried over to meet us. "Where to, Fess?" the first inquired, smiling.

"Europe, like always," the other cut in.

Pittsburgh at the Nixon Theater, where John Lee Hooker was booked as the featured attraction.

"Y'all forgotten already? Only got back last week," T-Bone replied, playing the game.

"See, that's my due," he told me, his voice self-assured. But he let
me go forward and lead the way into the lounge. We sat ourselves
down, an odd pair. "I wouldn't want Bernita's job," I said.

"Why?" He asked puzzled.

"Playing policeman could be tough."

"Maybe you like nursemaid better?" he asked.

We smiled at each other, and I shook my head. "No. But you're
about to get up and head for the bar, right?"

"Damn right." He grinned.

After a time I decided to see if we could get on ahead of the rest.
That way T-Bone could take his time.

"Would a chair be best?" the operations clerk suggested.

I nodded. "I'll be back for it in a minute." T-Bone was just downing a drink when I came up behind him in the bar. He winked at
the bartender.

"Will you squeeze another juice?" he asked. "Maybe the lady
would care for an orangeade." The barman laughed as I grabbed
T-Bone by the elbow, shaking my head.

The airline hostesses on the 747 were still busy tidying when we
went aboard. Sizing up T-Bone in friendly fashion, they assumed
he was a celebrity of sorts. He leaned toward me, straightened his
jacket, and smiled. "Guess I'm not out in left field yet."

On the stopover in Dallas we had an hour and a half to wait.
"How long?" T-Bone asked.

"Not long," I lied. I was afraid it was time enough for some of his
hometown cronies to gather and drink his health. We sat side by
side in the crowded lounge where cold looks soon told us this was
Dallas, not L.A. His face indifferent, T-Bone held his temper in.
From time to time I was aware he was watching me from the corner
of his eye. Suddenly he made up his mind. He got to his feet smiling and announced that he was off to the bar.

"And I make bold to inquire, what's *yours?*" he said. Although it
might have been as well to keep a straight face, I laughed. When we
eventually boarded the plane, T-Bone was sandwiched between a

cowboy and me. We soon traded places because he had to make several trips into the back. He hardly touched dinner, though he had had nothing to eat all day. Sometimes at home, too, his mouth hurt and he went without food.

"Don't worry. I'm not hungry," he said, adjusting the headphones and closing his eyes. I wasn't happy for him, but I knew enough not to let on.

When we landed in Pittsburgh, it was 10:30 P.M. and raining hard. We looked around, but there appeared to be no one to meet us and nowhere to sit. At the carousel I was hunting for T-Bone's guitar because the case was so battered that it could easily be lost. When I hauled it off the roundabout and T-Bone was reunited with it, I felt better. We had no phone number to call, and at that hour the theater, the only address we had, would be closed.

"Well, you stay here. I'll go to Information," I told him. I left him surrounded by our things, and a half hour later when I started back, I stopped to hear an announcement over the loudspeaker and saw a girl in t-shirt and jeans whom I had not noticed before.

"Did you catch what was said?" I asked.

She nodded. "We've asked Information to help us page T-Bone Walker," she said.

And about time, I thought. "He was getting ready to head back to L.A.," I told her. I went off to fetch T-Bone, and when we returned, Brian Cleland was approaching, hands outstretched. Cleland headed Unity Plus Attractions, which had hired the groups the Nixon Theater was advertising for Saturday night. After introducing himself, he beckoned to Leslie Hammer, the girl I'd met. "She's our Girl Friday," he said. "Handles the press."

Behind her a beefy man pushed past and pumped T-Bone's hand. He was a flashy dresser who looked like an advance man for a rock attraction.

"How're you doin', kiddo," he boomed, slapping T-Bone on the back. "Betcha a drink wouldn't hurt. Just leave it to me."

"Let's get everyone down to the William Penn first," Cleland suggested. "If T-Bone's not too tired, you can make it to the bar there."

"*I'm* tired," I said.

But T-Bone shook his head.

"Never too beat for a quick one," he replied. The booking agent laughed and punched him on the arm.

Apologizing for being late and blaming the rain, which had shown no signs of letting up, Cleland led us to a limousine and began to talk of the show he had booked.

"Aw, forget business," the other man said. "T-Bone's set his heart on a little fun tonight." I stared out the window and, when we pulled up at the hotel, went straight to the desk for the key to my room, stopping at the elevator just long enough to catch T-Bone's eye.

"They've left your guitar in the middle of the lobby," I remarked. He nodded, but headed for the bar with the other three.

On my own at last, I hoped to fall asleep right away. I figured whatever might go wrong would be easier to cope with the next day. But I kept waking with a start, concerned about the guitar. And I was afraid if I called T-Bone's room, he might have just turned in.

I need not have worried. At 9 A.M., the phone rang, and T-Bone's approach was disarming. "How're you doing?" he said. "Hooker is here, and I've been down to see the guys."

The evening was programmed to start with a local outfit playing rock, and after T-Bone, John Lee Hooker would close the show. Hooker at that time was not in such great shape either, and T-Bone remembered that when he agreed to come. They would not show each other up. They went back a long way together.

"I've met his fellows before," T-Bone said. "They're all good guys."

When time came for rehearsal, he knocked on my door, and we headed downstairs. "I already called Hooker," T-Bone informed me. "We'll stop by his room first."

John Lee lay propped up on pillows, watching baseball on TV. "This is how I take care of things, Bone," he explained. "Plenty, plenty rest. Kenny's in charge of my group and knows what to do. They'll help you, man. Everything will be cool."

"Good. I'm not worried." T-Bone waved as we went out the door.

The group waited for us in the lobby, and we went back to where the pickup waited, loaded and all ready.

"My drums OK?" Kenny Swake inquired routinely as he climbed back of the wheel. Kenny and Skip Olsen, the fender bass, exchanged some fast repartee with Joel Selvin and Charlie Grimes, Hooker's backup guitars.

"I see the brothers have a time keeping up with those two cats," T-Bone informed me.

Joel took charge of T-Bone's guitar. "I'll tune it when we get there," he said. Leo Blevins had tuned it before we left, tightening the strings, but T-Bone knew it would need going over again.

Inside the theater the blind pianist, Butch Martin, and his unit were rehearsing. Martin was at center stage, hammering the piano keys and shouting encouragement to a backup vocal group. T-Bone had disappeared. Serious on arrival, he had walked into the wings and, lifting up his case, had taken out the guitar. I located the door of the auditorium and went out front. Besides the lighting and acoustic crews, there were not many people around. Flanked by groupies, the agent I had met the night before was seated well in the back. Coming down front, T-Bone nodded in his direction and crossed over to me. We sat listening for a while.

"Pretty soon the guys will get set up for Hook," he said. "I explained a couple of things, so I can rest easy now."

In a moment Brian Cleland, Leslie Hammer at his side, left the stage and approached us. Pleased, seeing us wave, they smiled. "Everything under control?" Brian asked.

T-Bone nodded. "No sweat."

After we returned to the stage, we had to stand about for a time. T-Bone stretched and flexed his fingers, and perspiration dampened his face.

"Why not do like Hooker and use a chair onstage?" I suggested. At home Lowell Fulson had urged him: "Take a chair. It will make it easier to fake if you have to. And you won't have the weight on your hands."

"*No way.*" T-Bone had silenced him, frowning, and the idea had been shelved. Now he looked irritated and did not answer. Then he stepped forward to meet Joel, who was coming across with his guitar.

"Band's ready, boss," he said.

"OK. Just play me the changes. You know what I need." Striking a couple of chords, T-Bone went to the mike and set the tempo for

"Bobby Sox Blues." "OK, that's fine," he said a moment later. "Rehearsal is only for tempo, right?" He took "Party Girl" a bit brighter, and the band fell in behind. T-Bone gave them no time to stretch out. This was part of the smoke screen he had going. "We'll change the pace after that," he said, "and I'll do 'Evenin'' next. Tonight you pick up the beat from my intro," he told Kenny.

"Then what?" Kenny replied.

"Well, we'll shuffle a while, like so." With "T-Bone Shuffle," the band got into its stride, aware this was the territory T-Bone had made his own.

"And 'Stormy Monday' closes the show, I guess?" Kenny called out as T-Bone strolled away into the wings, and the guys, smiling, came across to him.

"Thanks, fellas," T-Bone said. "Who gets to go to the liquor store?"

Joel grinned. "I don't mind."

"You call it then," T-Bone said.

When I heard from him next, it was 7:45 P.M. He was at my door looking sharp, wearing a new black-and-white checked suit. At the theater the first show had started, and Butch Martin was into his act. Coming up through the stage door from the front, Brian Cleland and Leslie looked relaxed. I hoped that meant the house was OK.

"How is it?" I said.

"Fair." Brian was noncommittal, but he had a smile for T-Bone. "It's the early show after all. How are things with you?"

"Just fine." T-Bone made it sound like "What else?" Crossing to where the instruments were stashed, he located his case and lifted out his guitar. After a moment, he nodded. Joel had tuned it just right.

"You don't have to do a full forty minutes," Brian said, following him across. "Whatever suits is OK." He was taking trouble to let T-Bone see his mind was easy, and this confirmed my impression of him. The agency's man was nowhere to be seen, but I was not surprised by that.

Butch Martin finished his set, and Hooker's musicians filed onto a darkened stage to set up. When the lights reappeared, Cleland walked out to the mike.

"We're pleased to bring you T-Bone Walker," he said. "You know him. You've heard 'Stormy Monday.' Now you can tell your friends you've seen him. A big hand for T-Bone, please!"

Negotiating a maze of cables attached to amplifiers and mikes, T-Bone moved ahead carefully in the direction of the footlights. The applause was fair. The audience was young, and not many knew his name. But opening up with "Mean Mistreater," T-Bone registered at once.

"We hear you, mister!" a voice hollered. T-Bone smiled and his delivery picked up. Before the applause died down, he made a switch, introducing "Teenage Baby." Sensing a great number of kids out front, he knew what to call. The audience was custom-made for him. He might not have to worry at all. The next tempo was a jump, and the band was swinging all out. From there he could move to a shuffle or to any one of the tempos he had made his own. I was starting to think he would make it home free, when suddenly he seemed to recollect his circumstances and his concentration slipped.

"I'll try 'Evenin','" he told the band. He needed time to think, but he had made a bad choice. With the slower tempo the momentum died down and some of the excitement as well. Aware of the change, he cut "Evenin'" short and, altering the beat, slid into "T-Bone Shuffle." The audience would have had to be stone deaf to resist. Couples in the front stood up and eased into the aisles to dance. Glancing back over his shoulder, T-Bone called Joel to the mike to swap fours, then stood back and smiled, letting Joel stretch out. He kept flexing his hands. He could not carry on much longer, I knew. Kenny sensed the same thing, and raising a finger to indicate the last chorus, he let the band know they were winding it up. Waiting for the applause to die down, T-Bone stood silent, his mind a blank.

"'Stormy Monday'?" Kenny called, and T-Bone nodded, hands automatically fingering the opening chords. He had to move closer to the mike to be heard above the applause. Although his fans did not want him to stop now, he was soon through and heading for the wings. Hands in the air, he was waving good-bye.

Brian Cleland moved quickly past him and, going to the mike, tried to introduce John Lee Hooker and sidetrack the applause. T-Bone stood on the sidelines confronted by cables. Reaching out our hands, Joel and I hauled him in. "You were sensational, man," Joel told him, but T-Bone seemed not to hear. He started for the dressing room in a daze. Still, all that mattered was how it had looked from out front. I hoped he would remember that.

Between the two shows things quieted down. In John Lee's dressing room a TV crew was completing a documentary on blues artists for educational television. Jane Dennison, the producer, beckoned me in. "You'll want to hear this, I think—John Lee Hooker talking about T-Bone," she said.

John Lee's recollections were vivid, and this was a story he must have told many times before. "He's the man gave me my start, no kidding—T-Bone Walker. He was playing the Flame Show Bar in Detroit. A big draw, booked in twice a year. People were crazy about him. I was nothin' but a kid, and I'd never heard anyone play that much guitar." John Lee shook his head. "I was under age, but somehow I'd get inside. I couldn't stay away. He would spot me, and so one time he said, 'Kid, you know how to play?' I could do no more than nod. First thing you know, he was *announcing* me. 'Listen, everybody, the kid here can play. I hunch he really can *play*.' I had to come up to the mike alongside him, scared to death. I figured he'd cut me into his solos, but not Bone!

"'It's all yours,' he told me, and grinning, he walked right on out of the place. How I made out, I don't know, but after the engagement was finished, they had me come back later on.

"But the night he had me play, there must have been a hot game on. T-Bone gambled pretty heavy those days. But anytime he thought you could play, you'd get your chance."

"I didn't know all that much about T-Bone," Jane Dennison said.

"Well, they don't come any better," John Lee assured her. "Listen to the fellows that play. You'll always hear some T-Bone in there someplace."

"Well, I've got a little footage left," Jane told me. "Shall we put the camera on him a few minutes?"

"Great!" I hurried off to find him. He was in the corridor signing autographs for some fans.

"Something up?" he said.

"Hooker's paying a debt. The way he's talked about you, the camera-men want you inside."

T-Bone looked doubtful. "I've never done no TV," he said.

"You'll be fine," I told him and, taking him by the arm, brought him to Jane.

"Helen will feed you the questions," Jane explained. "You just talk, that's all." A chair was set up, and lights focused on it, but the preparations made T-Bone nervous.

"Let's clear the room," Jane decided. I debated asking Hooker to stay, but they had already talked with him at the hotel, and perhaps this should be T-Bone all the way.

When the camera switched on and he sat down, he said, "I never tried this before."

"Where do you want to start, Bone?" I asked. "What about the Rhumboogie?"

He searched for the right words. "Yeah, I played there . . ."

"Tell us about Little Harlem then, the early days. Maybe that's better."

His mouth was dry, and he grimaced. "Sure, Little Harlem was OK," he said, trying to think of something more to offer.

"Didn't you do a dance routine at that time?"

The heat was making him perspire, and the camera seemed to have a mesmerizing effect. "Yes, I had a nice act," he agreed. "I'd do the splits," he added before clamming up again. Jane was obviously disappointed, and the cameraman doused the lights. T-Bone turned to her smiling, apologetic. I would have given a lot then to have had the lights back on. *This* was the performer the camera needed to capture—humorous, appealing, ingenu-ous, and unassuming. Jane signaled to resume filming, but the cameraman had become impatient and did not wait for me to speak.

"So 'Stormy Monday' is your number?" he inquired.

T-Bone, I thought, *please don't tell about that boy again.* But he could not be stopped. He had never forgotten a raggedy kid who had once leaned on his piano, improvising a new set of lyrics to his piece.

"The way he built it up was so great," T-Bone said. "I use some of it to this day."

Jane looked at me and smiled. "Well, let's see if we can get some other shots from the front during the second show," she said.

Returning to the wings, T-Bone seemed more relaxed. If he had not downed too much, it might go better this time. Not long before, he had been able to drink all day and still carry it off. When Brian Cleland brought him out again, he was acting more like himself. Some of the audience must have caught the first show, because he got a warmer welcome this time.

He opened up with "West Side Baby," and the gallery started shouting requests for his hits. Changing the routine seemed to be a good idea, and for a time he appeared to be enjoying himself. All of a sudden he turned around, and I thought the band must have fluffed. But it wasn't that. From the way he was examining the guitar, he seemed to think a string had snapped.

"Go on, man. You're all right," Joel said, and turned him back to the mike, but T-Bone continued adjusting the screws. "You take it on out," he told Joel. A moment later he seemed satisfied and resumed control with a beat that frenzied the crowd. After rousing cheers, he moved to the mike to introduce "Evenin'." As the intro got under way, he felt his grip on the neck slacken and, suddenly dismayed, knew the chord sequence would be wrong. He stared in disbelief as his fingers froze on the strings.

Laughter broke out as he shouted: "Now I *know* I'm drunk! Here, I'll sing one instead." To applause from the gallery, he started up "Evil Gal Blues" and then segued into "Sail On, Little Girl." The band kept swinging behind him, but his legs were giving out. The house was still rocking when he disappeared into the wings. As Kenny's eyes searched for him in the shadows, the audience clamored for more. Over the persistent clapping, he recognized shouts for "Stormy Monday" and sent Joel to the mike to play the introduction, which forced T-Bone to return.

Standing beside me, John Lee Hooker muttered: "Don't apologize, man. Don't open your mouth."

But T-Bone was already clearing his throat. "Sorry," he was saying. "I've been sick, you know." As Brian Cleland approached, he was promising, "I'll do better next time."

When the show finished and Cleland was getting ready to leave after paying up, he led T-Bone off to one side and said, smiling, "You did just fine."

Twenty-four

Going Down Slow

Photograph by Harry J. Adams. Property of the author

When I had been home a few days, I received a letter from Vi. "T-Bone is still out on the road!" she wrote. "He stopped in Fort Worth to visit a friend. Then he got together with Bobby Blue Bland, and spent time with the band. You know, whenever he's back home he's having a ball."

Near the end of July, I had another letter. "We're happy because T-Bone's appointment with the clinic finally came through. We've been waiting on it, like four months. I certainly hope and pray the doctors will find out what is wrong."

Vi did not have much to add when I called her some weeks later. "I wonder do these doctors themselves know the trouble for sure," she said. "If it's his nervous system, like they say, you'd think they could do him a little better than they do. He moves so slow he can hardly get his clothes on by himself."

"I won't come out your way for a while, then," I told her. "Maybe Thanksgiving week."

"That's best. He can look forward to that. He should be better by then."

In early December, when I had heard nothing more, I called Pee Wee Crayton in Los Angeles. "He's not doing that good," he said. "I was hoping I'd see him on my birthday, December 18. I was playing a gig at Lucille's, and I was hoping he might show and do a couple of numbers with me. But it was really foggy that night, and so he phoned me at work to say they wouldn't let him go out—else he would have been there for sure. Esther says to tell you she's got a great idea. She wants everyone to get together to play a concert at the Union Hall to help pay T-Bone's bills. We're looking for you to come out."

This, the first of several calls about the concert, gave me an excuse to telephone Vi again. Babs, T-Bone's other daughter, answered the phone.

"I'll fetch Vi," she said.

"At times it seems Daddy's better," Vi said. "He's making plans with Kelie for Christmas, and he's got so he can dress himself again. Esther had told him her idea. The concert sounds fine. He's looking forward to it, and to seeing you."

Christmas came and went without any change, but on December 31 I heard from Vi again. "He was all right this morning when I went to work, but I thought I'd call him like always. He didn't answer when I phoned him at eleven, so I tried M'Dear out back and reached Babs there. She found him on the living room floor, near his chair. When he'd got that far, he'd fallen, and then he couldn't move, or speak. He's so thin Babs just swept him up and carried him off to his bed. Then she located Bernita, and by the time I arrived, the doctor and ambulance had been. Daddy was gone, back to the hospital again.

"They made all the tests once more and said he was paralyzed all right, even down to his hands, but the specialist, who is a neurologist, decided it wasn't a stroke. It was his nervous system, he thought. He said, 'You know what liquor can do to a man.'"

During January and February I heard often from T-Bone's friends. "I went to see him two, three times when he moved to the rest home," Joe Turner said. "My wife, Pat, and I saw him in the hospital even. We went to the desk and asked where he was. They said Room 13 or somethin', but I said: 'No, he's not. I see him lyin' here right now.' They had him in a booth on a table, facing the other way. 'That ain't T-Bone,' they said. 'Yes, it is,' I replied. 'I'd know him any place.' I'd recognized the back of his head.

"So Pat went up to kiss him, and he smiled and said: 'Doggone! Where y'all come from?'

"'We're here to see you. When you goin' to get out of bed?' we asked him then."

"Joe will play the benefit, of course," Esther wrote, "and Pee Wee, Cleanhead, and Lowell Fulson as well. A whole lot of others. George 'Harmonica' Smith, Johnny 'Guitar' Watson, Nellie Lutcher and the band, Joe Liggins and his Honey Drippers, and a bunch besides."

The next time I called Vi, it sounded as though all of his friends would perform. "That pleases him," she said, "and he was thrilled with what Carmella DiMilo did.[1] She and her friends ordered him a beautiful gold trophy shaped like a guitar. She brought it to the rest home where we've got him now.

"The hospital only kept him three weeks and wouldn't allow me to carry him back to the house. He needs day-and-night care. He's

1. Carmella DiMilo was a singer with Roy Milton's band.

at the West Vernon Convalescent Home, where his Uncle Jack stays. It's close by, and I can stop in at any time. I think he's looking better now. His color's coming back, and he's eating again. Uncle Jack feeds him breakfast, checks on him every hour, and calls me each day. Junior gets in to do lunch, and I go straight there after work.

"He's beginning to use his hands again and sometimes feeds himself. In the evenings it's Bernita and Kelie and I. Kelie climbs up on the bed and makes him laugh. But M'Dear is not doing so good.[2] Although he's called her on the phone, she's not seen him since he left. It's not as if he were coming back soon. She doesn't say anything, but it's like she knows."

"But *he* don't know. He doesn't understand," Pee Wee Crayton explained when he called. "That's what upsets me. He wants my help. When he gets confused, he says he's stranded and his guitar is lost. He thinks I should do something, and that gets me down. So right now I have Esther go in my place. Because there is *nothing* I can do. If there was, I would have—you have to know that. Anything. He told Esther last time, 'Pee Wee doesn't like to see me like this.'" Listening in on an extension, Esther interrupted her husband.

"I disagreed. I said: 'You wrong. He's just busy. We both *love* being with you, always have.' And that was the truth. I wish we could have known how to show our appreciation and gratitude to that man while he could still understand. I don't think he really knows how we feel, why we're doing the benefit and all."

"Well, he knows how *I* feel," Pee Wee countered. "A brother couldn't love him more. And I need to repay him for what he's done for me."

"T-Bone was always lookin' out for Pee Wee," Esther said. "Like the time he went to Alaska and Pee Wee said, 'Boy, I wish *I* could go.' When T-Bone came back, he had a contract for Pee Wee in his hand! It happened like that so many times. Someone said the other day that people would go up to T-Bone on the street sayin', 'I need a job.' Bone would tell them, 'I'll see what I can do,' and before he got through with his engagement, he'd have a job for someone who hadn't been working all year."

2. Surprisingly, T-Bone's mother outlived him by seven years, dying in 1982.

"When he was busy," Pee Wee went on," he'd tell a contractor, 'I'm sorry, I can't make it, but my friend Pee Wee Crayton can.' He's the cause of my playin' the Parisian Room right now. But I paid him back in 1973. His last booking there he was sickly, so I'd go every night and help with his show. He was playing, but he was shaky, and it made me nervous to see him working like that. So then sometimes after he finished a song, he'd be able to say, 'Tell you what, I'm goin' to let Pee Wee sing one, and I'm goin' to get down and listen myself.'"

A short time later I received another note from Vi. "He's trying hard," she wrote. "His mind functions pretty good at times. But don't come for a while. He'd hate for you to find him this way. Still, you're needed for the benefit, so please tell Esther OK."

Stanley felt I should go as soon as they called, so I contacted Pee Wee and asked him to keep in close touch. For a time I heard nothing more, and I'd started to hope again when on Sunday morning, March 16, 1975, Lois Badsen phoned from New York.

"We just got through talking with the family in L.A. Harold wanted to check things. . . ." She paused.

"Go on," I said.

"Yes. Well, T-Bone . . . he just died. This morning, two hours ago. Junior says can you come?"

"Thank you, Lois," Stanley said, taking the receiver from me. "We'll call him right away."

After writing the obituary for the New York *Times*, I left for Los Angeles and an appointment with Junior at the house.

"Dad hadn't seemed much different," Junior said. "But the nurse serving him breakfast explained he suddenly waved her away. 'Somethin' ain't right,' he said, and next moment his temperature had jumped to 106. He lapsed into a coma after that, and they couldn't raise a pulse. Next thing you know, *bam.*"

Babs overheard him and said: "You know he didn't want to hang on like that. A burden to all."

"He was too lively." Junior nodded. "With him, it was like a car he would keep driving until the motor had had it and gone. Only difference, his motor they couldn't repair. He was a contradiction of sorts. So extroverted, but really a family man. When I would walk into that hospital, sick as he was, you would hear him proclaim in that big, stiff voice, 'That's my boy come to see me, the one I was telling you about.'

"I'm gonna miss Dad, that's for sure. Some people figured that because we weren't always together, we weren't that close. They'll never know how far they were from the truth. I don't want to harp on this, but what got him the most respect was that thing, believing he should help anyone down and out. He lived up to that. And then when it came his turn, he *never* sang the blues. I never heard him complain."

Junior could not remain to talk. He told me that Vi, who had been sedated, was resting and that I should leave for Curzon Street, where viewing had already begun in the Angelus Funeral Home.

In the front room where T-Bone lay, attendants were bringing in wreaths and floral tributes wherever space would allow. A file of mourners moved slowly past the bier. Suffering appeared to have left T-Bone unchanged. Imagining for a moment that if I waited I might hear him speak, I hesitated before moving on. For me one thing was paramount: the vacuum that existed, that would persist now that T-Bone was gone. No more "going along with the program, see."

In the rear flustered attendants attempted to cope with a situation that had not been foreseen. Flowers continued to arrive and for lack of space remained in containers. Telegrams and condolences, many of them still unopened, were stacked a foot high. A press release was required, and I transmitted it when calls came in from London, Paris, and Berlin. Calls also came from Tokyo, where T-Bone had been invited to tour later in the year. So much public grief and concern threatened the funeral arrangements the family had made.

"Who knows how many will show up tomorrow?" Junior groaned. "We'll have to hope for the best. No one expected this. Five hundred, yes, the chapel could handle that, but . . ." It was too late now for alternative plans. Friends and fans discussed the coming benefit, now a memorial concert scheduled for May 5. At home contributions had come in from B. B. King, the Copasetics, Stevie Wonder, Ray Charles, Freddie King, Dizzy Gillespie, and others.

The parlor was scheduled to close at nine o'clock. However, a crowd of friends remained, hoping to speak with family members still standing by the coffin. The funeral director had to promise viewing could be resumed the next morning in the church before the service began.

By noon the following day traffic had come to a halt around West Forty-third Place. Four limousines drew up in front of the house, and behind the hearse a lengthy cortege formed. An hour and a half passed while attendants marshaled vehicles into single file. Finally, preceded by motorcycle police, the procession pulled away from the curb, and a long file of cars—Lester, who was riding with me, counted fifty—snaked its way slowly across town to the funeral home. Its passage was slowed by crowds overflowing pavements still some distance from the funeral home.

Since resumption of the viewing had awaited the arrival of the hearse, the chapel was now filled to capacity, and hundreds of mourners remained outside, unable to get in. As the cortege inched its way into the yard, I glimpsed a dispirited Joe Turner standing some distance from the doors. I learned later that other honorary pallbearers also had not managed to get in.

It was past two by the time police enabled funeral personnel to open a path for the family so they could enter by a door in the rear of the church. Shepherded back of the altar, we were directed to a glassed-in enclosure overlooking the casket, which was almost obscured by wreaths and crosses and floral guitars. Junior struggled to seat dignitaries and family members and performers from out of town. When he found a place for me, Lester remained at my side. A uniformed nurse was stationed beside M'Dear. By 3:30 people in the packed pews were restless; yet outside hundreds still waited, determined to file by the bier.

Junior told me later that five hours had elapsed from the time the hearse arrived at the funeral home until the memorial at the graveside was finally over. "With my grandmother in mind," he said, "I'd wanted to keep both services brief, but who could have looked for such crowds. I doubt if some of those strangers whom I saw trying to force their way in even knew my father. For a time it looked as though we might have a circus on our hands. Poor Bernita. She had wanted the greatest respect for Dad and took it hard. At one point an attendant approached me about a fellow by the organ who demanded to sing. Since he was unknown to us all, I had to go back and explain that arrangements for the service had already been made.

" 'This is not an impromptu affair,' I told him. 'If I let you up, others would want to do the same. My father is being buried today. This is not a performance.' But I thanked him for being there, and like the rest of the family, I was very moved so many had thought to come, although never for a moment had we expected the day to turn out like this. We knew Dad had many friends, but we'd thought to see mostly people he'd known during the last few years of his life. There were others there he must have known decades ago, people he might well not have recalled. But *they* hadn't forgotten.

"Of course, there were some . . . well, *others*—people hoping to draw attention to themselves at all costs. I'm not referring to that lady who called from Denver this morning. Hers were feelings we respected. But we couldn't say as much for quite a few folks. Maybe they were hoping for a spectacle, something different from the ceremony the family had planned. But we wouldn't allow anything like that."

The service in the chapel had not been elaborate. Two hours after the hearse had arrived, Junior indicated he wished the casket closed and Bible readings begun. Following a selection of church music, one by one the ministers whom the family had invited to speak proceeded to the front of the chapel and stood, solemn, erect, in purple and black, before the expectant congregation. Those who anticipated a storybook account of his career were instead exhorted to pray, as T-Bone, no longer a public but now a private man, was consigned to his Maker and laid to rest. This was perhaps fitting, for in his own estimation T-Bone was indeed a family man.

Epilogue

Photograph courtesy Bruce Ricker

The memorial concert was presented by Esther Crayton at the Musicians' Union Auditorium in Los Angeles on May 5, 1975.[1] Well publicized and sold out, it was a lengthy affair featuring outstanding blues artists of yesterday and today. T-Bone's life and achievements were repeatedly recalled with affection and humor.

Pee Wee Crayton opened the proceedings as leader of his own group. He played a selection of T-Bone's hits, and Patty Jack said, "He sounds good enough for you to think T-Bone is up there beside him." Lowell Fulson followed, backed by the same musicians. When one of his strings snapped, Pee Wee handed him his own guitar.

"Can you believe that?" Esther remarked. "My husband has never let anyone touch his box—no one except Bone."

Fulson was warmly received, and the applause continued when Eddie "Cleanhead" Vinson was announced. He was on sure ground with "Kidney Stew" and "Cherry Red," two of his biggest hits.

In the wings routining the presentation were the comedian Bill Murray, who had worked with T-Bone in the 1950s at Idlewild, and tenor saxophonist Red Holloway, who was responsible for talent in the Parisian Room.

Marl Young, conductor, arranger, and a prominent member of the union board, who retained vivid memories of T-Bone at the Rhumboogie Club in Chicago in 1943, had been asked to deliver the memorial address. He recalled T-Bone's accomplishments over the years, his advocacy of the electric guitar in the early 1940s, and the influence he had exerted on generations of blues and jazz guitarists. "But what impressed me most," he said, "was the kick he got out of giving other people a leg up, seeing them make it to the top."

Later in the program, after Nellie Lutcher and her trio, Joe Liggins and the Honey Drippers, Johnny "Guitar" Watson, George "Harmonica" Smith, and others had performed, Young returned to the mike and called Vida Lee, Junior, Bernita, and R. S. to the stage, where Pee Wee and Esther waited. Vi, tears in her eyes, shaky and spent, turned to Junior for help. It was a difficult moment for Junior as well. He had not rehearsed what the family might say to

1. The concert raised four thousand dollars, which helped defray T-Bone's hospital bills.

this crowd of people that had packed the hall out of respect for his father.

"All of us here tonight," he began, "my mother and sister, my gran, you know I can't forget *her*, thank every one of you for this tribute to my father. Were he here, he would have been very proud. And we are grateful to Esther and Pee Wee for working so hard to put on this wonderful show. We are so grateful, too, to all Dad's friends who have performed tonight. Will it show our appreciation if we can get R. S. to play for you now? But remember," he added, as clapping broke out, "he'll be very nervous, you know, trying to sound like the boss. You be *kind.*" He smiled.

In the auditorium Patty Jack and I stood side by side listening to people cheer as R. S. went to the mike to start up "Stormy Monday," T-Bone on his mind. "See that?" Patty Jack grimaced. "*Who* do he take after? Been drinkin' all day!"

Then it was time for Joe Turner to wind up the affair. "How does he seem?" Esther looked to Patty Jack for reassurance. She had tried all evening to forestall the fans who kept bringing Joe drinks. She remembered an evening at the Parisian Room the week before. Around midnight, as Joe finished a set, he called someone over to help him get down off the stand. He suddenly lost his balance and collapsed on the floor. Trying for a brief moment to regain his feet, he gave up and lay back. "Aw, forget it," he cried. "Bring me the drinks over here!"

Pee Wee was encouraging people in the front row to get Joe onto the stage. They led him to a stool in front of the band. "OK, you know what to do," Pee Wee told him. "Figure he's here beside you, waiting to break into your act!"

Joe leaned forward and grabbed the mike. As he started to holler, his mouth opening wide, Pee Wee turned away, tears stinging his eyes. "*Listen.*" Patty Jack grabbed my arm. "All them verses you never heard before! Bone is putting somethin' special into his head."

Much later, as the maintenance men were dimming the lights to get people to their feet, Joe was still going strong. "I got a right," he was shouting, "to sing the blues tonight!"

Appendix A

Recommended Recordings

Some of the most inspired records T-Bone Walker ever made came from the early sessions Ralph Bass produced for the Black and White label beginning in 1946. For the first date T-Bone, possibly urged on by Bass, hired Jack McVea on tenor, Red Kelly on trumpet, Crow Kahn on piano, Frank Clarke on bass, and Rabon Tarrant on drums. With the exception of using Al Killian as a replacement for Kelly, the personnel for the second session of 1946 was identical. Of the four titles issued, the one best remembered was "I'm in an Awful Mood."

By 1947 T-Bone felt sufficiently at home in the studio to engage musicians who particularly impressed him. Two he had known in Les Hite's band—drummer Oscar Lee Bradley and tenor saxophonist Hubert Maxwell "Bumps" Myers—participated in every session he made for Black and White from that first 1947 session on. Although Myers was born in Clarksburg, West Virginia, in 1912, his family moved to California a few years later, and by 1934, his apprenticeship completed, Myers had accompanied Buck Clayton and Teddy Weatherford to China and played for eighteen months in Shanghai. At that time air travel was not commonplace, and between East and West Coast musicians there was not much interchange. So Bumps was never as well known in the East as in the West. He was a swinging tenor with an enviable sound and was endowed with that feel for an effortless beat projected also by Texans of the same generation such as Illinois Jacquet and Buddy Tate.

Among the titles recorded during that first session in 1947, when the group also included Teddy Buckner on trumpet, Lloyd Glenn on piano, and Arthur Edwards on bass, were a classic "Stormy Monday" and also "T-Bone Jumps Again," the latter an instrumental on which Buckner shines. Buckner, born in Sherman, Texas, worked during the 1930s with Lionel Hampton, Benny Carter, and Horace Henderson. While he was with Hampton, the band sometimes backed up Louis Armstrong, who, then in his prime, was a noticeable influence on instrumentalists of every kind. This influence can be seen even in T-Bone's vocal rendition, on a later session, of his own "Still in Love with You." Buckner's style was rooted in Armstrong, and he was fortunate in producing a tone that complemented the type of jazz he expressed so well and that he continued to exemplify in the 1970s as leader of a small band featured at Disneyland for several years. On piano, Lloyd Glenn was a favored accompanist for most of the blues singers centered in Los Angeles. He made all Lowell Fulson's sessions and was T-Bone's choice whenever Willie McDaniels was unavailable. During the 1970s, Lloyd Glenn enjoyed renewed prestige as a purveyor of vintage blues and boogie piano behind blues singer Joe Turner in prime nightclub bookings.

When T-Bone made another session with Buckner and Myers, on November 6, 1947, the rhythm section included McDaniels on piano and Billy Hadnott on bass. "McDaniels was heavy-handed, but he was a good piano player," recalled bassist Red Callender, who used him in a trio extensively recorded by Exclusive Records. Hadnott appeared first in Kansas City playing with Jay McShann at Lucille's Band Box (Piney Brown's erstwhile Subway Club), in a band that included Fred Beckett on trombone, Jimmy Keith on tenor, and, on altos, Professor Smith, from the Oklahoma City Blue Devils, and Charlie Parker. An excellent section man, Hadnott was always in demand in Los Angeles recording studios and more recently has been a member of Nellie Lutcher's group. In a session that followed, T-Bone recruited yet another Hite alumnus, trumpet player George Orendorff. Orendorff also was influenced by Armstrong and contributed enormously to the success of dates on which he appeared. Later T-Bone was to feature Jack Trainor, a musician with a beautiful tone and effective style reminiscent of Frankie Newton's. Trainor's career ended in suicide after he had suffered for years with crippling arthritis.

However, of the fifty titles T-Bone recorded during 1946 and 1947, the trumpet player most often featured was Orendorff, who can be heard to advantage on the Capitol album of reissues. Jazz historians appreciate "Inspiration Blues" (retitled "Born to Be No Good") and "T-Bone Shuffle," but Orendorff is, in addition, marvelously well represented by "Go Back to the One You Love," "I Wish You Were Mine," and "Wise Man's Blues." Born in Atlanta, he started out on guitar and switched to trumpet when his family moved to Chicago and enrolled him in Wendell Phillips High School, where he met Lionel Hampton, Eddie South, and Wallace Bishop. He joined Les Hite in 1930 and recorded with him behind Armstrong, appearing as well in films that featured Hite. After a stint in the army in the 1940s, he returned to Los Angeles, where he was in demand as a sideman and continued to make records, ultimately combining gigs with his duties as an official in the American Federation of Musicians. Orendorff had a number of poems published, which is not surprising, given his inventive trumpet style.

Although T-Bone never said much about it, he was proud of his association with jazz musicians. He knew that among blues men he was unique in this regard. Like many of his friends in Lawson Brooks's band, he could have settled for a career as a sideman playing jazz had he been less talented. But his potential as a singer and his personal magnetism meant wider horizons from the start. Still, he was aware that the status he enjoyed among musicians was based on what he accomplished on guitar. This was his first priority and characterized him as an artist. Playing took precedence over everything, just as it had when he first encountered Charlie Christian in Oklahoma City and they shared veteran guitarist Chuck Richardson's instruction before proceeding on journeys of exploration at those jam sessions that proliferated in Kansas City during the 1930s.

Speaking of the Black and White sessions, T-Bone said: "Rehearsing wasn't too big a thing. We didn't get to play all that much, you know. The fellows understood one another, and we'd pool our ideas. McDaniels was something else. He did a lot of those things for me, such as 'Crime Doesn't Pay' and 'I Miss You, Baby.' And there was another McDaniels—Grover, from Dallas, who also wrote a lot of the lyrics I sang. Sometimes we would rehearse before a session, like when we made 'Stormy Monday.' Lloyd Glenn had a machine, the kind you can make records with. It cuts a disc and plays it back. So instead of writing anything out, we rehearsed and recorded and then played it to see how it sounded. Lloyd brought that heavy thing to the studio the following day to make sure that when we got ready to record, we could get that same tempo, that feeling. He's a terrific musician. When it comes to blues, he can play anything you want, and he's made a lot of sessions himself, recording his own numbers. I never wrote down my own stuff. Mostly worked things out beforehand, or on the job, and the beat was always big with me."

Possibly more than anyone else, T-Bone was responsible for the wave of popularity for the shuffle beat. His "T-Bone Shuffle" and "T-Bone Boogie" made him instantly recognizable. "We called those 'jumps,'" he said. "They were always in demand. But there were other kinds of things we did with the blues. I classify them three ways: there's *sweet* blues, like 'First Love Blues' or 'That Old Feeling Is Gone'; then there's *deep* blues, way down, like 'I'm in an Awful Mood.' And then the blues you come on with when you let your chick find out she's through. You know, like 'Got Bad News for You, Baby.'" Because his public identified him more closely with that category than any other, he laughed, adding, "Remember what they used to sing? 'Go Back Where You Stayed Last Night.'" But the element of double entendre implicit there, so traditional in the blues, was something T-Bone did not care for and carefully avoided.

The format used in the Capitol reissues was simple, necessarily so because of the skeletal instrumentation and the fact that the length of selections was governed by the three-minute time limit imposed by 78s. When the tempo was leisurely, as in "I Want a Little Girl" and "I'm Still in Love with You," it allowed little more than a thirty-two-bar chorus for T-Bone to sing, accompanying himself on guitar and eliciting responses from Myers or one of the other horns. Often Orendorff or Trainor could be heard playing a muted lyrical solo in the background, one of those effective devices too soon abandoned. T-Bone usually wound up this kind of number with a reprise of the final eight bars, concluding with a flurry of chords. On a fast blues, like "West Side Baby" or "T-Bone Jumps

Again," after introductory choruses on guitar by T-Bone, customarily Myers would stretch out for twenty-four bars before T-Bone came back propelled by a riffing ensemble. Then he would move aside to let the trumpet player in, and finally he would cue the group into the take-out pattern, going for as many repeats as time allowed. And this became more or less standard procedure for the R and B groups then evolving.

In 1946 and 1947 the style of the period dominated by the trumpets of Louis Armstrong, Roy Eldridge, Harry James, and Dizzy Gillespie was being challenged by the assertive sound of the tenor saxophone. First suggested by Coleman Hawkins, this sound was subsequently emphasized by Ben Webster, Don Byas, and others who modeled their style on that of Hawkins. Later, despite Lester Young's cooler approach in the 1940s, its aggressive potential was realized in the exciting solos of Arnett Cobb and Illinois Jacquet in Lionel Hampton's band. This led inevitably to a honking tenor and the coating of corn that characterized rhythm and blues, a field in which King Curtis was to excel. Thus a good deal of T-Bone's growing reputation reflected the popularity of a style he had unwittingly helped to create, but what was still more significant was the way his sound presaged the guitar age ahead.

Appendix B

Duke Robillard on T-Bone Walker

Duke Robillard, a Rounder recording artist, attained national prominence during his years as star guitarist with the popular group Roomful of Blues. He played and sang with such authority that whenever veteran blues artist Muddy Waters spied him in his audience, he was invited to sit in, an honor few were accorded.

In more recent years, heading his own trio, he has established an enthusiastic following at home and abroad. The degree of admiration and understanding he manifests for T-Bone Walker's talents in the following excerpts from an interview demonstrates the influence T-Bone exerted not only on contemporaries but on younger generations as well.

When T-Bone's double album came out on Blue Note in 1976, I realized I'd had to go through a period of listening to swinging jazz before I could understand his guitar playing. Because his timing, phrasing, and tone—everything—was really complex compared to any other blues guitarist I can think of. By now I could hear what it was everyone had picked up from him, everyone from B. B. King to Gatemouth Brown, Lowell Fulson, all the greatest single-string guitarists. T-Bone played much more on chords than the other players. He used sixth and ninth chords a lot, working around them and playing lines that would sound great on a horn. His playing is amazingly musical. His timing reminds me in some ways of Charlie Christian. Although they are different as musicians, they both had this way of playing *ahead* of the beat. Both would also, in a solo, say, wind up at the end of one chord ahead of the beat, so that if you were following the solo, you might think he was in one place while actually he's in another. Something like the feel of Lester Young. What else he and Charlie had in common was a superaccurate feel for tempo. I doubt you could find any record they made where from the first note they are not swinging.

The kind of guitar T-Bone used was a Gibson ES5, a big one, an arch-type guitar with three pickups. It's got a sound unlike any other. It was probably the first Gibson guitar with a pickup, now known as the Charlie Christian pickup. I think a big part of T-Bone's sound is because he played that kind of guitar, an acoustic guitar amplified. From that you can get a lot of tonal colorings just by where you pick. T-Bone may pick one phrase down by the neck, and for accent for another he may go up by the bridge. Guitar players today don't do that at all, not in rock, anyway—none of the guitar players that I've heard in twenty years. Today the effects are almost all electronic, and something gets left out.

Besides, T-Bone was really the first to use *sustain*, which all guitarists use today, but electronically—that is, by feedback. He had a way of strumming a chord—like when he'd go from one change to another in a blues, from 1 to the 4, say. If he used an A-flat, he might hit a D and then slide down to a B-flat and have the guitar up loud enough so that it would ring and the note would carry. The chord would carry enough to give it the effect of a whole horn section. On his early records it sounds beautiful, two or three saxophones and maybe a trumpet, and T-Bone playing those chords. He was the first to do that, I think, though a million guitar players thought of doing it after.

Something different about T-Bone, something original, was the way he held the guitar. It takes some getting used to at first, but it's a comfortable way of playing. When you hold the guitar out from yourself, like he did, against your chest, your hand just rests on the strings, and it seems good. You get a real loose feeling. T-Bone was a great influence on other guys, especially the way he worked the guitar in with the lyrics he sang. That had a definite influence on B. B. King, I feel sure. He says so, and it's real easy to hear—that playing obligato to your own vocal lines. Another thing: what other guitarist was equally at home playing *either* jazz or blues? If you don't count George Benson, that goes for today as well. This gives T-Bone an eminence all his own.

Besides, for me, he typifies one of the things I love most about the music of the thirties and forties. Just by *playing* music, they were entertainers as well. That is recognizable on their records. You can hear that joy in the music, that feeling good. How come this approach is frowned on today? *Lese-majesté,* maybe? Well, music was *fun* back then. You know, T-Bone hit it right on the head:

> Let your hair down, baby
> Let's have a natural ball.

Appendix C

"Call It Stormy Monday"

CALL IT STORMY MONDAY

Words and Music by
ARON T. WALKER

Call It Stormy Monday - 1
0012CSM - 2 - 1

EXTRA LYRICS

2

Yes, the eagle flies on Friday,
And Saturday I go out to play ___
Eagle flies on Friday,
And Saturday I go out to play..
Sunday I go to church,
Then I kneel down to pray.

3

Lord have mercy,
Lord have mercy on me ___
Lord have mercy,
My heart's in misery.
Crazy 'bout my baby,
Yes, send her back to me.

Selected Bibliography

BOOKS

Arnaudon, Jean-Claude. *Dictionnaire du Blues*. Paris, 1977.

Bruynoghe, Yannick. "T-Bone Walker." In Stanley Dance, ed. *Jazz Era*. London, 1961.

Case, Brian, and Stan Britt. *The Illustrated History of Jazz*. New York, 1978.

Charles, Ray, and David Ritz. *Brother Ray*. New York, 1978.

Chilton, John. *Who's Who of Jazz*. Philadelphia, 1972.

Dance, Stanley. *The World of Count Basie*. New York, 1980.

Feather, Leonard. *The Encyclopedia of Jazz*. New York, 1960.

Feather, Leonard, and Ira Gitler. *The Encyclopedia of Jazz in the Seventies*. New York, 1976.

Fox, Ted. *Showtime at the Apollo*. New York, 1983.

Gillespie, Dizzy, and Al Fraser. *To Be or Not to Bop*. New York, 1979.

Gillett, Charlie. *The Sound of the City*. New York, 1970.

Guralnick, Peter. *Lost Highway*. Boston, 1979.

Haralambos, Michael. *Right On: From Blues to Soul in Black America*. New York, 1975.

Harris, Sheldon. *Blues Who's Who*. New Rochelle, N.Y., 1979.

Keil, Charles. *Urban Blues*. Chicago, 1966.

Kozinn, Allan, et al. *The Guitar: The History, the Music, the Players*. New York, 1984.

Leadbitter, Mike, and Neil Slaven. *Blues Records, 1943–1966*. London, 1968.

McCarthy, Albert, et al. *Jazz on Record: A Critical Guide, 1917–1967*. London, 1968.

Mongan, Norman. *The History of the Guitar in Jazz*. New York, 1983.

Oakley, Giles. *The Devil's Music: A History of the Blues*. New York, 1977.

Oliver, Paul. *The Story of the Blues*. Philadelphia, 1969.

Panassié, Hugues, and Madeleine Gautier. *Dictionnaire du Jazz*. Paris, 1971.

Sawyer, Charles. *The Arrival of B. B. King*. New York, 1980.

Shapiro, Nat, and Nat Hentoff. *Hear Me Talkin' to Ya*. New York, 1955.

Shaw, Arnold. *Honkers and Shouters*. New York, 1978.

Schiffman, Jack. *Harlem Heyday*. Buffalo, 1984.
Southern, Eileen. *Biographical Dictionary of Afro-American and African Musicians*. Westport, Conn., 1982.
Travis, Dempsey J. *An Autobiography of Black Jazz*. Chicago, 1983.

PERIODICALS

Excellent sources of information on the blues are Blues Unlimited, *published at Bexhill-on-Sea, England, and* Living Blues, *published in University, Mississippi. The following list consists of only the most important articles used in the researching of this book.*

Bas-Raberin, Philippe. "T-Bone Blues." *Jazz* (Paris), January, 1974.
Crayton, Pee Wee. "Living Blues Interview." *Living Blues*, Nos. 56 (Spring, 1983) and 57 (Autumn, 1983).
Demetre, Jacques, and Bernard Niquet. "T-Bone Walker." *Jazz Hot* (Paris), May, 1969.
Fiofori, Tam. "The Blues: T-Bone Walker and Big Mama Thornton Talk." *Melody Maker*, April 29, 1972.
Gayer, Dixon. "Gotta Feel the Blues to Play 'em." *Down Beat*, October 15, 1942.
Gleason, Ralph. "Should Happen to T-Bone, He's Ready." *Down Beat*, December 31, 1947.
Jones, Max. "Thorny Problem of Mixing Blues with Modern Jazz." *Melody Maker*, December 17, 1966.
Jones, Max. "T-Bone—Showman and Guitar Pioneer." *Melody Maker*, April 5, 1975.
Millar, Bill. "Big Jim Wynn." *Blues Unlimited*, No. 115 (May–June, 1975).
Morgantini, Jacques. "Avec T-Bone Walker." *Bulletin H.C.F.* (France), No. 153 (December, 1965).
O'Neal, Jim and Amy. "T-Bone Walker." *Living Blues*, Nos. 11 (Winter, 1972) and 12 (Spring, 1973).
Sheridan, Kevin and Peter. "T-Bone Walker: Father of the Electric Blues." *Guitar Player*, March, 1976.
Stolper, Darryl. "R. S. Rankin: T-Bone Walker Junior." *Blues Unlimited*, No. 115 (May–June, 1975).
Vernon, Mick. "Aaron T-Bone Walker." *R & B Monthly*, April 15, 1965.

OBITUARIES OF T-BONE WALKER

Blues Unlimited, No. 113 (May–June, 1975).
Living Blues, No. 21 (May–June, 1975).
New York *Times*, March 18, 1975.

LINER NOTES

Many liner notes to record albums are essentially blurbs, but some provide useful biographical data as well as helpful insights into the music. In the latter category, the following are recommended.

Adler, Danny. *T-Bone Jumps Again*, Charly 1019.
Britt, Stan. *Plain Ole Blues*, Charly 1037.
Burkhardt, Werner. *American Folk Blues Festival*, Decca DL 74392.
Gleason, Ralph. *T-Bone Blues*, Atlantic 8020.
Harris, Sheldon. *Funky Town*, Bluesway 6014.
Morgantini, Jacques. *Feeling the Blues*, Black & Blue (France) 33-019.
Notini, Per. *The Inventor of the Electric Guitar Blues*, Blues Boy BB-304.
Welding, Pete. *Classics of Modern Blues*, Blue Note LA-533-H2.
White, Cliff. *The Natural Blues*, Charly 1057.

Discography

This discography is reprinted from the French magazine *Soul Bag* (No. 100, September–October, 1984) by kind permission of the editor, Jacques Périn. It was compiled by Daniel Groslier, assisted by Christian Bresnier, Jean Buzelin, Guy Durand, Gérard Herzhafti, Dominique Fanger, Daniel Garçon, Jacques Périn, and, especially, Kurt Mohr. Mike Leadbitter and Neil Slaven's *Blues Records, 1943–1966* (London, 1968), and Michel Ruppli's admirable discographies were also helpful.

The discography is divided into two main sections. The first consists of a chronological listing of all of T-Bone's known recordings, take by take. The second section lists T-Bone's albums, anthologies in which he appeared, and albums on which he was an accompanist.

The format employed here is the customary one for jazz and blues discographies. That of the first section requires some explanation. First provided is the name of the individual or group who made the record. Then come details concerning personnel. The following abbreviations indicate the instruments used.

vo—vocal	dm—drums
g—guitar	hca—harmonica
tp—trumpet	org—organ
tb—trombone	fl—flute
cl—clarinet	vln—violin
as—alto saxophone	bg—bass guitar
ts—tenor saxophone	fem vo—female vocal
bs—baritone saxophone	el p—electric piano
p—piano	arr—arranger
b—string bass	

After the personnel listing come the place the record was made and the date.

The remainder of each entry consists of three columns. The middle column lists the titles in the order in which they were recorded. The numbers to the left are the master numbers given each take. To the right are the names and numbers of the different labels on which each title has appeared, as nearly in chronological order as possible. Almost all of the earlier recordings were released two at a time on 78s or 45s, but most of them were subsequently reissued on LPs, as indicated. Capital letters in parentheses refer to the record's country of origin if other than the United States:

(E)—England
(F)—France
(G)—Germany
(S)—Sweden
(I)—Italy
(A)—Austria
(J)—Japan
(SP)—Spain

Several of the entries have numbers following abbreviations for instruments, *e.g.*, vo 1, g 2, dm 10. In each case the number is to be matched up with the numbers in parentheses following the titles in that entry. The numbers thus help indicate which instruments were used on which titles in the session.

Oak Cliff T-Bone: T-Bone Walker (vo, g); Douglas Fernell (p)
Dallas, December 5, 1929

149548-1	TRINITY RIVER BLUES	Columbia 14506-D; Roots (A) LP 327
149549-2	WICHITA FALLS BLUES	Columbia 14506-D; Blues Boy (S) LP 304

Les Hite and His Orchestra: T-Bone Walker (vo); Paul Gydner Campbell, Walter Williams, Forrest Powell (tp); Britt Woodman, Allen Durham (tb); Les Hite (as, lead); Sol Moore (bs); Floyd Turnham (as); Quedillis Martin, Roger Hurd (ts); Nat Walker (p); Frank Pasley (g); Al Morgan (b); Oscar Bradley (dm)
New York, *ca.* June, 1940

| US-1852-1 | T-BONE BLUES | Varsity 8391; Blue Note 530; Elite X 10 |

Freddie Slack and His Orchestra: T-Bone Walker (vo 2, g); Charles Gifford, Clyde Hurley, John Letman, Bill Morris (tp); Bruce Squires, Gerald Foster, Bill Lawlor (tb); Barney Bigard (cl, ts); John Huffman, Willie Martinez (as); Ralph Lee, Les Baxter (ts, bs); Freddie Slack (p); Jud De Naut (b); Dave Coleman (dm); Ella Mae Morse, Johnny Mercer (vo 1)
Hollywood, July 20, 1942

CAP-50	HE'S MY GUY (1)	Capitol 113; Ajaz LP 281; Big Band Archives LP 1202
CAP-51	MISTER FIVE BY FIVE (1)	Capitol 115 LP 1802 LP 11971; Ajaz LP 281; Electrola (G) 056-85611; Ember LP 6605
CAP-52	THE THRILL IS GONE (1)	Capitol 115; Ajaz LP 281; Big Band Archives LP 1202
CAP-53	RIFFETTE (1)	Capitol 129 15239 LP1082; Ajaz LP 281; Big Band Archives LP 1202
CAP-54-A	I GOT A BREAK BABY (2; no horns, rhythm only)	Capitol 10033 15033 LP 8185; Charly (E) LP 1019
CAP-55-A	MEAN OLD WORLD (2; no horns, rhythm only)	Capitol 10033 15033 LP 8185; Charly (E) LP 1019

Freddie Slack and His Orchestra: Charles Gifford, Clyde Hurley, John Letman, Bill Morris (tp); Bruce Squires, Gerald Foster, Bill Lawlor (tb); Barney Bigard (cl, ts); John Huffman, Willie Martinez (as); Ralph Lee, Les Baxter (ts, bs); Freddie Slack (p); T-Bone Walker (g); Jud De Naut (b); Dave Coleman (dm); Ella Mae Morse (vo 1), Johnny Mercer (vo 2)
Hollywood, July 31, 1942

CAP-70	THAT OLD BLACK MAGIC	Capitol 126; Ajaz LP 281
CAP-71	OLD ROB BOY (1)	Capitol 133; Ajaz LP 281
CAP-72	WAITIN' FOR THE EVENING MAIL (2)	Capitol 137; Ajaz LP 288
CAP-73	WRECK OF THE OLD '97	Capitol 122; Ajaz LP 288
CAP-74	HIT THE ROAD TO DREAMLAND	Capitol 126; Ajaz LP 288
CAP-75	GET ON BOARD LI'L CHILDREN (1)	Capitol 133; Ajaz LP 288
CAP-76	I LEFT MY SUGAR (2)	Capitol 122 LP 907; Ajaz LP 288

Freddie Slack and His Orchestra: Charles Gifford, Bill Morris, George Went (tp); Gerald Foster, Bill Lawlor, Jim Skiles (tb); Barney Bigard (cl); Clyde Hylton, Neely

Plum (as); Les Baxter, Ralph Lee (ts); Karl Leaf (bs); Freddie Slack (p); T-Bone Walker (g, vo 1?); Phil Stephens (b); Dave Coleman (dm)
Hollywood, March 9, 1944

CAP-219	SWINGIN' ON A STAR	Capitol 160; Ajaz LP 288
CAP-220	THE GEE CHI LOVE SONG	Capitol 203; Ajaz LP 288; Big Band Archives LP 1202
CAP-221	CUBAN SUGAR MILL	Capitol 172 15239 LP 83 LP 6529; Ajaz LP 288; Big Band Archives LP 1202
CAP-222	SIT AND SIP (1)	Unissued

T-Bone Walker (vo, g); remainder unknown: tp, as, ts, bs, p, b, dm
Los Angeles, December, 1944

	LOW DOWN DIRTY SHAME BLUES (MAR- RIED WOMAN BLUES)	Swing House (E) LP 30

T-Bone Walker with Marl Young's Orchestra: T-Bone Walker (vo, g); Marl Young (p); remainder unknown: tp, as, ts, b, dm
Chicago, possibly May, 1945

3305-1	SAIL ON BOOGIE	Rhumboogie 4000; Blues Boy (S) LP 304
3306-1	I'M STILL IN LOVE WITH YOU	Rhumboogie 4000; Blues Boy (S) LP 304
3307	[Unknown take]	
3308-2	YOU DON'T LOVE ME BLUES	Rhumboogie 4003; Blues Boy (S) LP 304
3309-2	T-BONE BOOGIE	Rhumboogie 4002; Blues Boy (S) LP 304
3310-1	MEAN OLD WORLD	Rhumboogie 4003; Blues Boy (S) LP 304
3311-2	EVENING	Rhumboogie 4002; Blues Boy (S) LP 304

T-Bone Walker with Marl Young's Orchestra: T-Bone Walker (vo, g); Marl Young (p); remainder unknown: tp, as, ts, b, dm
Chicago, possibly 1945 or 1946

409-2/ 1036-SW	IM 453	MY BABY LEFT ME	Mercury 8016; Old Swing- master 11; Imperial (F) LP 1561451
410-2	IM 454	COME BACK TO ME BABY	Mercury 8016; Constellation LP CS 6; Imperial (F) LP 1561451
1040-SW	IM 455	SHE IS GOING TO RUIN ME (entitled FAST WOMAN on Imperial)	Old Swingmaster 11; Con- stellation LP CS 6; Imperial (F) LP 1561451

IM456 I CAN'T STAND BEING Old Swingmaster 11; Con-
AWAY FROM YOU stellation LP CS 6; Imperial
(F) LP 1561451

T-Bone Walker and His Guitar with Jack McVea All-Stars: T-Bone Walker (vo, g); Joe "Red" Kelly (tp); Jack McVea (ts); Tommy "Crow" Kahn (p); Frank Clarke (b); Rabon Tarrant (dm)
Hollywood, 1946

BW 410-2/CAP-4373 NO WORRY BLUES Black & White 111; Capitol
LP 8185; Pickwick LP 3173;
Charly (E) LP 1037

BW 411-2/CAP-4374 DON'T LEAVE ME BABY Black & White 111; Capitol
LP 8185; Pickwick LP 3173;
Charly (E) LP 1037

BW 412-2/CAP-4371 BOBBY SOX BABY Black & White 110; Capitol
LP 1958; Charly (E) LP 1019

BW 413-4/CAP-4372 I'M GONNA FIND MY Black & White 110; Charly (E)
BABY LP 1037

T-Bone Walker with Al Killian Quintet: T-Bone Walker (vo, g); Al Killian (tp); Jack McVea (ts); Tommy "Crow" Kahn or Lloyd Glenn (p); Frank Clark (b); Rabon Tarrant (dm)
Hollywood, December, 1946

BW 504-2/CAP-4377 I'M IN AN AWFUL MOOD Black & White 121; Capitol
LP 8185; Charly (E) LP 1037

BW 505-4/CAP-4376 IT'S A LOWDOWN DIRTY Black & White 115; Charly (E)
DEAL LP 1037

BW 506-1/CAP-4375 DON'T GIVE ME THE Black & White 115; Pickwick
RUNAROUND LP 3173; Charly (E) LP 1057

BW 507-1/ HARD PAIN BLUES Black & White 121; Blues Boy
CAP-4370(?) (S) LP 304; Charly (E) LP
1057

T-Bone Walker (vo, g) with John "Teddy" Buckner (tp); Hubert "Bumps" Myers (ts); Lloyd Glenn (p); Arthur Edwards (b); Oscar Lee Bradley (dm)
Hollywood, mid-1947

BW 635-3/CAP-4378 I KNOW YOUR WIG IS Black & White 122; Capitol
GONE 57-70014 EP 2-370 LP
370 LP 8185 LP 80732;
Charly (E) LP 1019

BW 636-1/CAP-4383 T-BONE JUMPS AGAIN Black & White 125; Capitol
(instr.) EP 4-1958 LP 1958 LP
8185; Charly (E) LP 1019

BW 637-3/CAP-4379 CALL IT STORMY MON- Black & White 122; Capitol
DAY (BUT TUESDAY'S 57-70014 EP 1-370 LP
JUST AS BAD) T1958 LP H370 LP 8185

		LP 80732; Albatros (I)
		LP 8474; Charly (E) LP 1019
BW 638- /CAP-4396	SHE HAD TO LET ME DOWN	Black & White unissued; Charly (E) LP 1057

T-Bone Walker (vo, g) with Teddy Buckner (tp); Bumps Myers (ts); Willard
McDaniels (p); Billy Hadnott (b); Oscar Lee Bradley (dm)
Los Angeles, November 6, 1947

BW 643-2/CAP-4397	SHE'S MY OLD TIME USED TO BE	Capitol 944 EP 1-370 LP 80732 LP 8185 LP H370; Charly (E) LP 1019
BW 644- /CAP-4398	DREAM GIRL BLUES	MFP (E) LP 1043; Charly (E) LP 1037
BW 645-3/CAP-4387	MIDNIGHT BLUES	Black & White 127 LP 1043; Charly (E) LP 1037
BW 646-4/CAP-4399	LONG LOST LOVER BLUES	Capitol 57-70023 LP 80179 LP 1043; Charly (E) LP 1037
BW 647- /CAP-4400	TRIFLIN' WOMAN BLUES	Joker (I) LP 4023 LP 76/6 LP 1043; Charly (E) LP 1037
BW 648-3/CAP-4380	LONG SKIRT BABY BLUES	Black & White 123 LP 1043; Charly (E) LP 1037
BW 649-1/CAP-4381	GOODBYE BLUES	Black & White 123; Pickwick LP 3173; Charly (E) LP 1037
BW 650-3/CAP-4401	TOO MUCH TROUBLE BLUES	Capitol 944 LP 80732; MFP (E) LP 1043; Charly (E) LP 1019
BW 651-4/CAP-4384	I'M WAITING FOR YOUR CALL	Black & White 126; Pickwick LP 3173; Charly (E) LP 1057
BW 652-2/CAP-4402	HYPIN' WOMAN BLUES	Capitol 57-70025 EP 1-370 LP H370 LP 20642 LP 80732 LP 6681(?); MFP (E) LP 1043; Charly (E) LP 1019
BW 653- /CAP-4403	SO BLUE BLUES	Charly (E) LP 1057
BW 654-1/CAP-4404	ON YOUR WAY BLUES	Capitol 799; Charly (E) LP 1019

T-Bone Walker (vo, g) with George Orendorff (tp); Bumps Myers (ts); Willard
McDaniels (p); Billy Hadnott (b); Oscar Lee Bradley (dm)
Los Angeles, November, 1947

BW 655- /CAP-4405	THE NATURAL BLUES	MFP (E) LP 1043; Charly (E) LP 1057
BW 656-1/CAP-4385	THAT'S BETTER FOR ME	Black & White 126; Charly (E) LP 1057; Blues Boy (S) LP 304

| BW 657-2/CAP-4394 | FIRST LOVE BLUES | Comet T53; Capitol 70042 EP 2-370 LP H370 LP 8185 LP 80732; Charly (E) LP 1019 |
| BW 658-5/CAP-4389 | LONESOME WOMAN BLUES (alternate take on Charly) | Comet T50; MFP (E) LP 1043; Charly (E) LP 1057 |

T-Bone Walker (vo, g) with George Orendorff (tp); Bumps Myers (ts); Willard McDaniels (p); John W. Davis (b); Oscar Lee Bradley (dm)
Los Angeles, 1947

BW 659-3/CAP-4406	VACATION BLUES	Capitol 57-70012 LP 80732; MFP (E) LP 1043; Charly (E) LP 1057
BW 660-2/CAP-4391	INSPIRATION BLUES	Comet T51; Black Diamond EP 4509; Charly (E) LP 1057
BW 661-2/CAP-4392	DESCRIPTION BLUES (alternate take on Charly)	Comet T52; Ace of Spades LP 1001; Charly (E) LP 1057; Blues Boy (S) LP 304
BW 662-2/CAP-4395	T-BONE SHUFFLE	Comet T53; Capitol 70042 EP 1-370 EP 4-1958 LP T1958 LP 8185 LP 80732 85330 LP H370 LP 6681(?); Black Diamond EP 4509; Charly (E) LP 1019

T-Bone Walker (vo, g) with Jack Trainor (tp); Bumps Myers (ts); Willard McDaniels (p); Billy Hadnott (b); Oscar Lee Bradley (dm)
Los Angeles, 1947

BW 675-2/CAP-4393	THAT OLD FEELING IS GONE	Comet T 52; Capitol LP 8185; Charly (E) LP 1037
BW 676- /CAP-4407	THE TIME SEEMS SO LONG	Charly (E) LP 1057
BW 677-3/CAP-4408	PRISON BLUES	Capitol 57-70012 LP 80732; MFP (E) LP 1043; Charly (E) LP 1037
BW 678- /CAP-4409	HOME TOWN BLUES	Charly (E) LP 1057
BW 679- /CAP-4410	WISE MAN BLUES	Capitol LP T1958; Charly (E) LP 1019
BW 680- /CAP-4411	MISFORTUNE BLUES	MFP (E) LP 1043; Charly (E) LP 1057
BW 681- /CAP-4412	I WISH YOU WERE MINE (alternate take unissued)	Capitol LP T1958; Charly (E) LP 1019
BW 682- /CAP-4413	I'M GONNA MOVE YOU OUT AND GET SOMEBODY ELSE	Charly (E) LP 1057

BW 683- /CAP-4414   SHE'S THE NO   Charly (E) LP 1057
   SLEEPIN'EST WOMAN

BW 684-2/CAP-4386   PLAIN OLD DOWN   Black & White 127; Capitol
   HOME BLUES   LP 8185; Charly (E) LP 1037

BW 685-2/CAP-4415   BORN TO BE NO GOOD   Capitol 57-70025   EP 2-370
   LP T1958   LP 80732
   LP H370; Charly (E) LP 1019

BW 686-3/CAP-4416   GO BACK TO THE ONE   Capitol 799   LP T1958   LP
   YOU LOVE   H370; Charly (E) LP 1037

Note: BW 677 is mistitled on Capitol LP 80732 and MFP (E) LP 1043 as "Hometown Blues."

T-Bone Walker (vo, g) with Jack Trainor or George Orendorff (tp); Bumps Myers (ts); Willard McDaniels (p); Billy Hadnott (b); Oscar Lee Bradley (dm)
Los Angeles, December, 1947

BW 695-2/CAP-4382   I WANT A LITTLE GIRL   Black & White 125; Capitol
   EP 4-1958   LP T1958;
   Charly (E) LP 1057

BW 696-1/CAP-4390   I'M STILL IN LOVE WITH   Comet T 51; Capitol 70055
   YOU·   LP T1958; Charly (E)
   LP 1057

BW 697-1/CAP-4417   YOU'RE MY BEST POKER   Capitol 57-70023   EP 2-370
   HAND   EP 4-1958   LP 80179
   LP T1958   LP 80732
   LP H370   LP 8185;
   Charly (E) LP 1019

BW 698-3/CAP-4388   WEST SIDE BABY   Comet T 50; Capitol
   57-70055   LP T1958;
   Charly (E) LP 1037

Note: Capitol LP T1958 is also on Capitol (F) T 1958; Capitol LP H370 is also on Capitol (E) 6681.

T-Bone Walker and His Band: T-Bone Walker (vo, g); Eddie Hutcherson (tp); Edward Hale (as); Eddie Davis (ts); Jim Wynn (ts, bs); Zell Kindred (p); Buddy Woodson (b); Robert "Snake" Sims (dm)
Los Angeles, April 5, 1950

IM-174-5   GLAMOUR GIRL   Imperial 5071   LP 9116;
   Minit LP 40005; Imperial (F)
   1546761

IM-175-3   STROLLIN' WITH BONE   Imperial 5071   LP 9098; Blue
   Note LP 533; Polydor (F)
   46867; Imperial (F) 1546751

IM-176   THE SUN WENT DOWN   Imperial 5086   LP 9098   LP
   9210   LP 9257; Blue Note
   LP 533; Polydor (F) LP
   46867; Imperial (F) 1546761

IM-177	YOU DON'T LOVE ME	Imperial 5086 LP 9098; Blue Note LP 533; Polydor (F) LP 46867; Imperial (F) 1546751
IM-178	TRAVELIN' BLUES	Imperial 5094 LP 9210; Polydor (F) LP 46867; Imperial (F) 1546751
IM-179	THE HUSTLE IS ON	Imperial 5081; Cid/Omega (F) 78611; Blues Boy (S) LP 304
	THE HUSTLE IS ON (alternate take)	Imperial LP 9116; Blue Note LP 533; Polydor (F) LP 46867; Imperial (F) LP 1546761
IM-180BABY	BABY BROKE MY HEART	Imperial 5081; Cid/Omega (F) 78611; Blues Boy (S) LP 304
	BABY BROKE MY HEART	Blue Note LP 533; Imperial (F) LP 1546761
IM-181	EVIL HEARTED WOMAN	Imperial 5094 LP 9098; Blue Note LP 533; Polydor (F) LP 46867; Imperial (F) LP 1546751

Note: IM-178 is possibly an alternate take of IM-179.

T-Bone Walker with Marl Young's Band: T-Bone Walker (vo, g); Marl Young (p); Billy Hadnott (b); remainder unknown: brass, dm
Los Angeles, late September or early October, 1950

IM-221	I WALKED AWAY	Imperial 5103 (F) LP 1561451; Blues Boy (S) LP 304
IM-222	NO REASON	Imperial 5116 (F) LP 1561451; Blues Boy (S) LP 304
IM-223	LOOK ME IN THE EYES	Imperial 5116 (F) LP 1561451
IM-224	TOO LAZY	Imperial 5103 (F) LP 1561451

T-Bone Walker (vo, g) with tp; as; Maxwell Davis (ts); Willard McDaniels (p); Billy Hadnott (b); Oscar Lee Bradley (dm)
Los Angeles, August 15 and 20, 1951

IM-329	ALIMONY BLUES	Imperial 5153 LP 9116; Blue Note LP 533; Imperial (F) LP 1546761
IM-330	LIFE IS TOO SHORT	Imperial 5153 LP 9146; Blue Note LP 533; Imperial (F) LP 1561441
IM-331	YOU DON'T UNDERSTAND	Imperial 5147 5384 LP 9098; Blue Note LP 533; Imperial (F) LP 1546751

IM-332	WELCOME BABY (SAY PRETTY BABY)	Imperial 5147 5384 LP 9098 LP 9146; Polydor (F) LP 46867; Imperial (F) LP 1546751
IM-333	I GET SO WEARY	Imperial 5161 LP 9146 LP 9210 LP 94002 (F) LP 1561441; Post 2002; Blue Note LP 533; Liberty (E) LP 83215; Joker (I) LP 3592 LP 74/6
IM-334	YOU JUST WANTED TO USE ME	Imperial 5161 LP 9146 (F) LP 1561441
IM-335	TELL ME WHAT'S THE REASON	Imperial 5247 LP 9098; Post 2002; Blue Note LP 533; Imperial (F) 1546751
IM-336	I'M ABOUT TO LOSE MY MIND	Imperial 5261 LP 9116; Minit LP 40005; Blue Note LP 533; Imperial (F) LP 1546761

T-Bone Walker (vo, g) with unknown as; Maxwell Davis (ts); Willard McDaniels (p); Billy Hadnott (b); Oscar Lee Bradley (dm)
Hollywood (?), December, 1951

IM-383	COLD COLD FEELING	Imperial 5171 5652 LP 9098 LP 9210 LP 9257; Blue Note LP 533; Polydor 27722; Imperial (F) LP 1546751
IM-384	NEWS FOR MY BABY	Imperial 5171 LP 9116; Blue Note LP 533; Polydor (F) LP 46867; Imperial (F) LP 1546761
IM-385	GET THESE BLUES OFF ME	Imperial 5181; Blue Note LP 533; Imperial (F) LP 1546751
IM-386	I GOT THE BLUES AGAIN	Imperial 5181, LP 9098; Blue Note LP 533; Polydor 27722; Imperial (F) LP 1546751
IM-387	THROUGH WITH WOMEN	Imperial LP 9146 (F) LP 1561441; Blue Note LP 533
IM-388	STREET WALKING WOMAN	Imperial 5202 LP 9146; Blue Note LP 533; Polydor 27722
IM-389	BLUES IS A WOMAN	Imperial 5202 LP 9098; Blue Note LP 533; Imperial (F) LP 1546751
IM-390	I GOT THE BLUES	Imperial 5193 LP 9116; Blue Note LP 533; Polydor 27722 (F) LP 46867; Imperial (F) LP 1546761

Roy Hawkins (vo) with Maxwell Davis (ts); Jim Wynn (bs); Lloyd Glenn (p); T-Bone Walker (g); Billy Hadnott (b); "Snake" Sims (dm)
Los Angeles, January 8, 1952

MM-1771	HIGHWAY 59	Modern 859; Route 66 (S) LP 9; Ace (E) LP 103
MM-1772	WOULD YOU	Modern 859; Route 66 (S) LP 9; Ace (E) LP 103
MM-1823	DOING ALL RIGHT	Modern 869; Route 66 (S) LP 9
MM-1824	THE THRILL HUNT	Modern 869; Route 66 (S) LP 9

T-Bone Walker (vo, g) with unknown tp, as, ts, bs, p, b, dm
Los Angeles (?), January 5, 1942

IM-403	HERE IN THE PARK	Imperial 5239 LP 9146 (F) LP 1561441; Liberty (E) LP 12108
IM-404	BLUE MOOD	Imperial 5216 LP 9098; Blue Note LP 533; Imperial (F) LP 1546751
IM-405	EVERY TIME	Imperial 5247 LP 9116; Blue Note LP 533; Polydor (F) LP 46867; Imperial (F) LP 1546761
IM-406	I MISS YOU BABY	Imperial 5261 LP 9146; (F) LP 1561441

T-Bone Walker (vo, g) probably with _____ Smith (tp); Edward Hale (as); Maxwell Davis (ts); Jim Wynn (bs); Zell Kindred or Willard McDaniels (p); R. S. Rankin (g); Buddy Woods (b); Robert "Snake" Sims or Oscar Lee Bradley (dm)
Los Angeles (?), March 10, 1952

IM-409	LOLLIE LOU	Imperial 5193 LP 9146 (F) LP 1561441
IM-410	PARTY GIRL	Imperial 5239 LP 9146 (F) LP 1561441; Liberty (E) 12100; Blue Note LP 533
IM-411	LOVE IS JUST A GAMBLE	Imperial 5311 LP 9116; Minit LP 40005; Blue Note LP 533; Imperial (F) LP 1546761
IM-412	HIGH SOCIETY	Imperial 5311 LP 9146 (F) LP 1561441; Blue Note LP 533

T-Bone Walker (vo, g)
Hollywood (?), September 22, 1952

IM-493	MY BABY LEFT ME BLUE	Imperial (F) LP 1561451
IM-494	COME BACK TO ME BABY	Imperial (F) LP 1561451

| IM-495 | FAST WOMAN | Imperial (F) LP 1561451 |
| IM-496 | I CAN'T STAND BEING AWAY FROM YOU | Imperial (F) LP 1561451 |

T-Bone Walker (vo, g) with unknown tp, as, ts, bs, p, b, dm; Tiny Brown or Baby Davis (fem vo 1)
Hollywood (?), March 20, 1953

IM-519	I'M STILL IN LOVE WITH YOU (1)	Imperial LP 9116; Imperial (F) LP 1546761
IM-520	GOT NO USE FOR YOU (1)	Imperial 5216 LP 9146 (F) LP 1561441; Blue Note LP 533
IM-521	RAILROAD STATION BLUES	Imperial 5228; Blue Note LP 533; Imperial (F) LP 1546751
IM-522	LONG DISTANCE BLUES	Imperial 5228 (F) LP 1561451

T-Bone Walker with Jim Wynn and His Orchestra: T-Bone Walker (vo, g); 2 tp; Edward Hale (as); Maxwell Davis (ts); Jim Wynn (bs); Zell Kindred (p); R. S. "T-Bone Jr." Rankin (g); Buddy Woods (b); Robert "Snake" Sims (dm)
or

T-Bone Walker with T. J. Fowler's Band: T-Bone Walker (vo, g); John Lawton (tp); Lee Gross (as); Walter Cox (ts); T. J. Fowler (p); Henry Ivory (b); Clarence Stamps (dm) (this was the personnel probably used on previous and following sessions)
Detroit or Los Angeles, October 27, 1953

IM-644	VIDA LEE (no horns, ts only)	Imperial 5274 LP 94002; Liberty (E) LP 83215
IM-645	MY BABY IS NOW ON MY MIND	Imperial 5274 (F) LP 1561451; Blues Boy (S) LP 304
IM-646	DOIN' TIME	Imperial 5962 (F) LP 1561451
IM-647	BYE BYE BABY	Imperial 5284 LP 9116; Blue Note LP 533; Polydor (F) LP 46867; Imperial (F) LP 1546761

T-Bone Walker with Dave Bartholomew's Band: T-Bone Walker (vo, g); band probably comprised Dave Bartholomew (tp); Wendel Duconge (as); Lee Allen, Herb Hardesty (ts, bs); Walter Nelson (g); Frank Fields (b); Cornelius Coleman (dm); unknown p
New Orleans, November 6, 1953

| IM-651 | WHEN THE SUN GOES DOWN | Imperial 5264 (F) LP 1561441; Blues Boy (S) LP 304 |
| IM-652 | PONY TAIL | Imperial 5264 (F) LP 1561441; Blues Boy (S) LP 304 |

| IM-653 | WANDERIN' HEART | Imperial 5284 (F) LP 1561441 |
| IM-654 | I'LL ALWAYS BE IN LOVE WITH YOU | Imperial 5284 (F) LP 1561451 |

T-Bone Walker with Dave Bartholomew's Orchestra: Probably same personnel as before
Los Angeles, December 7, 1953

IM-738	I'LL UNDERSTAND	Imperial 5330 LP 9116; Imperial (F) LP 1546761
IM-739	HARD WAY	Imperial 5330 (F) LP 1561451
IM-740	TEEN-AGE BABY (band ensemble)	Imperial 5229 LP 9116; Polydor (F) LP 46867; Imperial (F) LP 1546761
IM-741	STRUGGLIN' BLUES	Imperial 5299 (F) LP 1561451

Note: Imperial LP 9098 is also on Liberty (E) LP 3047; Imperial LP 9116 also on Liberty (E) LP 9057; Imperial LP 9210 also on Pathé-Marconi (F) LP 83300. French Imperial (Pathé Marconi) will issue all Imperial sides.

T-Bone Walker (vo, g) with Andrew "Goon" Gardner (as); Eddie Chamblee (ts); McKinley Easton (bs); Johnny Young (p); Ransom Knowling (b); Leroy Jackson (dm)
Chicago, April 21, 1955

A-1517	PAPA AIN'T SALTY	Atlantic 1065 LP 8020 LP 4589 (F) 332006; Midi (F) LP 68005
A-1518	ALL I WANT IS ONE MORE CHANCE	Unissued
A-1519	WHY NOT	Atlantic 1074
A-1520	T-BONE SHUFFLE	Atlantic 1065 LP 8010 LP 8020 LP 1239 LP 2-506 LP 4589 (F) LP 332006 (F) LP 60095

T-Bone Walker (vo, g) with Junior Wells (hca); Jimmy Rogers (g); possibly Willie Dixon (b); possibly Francey Clay (dm)
Chicago, April 21, 1955

| A-1521 | PLAY ON LITTLE GIRL | Atlantic 1074 LP 8020 (F) LP 332006 |
| A-1522 | T-BONE BLUES SPECIAL | Atlantic LP 7226 LP 4589 |

T-Bone Walker (vo, g) with Lloyd Glenn (p); Billy Hadnott (b); Oscar Lee Bradley (dm)
Los Angeles, December 14, 1956

A-2272/A-2314	MEAN OLD WORLD	Atlantic LP 8020
A-2273/A-2315	YOUR WIG IS GONE	Unissued
A-2274/A-2317	T-BONE BLUES	Atlantic LP 8020 (F) LP 332006; Midi (F) LP 68005

A-2275/A-2316	STORMY MONDAY BLUES	Atlantic LP 8020 (F) LP 332006; Midi (F) LP 68005
A-2276/A-2319	BLUES FOR MARILI (instr.)	Atlantic LP 8020 (F) LP 332006
A-2277/A-2318	SHUFFLIN' THE BLUES (instr.)	Atlantic LP 8020 LP 4589

Note: Original master numbers 2272 to 2277 have been renumbered 2314 to 2319.

T-Bone Walker (vo, g); Plas Johnson (ts); Ray Johnson (p); R. S. Rankin (vo 1, g 2); Barney Kessel (g 2); Joe Comfort (b); Earl Palmer (dm)
Los Angeles, December 27, 1957 or 1959

A-2902	EVENIN'	Atlantic LP 8020 (F) LP 332006
A-2903	[INSTRUMENTAL] (2)	Unissued (?)
A-2904	TWO BONES AND A PICK (2; instr.)	Atlantic LP 8020 (F) LP 332006
A-2905	YOU DON'T KNOW WHAT YOU'RE DOING (1, 2)	Atlantic LP 7226
A-2906	HOW LONG BLUES	Atlantic LP 7226
A-2907	TWELVE BAR BLUES (2; instr.)	Unissued (?)

Note: A-2903 or A-2907 issued on Atlantic LP 8020 and (F) LP 332006 as BLUE ROCK (2:41). Atlantic LP 8020 is also on LP 8256, (F) LP 940027, (F) LP 40131.

American Folk Blues Festival: T-Bone Walker (vo 1, g 2, p 3); Memphis Slim (vo 4, p 5); John Lee Hooker (vo, g 6); Shakey Jake (vo, hca 7); Sonny Terry (vo, hca 8); Brownie McGhee (g 8); Willie Dixon (vo 9, b); Jump Jackson (dm 10)
Hamburg, October 18, 1962

	WE'RE GONNA ROCK (2, 4, 5, 10)	Brunswick (G) LP 009012
	I WANNA SEE MY BABY (1, 2, 5, 10)	Brunswick (F) EP 10644 (G) LP 009012
	I'M IN LOVE (1, 2, 5, 10)	Brunswick (G) LP 009012
	I'M CRAZY 'BOUT YOU BABY (3, 8)	Brunswick (G) LP 009012
	LET'S MAKE IT BABY (3, 6, 10)	Brunswick (F) EP 10644 (G) LP 009012; Polydor (F) 421/175; Excello LP 8029
	SHAKE IT BABY (3, 6, 10)	Brunswick (F) EP 10644 (G) LP 009012; Polydor (F) 421/175; Excello LP 8029
	THE RIGHT TIME (3, 6, 10)	Brunswick (G) LP 009012; Excello LP 8029
	HEY BABY (2, 5, 7, 10)	Brunswick (F) EP 10644 (G) LP 009012

LOVE MY BABY	Brunswick (G) LP 009012
(2, 5, 7, 10)	
BYE BYE BABY	Brunswick (G) LP 009012
(2, 4, 5, 9, 10)	
I'M NERVOUS (2, 5, 9, 10)	Polydor (F) EP 10644
I NEED YOU SO BAD (3, 6)	Excello LP 8029

Note: Brunswick LP 009012 is also on Polydor (F) LP 248204 and (F) 2310.296 and on L&R (G) 42017.

T-Bone Walker (vo 1, g); Shakey Jake (vo 2, hca 2); Memphis Slim (vo 3, p); Sonny Terry (hca 4); Brownie McGhee (vo, g 4); Helen Humes (vo 5); Willie Dixon (vo 6, b); Jump Jackson (dm)
Possibly Baden-Baden, West Germany (from unissued TV short), October, 1962

HEY BABY (2)	Rare Records LP RR02 (bootleg)
BLUES EVERYWHERE (3)	Rare Records LP RR02 (bootleg)
BOOGIE WOOGIE (3)	Rare Records LP RR02 (bootleg)
DON'T THROW YOUR LOVE SO HARD ON ME (1)	Rare Records LP RR02 (bootleg)
NERVOUS (6)	Rare Records LP RR02 (bootleg)
BABY WON'T YOU PLEASE COME HOME (5)	Rare Records LP RR02 (bootleg)
KANSAS CITY BLUES (5)	Rare Records LP RR02 (bootleg)
IMPROVISATION BLUES (1, 3, 4, 5, 6)	Rare Records LP RR02 (bootleg)
FAST BLUES (4)	Rare Records LP RR02 (bootleg)

Jimmy Witherspoon (vo) with Clifford Solomon (fl 1, ts); Bert Kendrix (p 3 or org); T-Bone Walker (g); Clarence Jones (b); Wayne Robertson (dm)
Los Angeles, August 15, 1963

GRAB ME A FREIGHT	Prestige LP 7300	
MONEY'S GETTIN' CHEAPER	Prestige 307	LP 7300
DON'T LET GO (band ensemble)	Prestige LP 7300	
I'VE BEEN TREATED WRONG	Prestige LP 7300	
CANE RIVER	Prestige LP 7300	LP 7713
BABY HOW LONG (3)	Prestige LP 7300	

GOOD ROCKING	Prestige LP 7300	LP 7713
KANSAS CITY	Prestige LP 7300	LP 7713
DRINKING BEER	Prestige LP 7300	LP7713
EVENIN' (1)	Prestige 307	LP 7300 LP 7713

Note: Prestige LP 7300 also on Prestige (F) FELP 10009 and Stateside (E) LP 10028.

T-BONE WALKER (vo, g) with unknown 2 ts, bs, org, g, bg, dm
Chicago, October, 1964

1004-1	HEY HEY BABY	Modern 1004; Trio (J) LP 3129
1004-2	SHOULD I LET HER GO	Modern 1004; Trio (J) LP 3129
	JEALOUS WOMAN	Unissued

T-BONE WALKER (vo, g) with Willard "Piano Slim" (p); unknown org 1, bg, dm
Houston, 1966

119101	TREAT YOUR DADDY WELL	Brunswick LP 754126; Home Cooking LP 103; Avco Embassy LP 33006
119103	LET YOUR HAIR DOWN BABY (NATURAL BALL)	Brunswick LP 754126; Home Cooking LP 103
119104	OLD TIME USED TO BE	Brunswick LP 754126
119105	YOU DON'T LOVE ME AND I DON'T CARE	Brunswick LP 754126
119106	IT AIN'T NO RIGHT IN YOU (AFRAID TO CLOSE MY EYES)	Brunswick LP 754126; Home Cooking LP 103
	PLEASE COME BACK TO ME (1)	Avco Embassy LP 33006

T-BONE WALKER (vo, g, p 1) with Willard "Piano Slim" (p 2); unknown org 3; Joey Long (g); unknown bg, dm; possibly Harmonica Fats (hca 4); Arnett Cobb (ts); Jimmy Ford (?) (tp 5); unknown tb
Houston, 1966

119102	YOU OUGHT TO KNOW BETTER (NO DO RIGHT) (2, 6)	Brunswick LP 754126; Home Cooking LP 103
119107/TBW 2	I AIN'T YOUR FOOL NO MORE (I'M NOT . . .) (1)	Brunswick LP 754126; Jet Stream 726
119108	DON'T LET YOUR HEARTACHE CATCH YOU (HEARTACHE) (3)	Brunswick LP 754126; 51 West LP 16013
119110/TBW 1	HATE TO SEE YOU GO (RECONSIDER BABY) (3, 5)	Brunswick LP 754126; Jet Stream 726
119111	IT TAKES A LOT OF KNOWHOW (3)	Brunswick LP 754126

TBW 4	BACK ON THE SCENE (T-BONE'S BACK) (longer version) (1, 3)	Home Cooking LP 103; Jet Stream 738; 51 West LP 16013	
	GOOD BOY (3, 4)	Home Cooking LP 103	
119109	I DON'T BE JIVING (3, 5)	Brunswick LP 754126; 51 West LP 16013	
TBW 3	(BABY) SHE'S A HIT (brass added) (1, 2, 3)	Home Cooking LP 103; Jet Stream 738; 51 West LP 16013	
	FARTHER UP ON THE ROAD (3)	Home Cooking LP 103	
	WHY WON'T MY BABY TREAT ME RIGHT (3)	Home Cooking LP 103	

Note: Brunswick LP 754126 is also on MCA (E) LP 331; a clipped version of it is on Jet Stream 726.

T-Bone Walker (vo, g) with Clark Terry (tp); Johnny Hodges (as); Paul Gonsalves (ts); Oscar Peterson (p); Sam Jones (b); Bobby Durham (dm)
Recorded live with Jazz at the Philharmonic, U.S. or Canada, June 28 or July 1, 1967

	WOMAN YOU MUST BE CRAZY	Pablo LP 2625 704
	STORMY MONDAY	Pablo LP 2625 704

T-Bone Walker (vo, g) with McKinley Johnson, Melvin Moore (tp); John "Streamline" Ewing (tb); Preston Love (as); John Williams (as, bs); Melvin "Tank" Jernigan (ts, arr); Lloyd Glenn (p); Mel Brown (g); Ron Brown (b, g); Paul Humphrey (dm)
Los Angeles, 1967 or 1968

14061	EVERY NIGHT I HAVE TO CRY	BluesWay 61008	LP 6008
	I'M GONNA STOP THIS NITE LIFE	BluesWay 61008	LP 6008
	LITTLE GIRL YOU DON'T KNOW	BluesWay 61008 LP 6058; MCA LP 1366	LP 6008
14064	CONFUSION BLUES	BluesWay 61008	LP 6008
	I'M STILL IN LOVE WITH YOU	BluesWay 61008	LP 6008
	COLD HEARTED WOMAN	BluesWay 61008 MCA LP 1366	LP 6008;
	TREAT ME SO LOW DOWN	BluesWay 61008 MCA LP 1366	LP 6008;
	I GOT A BREAK BABY	BluesWay 61008	LP 6008
	FLOWER BLUES	BluesWay 61008 LP 6058 LP 6061; MCA LP 1366	LP 6008

STORMY MONDAY   BluesWay 61008   LP
                        6008   LP 6058   LP 6061;
                        MCA LP 1366

Note: BluesWay LP 6008 is also on Stateside (E) LP 10223 and (F) 240691.

T-Bone Walker (vo, g) with McKinley Johnson, Melvin Moore (tp); John "Stream-line" Ewing (tb); Preston Love (as); John Williams (as, bs); Melvin "Tank" Jernigan (ts, arr); Lloyd Glenn (p); Melvin Brown (g); Ronald Brown (b, g); Paul Humphrey (dm); unknown hca 1, org 2
Los Angeles, 1968

GOIN' TO FUNKY TOWN (instr.) (2; no horns)	BluesWay LP 6014 LP 6058
PARTY GIRL	BluesWay LP 6014
WHY MY BABY (KEEP ON BOTHERING ME)	BluesWay LP 6014 LP 6058; MCA LP 1366
JEALOUS WOMAN (2)	BluesWay 6014 LP 6058; MCA LP 1366
GOING TO BUILD ME A PLAYHOUSE (2)	BluesWay 6014 LP 6058; MCA LP 1366
LONG SKIRT BABY BLUES	BluesWay 6014 LP 6058; MCA LP 1366
STRUGGLING BLUES (1)	BluesWay LP 6014
I'M IN AN AWFUL MOOD (2)	BluesWay LP 6014 LP 6058; MCA LP 1366
I WISH MY BABY (WOULD COME HOME AT NIGHT) (2)	BluesWay LP 6014 LP 6058 LP 1973; MCA LP 1366

Note: BluesWay LP 6014 is also on Stateside (E) LP 10265; BluesWay 6058 is also on MCA (F) 204932.

T-Bone Walker (vo, g, p 1) with Hal Singer (ts 2); George Arvanitas (p 3); Jacky Samson (b); S. P. Leary (dm)
Paris, November 13, 1968

I HATE TO SEE YOU GO (2, 3)	Black & Blue (F) LP 33019 LP 33376
AIN'T THAT COLD BABY (1)	Black & Blue (F) LP 33019 LP 33376
LEAVING YOU BEHIND (2, 3)	Black & Blue (F) LP 33019 LP 33376
FEELING THE BLUES (instr.) (2, 3)	Black & Blue (F) LP 33019 LP 33376
GEE BABY AIN'T I GOOD TO YOU (2, 3)	Black & Blue (F) LP 33019 LP 33376
I WANT A LITTLE GIRL (2, 3)	Black & Blue (F) LP 33019 LP 33376

SOMEONE IS GOING TO   Black & Blue (F) LP 33019   LP
MISTREAT YOU (3)   33376
LATE BLUES (instr.) (2, 3)   Black & Blue (F) LP 33019   LP
                                      33376

Note: Black & Blue LP 33019 is also on Black & Blue (F) LP 335 29 and (F) LP 33552, Barclay (F) LP 21688, and Delmark LP 633.

T-Bone Walker (vo, g) with collective personnel: unknown tp; Manu Dibango, Pierre Holassian, Francis Cournet (saxes); Bernard Estardy, Manu Dibango (p, org); Michel Sarbady (p); Slim Pezin (g); Jeannot Karl (b, g); Lucien Dobat (dm); Jean-Louis Proust, Bernard Estardy, Earl Lett (perc); backing vocals 1; T-Bone Walker only 2 (vo, p)
Paris, November, 1968

GOOD FEELIN' (2)   Polydor (F) LP 658158
EVERY DAY I HAVE THE   Polydor (F) LP 658158;
   BLUES (1)   Trump (F) 2104 001
WOMAN YOU MUST BE   Polydor (F) LP 658158
   CRAZY
LONG LOST LOVER   Polydor (F) LP 658158;
                                      Trump (F) 2104 001
I WONDER WHY   Polydor (F) LP 658158
VACATION (no horns)   Polydor (F) LP 658158
SHAKE IT BABY (1)   Polydor (F) LP 658158
POONTANG (instr.)   Polydor (F) LP 658158
RECONSIDER   Polydor (F) LP 658158
SAIL ON LITTLE GIRL (no   Polydor (F) LP 658158
   horns)
WHEN I GROW UP   Polydor (F) LP 658158
SEE YOU NEXT TIME (2)   Polydor (F) LP 658158

Note: Polydor LP 658158 is also on Polydor (F) 2393 007, Polydor 24-4502 (minus SHAKE IT BABY).

Eddie Vinson (vo, as) with Hal Singer (ts); Jay McShann (p); T-Bone Walker (g); Roland Lobligeois (b); Paul Gunther (dm)
Boulogne-Billancourt, France, April 28, 1969

KIDNEY STEW   Black & Blue (F) LP 33021
WAIT A MINUTE BABY   Black & Blue (F) LP 33021
OLD MAID BOOGIE   Black & Blue (F) LP 33021
SOMEBODY GOTTA GO   Black & Blue (F) LP 33021
   (GOT TO GO)   LP 950510
THINGS AIN'T WHAT   Black & Blue (F) LP 33021
   THEY USED TO BE
WEE BABY BLUES   Black & Blue (F) LP 33021
JUICE HEAD BABY   Black & Blue (F) LP 3302:
I HAD A DREAM   Black & Blue (F) LP 33021
I'M IN AN AWFUL MOOD   Black & Blue (F) LP 33021
(PLEASE) SEND ME   Black & Blue (F) LP 33021
   SOMEONE TO LOVE

Note: Black & Blue LP 33021 is also on Black & Blue (F) LP 33543 and Delmark LP 631.

Jay McShann (vo 1, p) with T-Bone Walker (g 2); Roland Lobligeois (b); Paul Gunther (dm)
Possibly Boulogne-Billancourt, France, April 28, 1969

	KEEP YOUR HAND OFF HER (1, 2)	Black & Blue (F) LP 33022
	HOOTIE IGNORANT OIL (2)	Black & Blue (F) LP 33022
	CONFESSIN' THE BLUES (1, 2)	Black & Blue (F) LP 33022
	ROLL 'EM (2)	Black & Blue (F) LP 33022 LP 950500
	KANSAS CITY (1,2)	Black & Blue (F) LP 33022
	OUR KINDA BLUES (2)	Black & Blue (F) LP 33022
	ROLLIN' WITH ROLAND	Black & Blue (F) LP 33022
	STOMPING IN K.C.	Black & Blue (F) LP 33022
	AFTER HOURS	Black & Blue (F) LP 33022
	HOOTIE BLUES	Black & Blue (F) LP 33022
	FOUR DAYS RIDER (1, 2)	Black & Blue (F) LP 33022
	DEXTER BLUES (2)	UNISSUED

Note: The first three titles, the fifth, and JAY'S BLUES (probably OUR KINDA BLUES) are on Curcio (I) CJ-59.

T-Bone Walker (vo, g) with Tom Scott (ts); Artie Butler (p 2, org 3); Louie Shelton (g); Max Bennett (b, g); Paul Humphrey (dm, p 1)
Los Angeles or New York, August 18, 1969

	EVERY DAY I HAVE THE BLUES (2)	BluesTime LP (2)9004 LP 29010
	VIETNAM (3)	BluesTime LP (2)9004
	SHAKE IT BABY (2)	BluesTime LP (2)9004 LP 29010
	COLD COLD FEELING (3)	BluesTime LP (2)9004
	T-BONE BLUES SPECIAL (1, 3)	BluesTime LP (2)9004
BT 29010	FOR B. B. KING (1)	BluesTime LP (2)9004 LP 29010; RCA (F) 3LP 42039
	SAIL ON (2)	BluesTime LP (2)9004

Note: BluesTime LP 29010 also on RCA LP 8427

Super Black Blues: T-Bone Walker (vo, g); Otis Spann (vo, p); Big Joe Turner (vo); Ernie Watts (ts); George Smith (hca); Arthur Wright (g); Ron Brown (b-g); Paul Humphrey (dm)
Los Angeles or New York, probably August, 1969

	PARIS BLUES (no ts)	BluesTime LP (2)9003

HERE AM I BROKEN   BluesTime LP (2)9003
HEARTED (vo Joe Turner
only)
JOT'S BLUES (no hca)   BluesTime LP (2)9003
BLUES JAM   BluesTime LP (2)9003

T-Bone Walker (vo, g) with Russ Andrews (ts); Lawrence Lucie (g); Wynton Kelly (p);
Al Hall (b); Elvin Jones (dm)
Recorded live at Carnegie Hall, New York, May, 1970

STORMY MONDAY   BluesTime LP (2)9009
BLUES
SAIL ON   BluesTime LP (2)9009

T-Bone Walker (vo, g) with Willard Burton (p); Johnny Copeland (g); Jimmy Jones (bg,
arr); unknown dm; female choir 1; unknown org 2
Pasadena, Tex. (?), 1970 (?)

STORMY MONDAY   Wet Soul 5   LP 1002
BLUES (1)
ALL NIGHT LONG   Wet Soul LP 1002; Charly (E)
                          LP 30107
MY PATIENCE KEEPS   Wet Soul LP 1002
RUNNING OUT
GLAMOUR GIRL   Wet Soul LP 1002
T-BONE'S WAY (instr.) (2) Wet Soul LP 1002
THAT EVENING TRAIN   Wet Soul 5   LP 1002
LOUISIANA BAYOU   Wet Soul LP 1002
DRIVE (instr.)
WHEN WE WERE   Wet Soul LP 1002
SCHOOLMATES
DON'T GO BACK TO   Wet Soul LP 1002
NEW ORLEANS
GOT TO CROSS THE   Wet Soul LP 1002
DEEP BLUE SEA
(YOU'LL NEVER FIND   Wet Soul LP 1002
ANYONE) TO BE A
SLAVE LIKE ME
LEFT HOME WHEN I WAS   Wet Soul LP 1002; 51 West LP
A KID   16013

Note: Wet Soul LP 1002 is also on Bellaphon (G) LP 1581 and Charly (E) LP 30144.

T-Bone Walker (vo, g) with Muddy Waters (vo, g); Mojo Buford (hca); Louis Myers (g);
Dave Myers (bg); Fred Below (dm)
Montreux, France, June 17, 1972

2478   (THEY CALL IT) STORMY   Chess LP 60015   LP 50023
                MONDAY
2543   SHE SAYS SHE LOVES ME   Chess LP 60015   LP 50023

T-Bone Walker (vo, g, el-p 1) with Hartley Sevens (vln 1, ts 3); Paul Pena (g, vo 4); Johnny Summers (bg); Vinnie Johnson (dm)
Montreux, France, June 17, 1972

CALL IT STORMY MON-DAY/RECONSIDER (3)	Polydor LP 5521; Verve (G) LP 2304.088
CHUTES DE PIERRES (instr.) (3)	Polydor LP 5521; Verve (G) LP 2304.088
WHY AM I TREATED SO BAD (2, 4)	Polydor LP 5521; Verve (G) LP 2304.088
WHEN I GROW UP (1, 3)	Polydor LP 5521; Verve (G) LP 2304.088
GOIN' BACK TO CHURCH (2)	Polydor LP 5521; Verve (G) LP 2304.088
SHAKE IT BABY (1, 2)	Polydor LP 5521; Verve (G) LP 2304.088
IN AN AWFUL MOOD/ GOODBYE BABY (3)	Polydor LP 5521; Verve (G) LP 2304.088
SAIL ON LITTLE GIRL (3)	Polydor LP 5521; Verve (G) LP 2304.088

T-Bone Walker (vo 1, p) with Edward Taylor (ts); Hartley Sevens (ts, tb, vln); Paul Lenark (Pena) (g); Phillip Morrison (bg); Vinnie Johnson (dm)
Munich, West Germany, October 26, 1972

SHAKE IT BABY (1)	Atlantic (G) LP 60036; L&R (G) LP 42018
GOIN' BACK TO CHURCH	Atlantic (G) LP 60036; L&R (G) LP 42018

T-Bone Walker (vo, g)
Montreux, France, and Los Angeles, 1973

WELL, I DONE GOT OVER IT	Reprise LP 2XS 6483
STORMY MONDAY	Reprise LP 2XS 6483
THE COMEBACK	Reprise LP 2XS 6483
EVERYDAY I HAVE THE BLUES	Reprise LP 2XS 6483
PERSON TO PERSON	Reprise LP 2XS 6483

Note: These five titles are from a 2-LP set entitled *Very Rare*, on which T-Bone Walker was given top billing, though he played on only five of the twenty numbers it contained. A strange collection of often inappropriate "guests" was responsible for the rest. Walker's contributions were recorded separately in Los Angeles and then dubbed in.

T-BONE WALKER'S ALBUMS

Label	Country of Origin	Number	Title	Alternative Releases
Blues Boy	S	BB-304	THE INVENTOR OF THE ELECTRIC GUITAR BLUES	
Capitol	US	T-1958	HIS ORIGINAL 1945–50 PERFORMANCES	Capitol (F) T 1958 and (F) 068-86523
Capitol	E	H 370	CLASSIC IN JAZZ	
Capitol 25cm	E	LC 6681	CLASSIC IN JAZZ	
Capitol	F	062-80732	TOO MUCH TROUBLE BLUES	
Capitol	J	8185	HIS ORIGINAL 1945–50 PERFORMANCES	
Charly	E	CRB 1019	T-BONE JUMPS AGAIN	
Charly	E	CRB 1037	PLAIN OLE BLUES	
Charly	E	CRB 1057	THE NATURAL BLUES	
Imperial	US	LP 9098	SINGS THE BLUES	Liberty (E) LBY 3047
Imperial	F	1546751	SINGS THE BLUES	
Imperial	US	LP 9116	SINGING THE BLUES	Liberty (E) LBY 3057
Imperial	F	1546761	SINGING THE BLUES	
Imperial	US	LP 9146	I GET SO WEARY	
Imperial	F	1561451	HOT LEFTOVERS	
MFP	E	1043	THE BLUES OF T-BONE WALKER	
Polydor	F	46867	HOME OF THE BLUES, VOLUME 3	
Blue Note	US	BN-LA-522-H2	CLASSICS OF MODERN BLUES	U.A./Imperial (J) LAX-140 (M) and (J) LAX-141 (M)

Label	Country of Origin	Number	Title	Alternative Releases
Atlantic	US	8020	T-BONE BLUES	Atlantic 8256, (F) 940027, and (F) 40131
Atlantic 25cm	F	332006	T-BONE BLUES	
Home Cookin'	US	HC-S-103	WELL DONE	
Brunswick	US	(7)54126	THE TRUTH	MCA (E) MUPS 331
BluesWay	US	BLS 6008	STORMY MONDAY BLUES	Stateside (E) SSL 10223 and (F) CSSX 240691
BluesWay	US	BLS 6014	FUNKY TOWN	Stateside (E) SSL 10265
BluesWay	US	BLS 6058	DIRTY MISTREATER	MCA 1366; BluesWay (F) 204932
Black & Blue	F	33019	FEELING THE BLUES	Black & Blue (F) 33529 and 33552; Barclay (SP) 21688; Delmark DS-633
Polydor	F	658158	GOOD FEELIN'	Polydor (F/G) 2393 007 and 24-4502
Wet Soul	US	1002	STORMY MONDAY BLUES	Bellaphon (G) BI 1581; Charly (E) CR 30144
BluesTime	US	(2)9004	EVERY DAY I HAVE THE BLUES	
Polydor	US	PD-5521	FLY WALKER AIRLINES	Verve (G) 2304 088 (LIVE FROM MONTREUX)
Reprise	US	6483	VERY RARE	Reprise (F) K 94001

ANTHOLOGIES IN WHICH T-BONE WALKER APPEARS

Label	Country of Origin	Number	Title	Alternative Releases
Roots	A	RL-327	TEXAS COUNTRY BLUES, VOLUME 3	
Swing House	E	SWH 30	R & B AND BOOGIE WOOGIE, VOLUME 2	
Constellation	US	CS 6	A BUCKET OF BLUES	
Capitol	Europe(?)	T 20642	JAZZ MEMORIES OF THE BLUES	

Label	Country of Origin	Number	Title	Alternative Releases
Capitol	F	154-85330/2	STORY OF SOUL (3-record set)	
Pickwick	US	3173	BLUES SHOUT!	
Ace of Spades	US	1001	CENTRAL AVENUE BLUES	
Albatros	I	8474	COMBOS BLUES	
Joker	I	4023	THE JAZZ GUITAR ANTHOLOGY, VOLUME 1	
Joker	I	76/6	THE JAZZ GUITAR	
Imperial	US	LP 9210	A WORLD OF BLUES, VOLUME 1	London (E) H4P-8099; Imperial (F) 068-83300
Imperial	US	LP 9257	THE BEST OF THE BLUES, VOLUME 1	Imperial LP 12257
Imperial	US	LM 94002	URBAN BLUES, VOLUME 1: BLUES UPTOWN	Liberty LBL 83215
Minit	E	MLS 40005	DIRT BLUES	
Minit	E	MLS 40009	CLASSIC R & B HITS, VOLUME 2 (COLD CUT FEELING)	
Joker	I	74/6	THE BLUES (6-record set)	
Joker	I	3592	THE BLUES, VOLUME 10: THE GREAT VOCALISTS	
Atlantic	US	1239	ROCK 'N' ROLL FOREVER, VOLUME 1	Atlantic 8010; Versailles (F) STVX 8003
Atlantic	US	SD 7226	TEXAS GUITAR FROM DALLAS TO L.A.	
Atlantic	US	SD2-506	ATLANTIC 25TH ANNIVERSARY: THE BLUES YEARS	Atlantic (F) 60095 (?)
Atlantic	J	P-4589-A	ATLANTIC BLUES SPECIAL	
Midi	G	68005	BLUES STORY	
Midi	G	60034	BLUES STORY, VOLUME 2	
Brunswick	G	009012	AMERICAN FOLK BLUES FESTIVAL 1962	Polydor (G) INT 109012, (F) 658017, (F) 248204, (F) 2310 296; L & R (G) 42017

Label	Country of Origin	Number	Title	Alternative Releases
Rare Records	F	RR 02	AMERICAN BLUES FESTIVAL JAM SESSION	
Excello	US	EX 8029	AFBF 72[?]	
Trio	J	PA-3129	MODERN BLUES ANTHOLOGY: BLUES GREAT ARTISTS, VOLUME 10	
Avco Embassy	US	AVE 33006	SOUL IN THE BEGINNING	Avco Embassy (F) 33006
51 West	US	Q-16013	PLAIN AND SIMPLE	
BluesWay	US	BLS 1973	A TASTE OF BLUESWAY	
Black & Blue	F	33375/7	BLUES ANTHOLOGY (2-record set)	
Black & Blue	F	950500	THE BLACK AND BLUE JAZZ HISTORY	
Black & Blue	F	950010	LA GRANDE PARADE DU JAZZ, VOLUME 1	
BluesTime	US	(2)9003	SUPER BLACK BLUES	
BluesTime	US	29009	SUPER BLACK BLUES, VOLUME 2	
BluesTime	US	29101	BLUE ROCKS	RCA SF 8427
RCA	F	PM4239	THE BLUES (3-record set)	
Charly	E	CR 30107	MUSIC CITY SOUL	
Chess	US	2CH 60015	BLUES AVALANCHE	Chess/Musidisc (F) CH 50023

Label	Country of Origin	Number	Title	Alternative Releases
Pablo	US	2625 704	THE GREATEST JAZZ CONCERT IN THE WORLD	
Atlantic	G	60036	AMERICAN FOLK BLUES FESTIVAL 1972	L & R (G) 42018
			T-BONE WALKER, ACCOMPANIST	
Big Band Archives	US	1202	FREDDIE SLACK/RIFFETTE	
Ajaz	US	281	FREDDIE SLACK/THE COMPLETE, VOLUME 1	
Ajaz	US	288	FREDDIE SLACK/THE COMPLETE, VOLUME 2	
Route 66	S	KIX-9	ROY HAWKINS/WHY DO EVERYTHING HAPPEN TO ME	
Ace	UK	CHA 103	ROY HAWKINS/HIGHWAY 59	
Prestige	US	FELP 7300	JIMMY WITHERSPOON/EVENIN' BLUES	Stateside (E) SL 10088; VSM/Prestige (F) FELP 10009
Black & Blue	F	33021	EDDIE VINSON/WEE BABY BLUES	
Black & Blue	F	33022	JAY McSHANN/CONFESSIN' THE BLUES	Black & Blue (F) 33543; Delmark DS 631

OTHER ANTHOLOGIES

FREDDIE SLACK: Capitol 11991, T 907, (E) H 83, (E) 6529, 1962; Ember (E) 6605
ELLA MAE MORSE: Capitol (F) 1553041 ("Riffette")
JIMMY WITHERSPOON: Prestige 7713

Index

279

Other DACAPO titles of interest

THE ARRIVAL OF B. B. KING
Charles Sawyer
274 pp., 99 photos
80169-8 $9.95

BILLIE'S BLUES
The Billie Holiday Story
1933-1959
John Chilton
Foreword by Buck Clayton
272 pp., 20 photos
80363-1 $12.95

BLUES FROM THE DELTA
William Ferris
New introd. by Billy Taylor
226 pp., 30 photos
80327-5 $10.95

BLUES WHO'S WHO
Sheldon Harris
775 pp., 450 photos
80155-8 $29.50

EVERY DAY
The Story of Joe Williams
Leslie Gourse
208 pp., 26 photos
80275-9 $9.95

GIANTS OF BLACK MUSIC
Edited by Pauline Rivelli
and Robert Levin
Foreword by Nat Hentoff
128 pp., 14 photos
80119-1 $7.95

I AM THE BLUES
The Willie Dixon Story
Willie Dixon with Don Snowden
288 pp., 44 photos
80415-8 $12.95

THE LEGACY OF THE BLUES
Art and Lives of Twelve
Great Bluesmen
Samuel B. Charters
192 pp., 15 photos
80054-3 $8.95

SCREENING THE BLUES
Paul Oliver
302 pp., 8 photos
80344-5 $11.95

STOMPING THE BLUES
Albert Murray
272 pp., 127 illus.
80362-3 $11.95

Available at your bookstore

OR ORDER DIRECTLY FROM

DA CAPO PRESS, INC.
233 Spring Street, New York, New York 10013